Location Behaviour and Relationship Stability in International Business Networks

Location Behaviour and Relationship Stability in International Business Networks investigates how buyer-supplier relationships within international business networks develop over time, looking at them from a geographical angle and from an actor composition point of view. Many existing theories assume that the application of lean logistics and modular production methods lead to uniform location behaviour on behalf of suppliers vis-à-vis their clients. Similarly, standing theories emphasize stability in terms of actor composition of business-to-business relationships and business network constellations. This book challenges the wisdom of these claims.

To put these claims to the test, a critical review of conceptual network literature is presented leading to an own conceptual framework for analysis. This framework is used for longitudinal empirical research on two cases of one buyer-multiple suppliers networks from the automotive industry. Reconstructions are provided of the networks of first tier suppliers that two car assembly plants engage for the delivery of components and the location dynamics these supplier networks display towards the two plants over a period of +/− 15 years. The detail with which the various (actor composition and geographical) network analyses are conducted and reported on is of a level that can be considered unique.

Based on these reconstructions, **Bart Kamp** obtains ample indications to argue that business networks go through significant changes over time, both as regards their actor composition and their geographical articulation. Also, he shows that location patterns of suppliers around buyer firms do not necessarily follow a deterministic one-best-way trajectory. A final merit of this book is that it is one of the few to form a bridge between and to integrate theoretical and conceptual fundaments from network research traditions from either side of the Atlantic Ocean.

Bart Kamp is Senior Policy Adviser at Resource Analysis (a division of Technum/Tractebel-Suez), one of the largest Belgium consulting firms in strategic policy and industry matters. He is project manager of a major European research assignment called 'Benchmarking car manufacturing performance and supportive public policy in European regions dependent on car industry'. In addition, he is a member of the GERPISA International Network of Researchers on the Automotive Industry and a visiting lecturer at the University of Antwerp Management School, Belgium. He has an ample track record of articles on the automotive industry and business-to-business relationships published in refereed journals, financial newspapers and automotive research associations' periodicals.

Routledge studies in business organizations and networks

Location Behaviour and Relationship Stability in International Business Networks

Evidence from the automotive industry

Bart Kamp

 Routledge
Taylor & Francis Group

LONDON AND NEW YORK

First published 2007
by Routledge
2 Park Square, Milton Park, Abingdon, Oxon OX14 4RN

Simultaneously published in the USA and Canada
by Routledge
270 Madison Ave, New York, NY 10016

Routledge is an imprint of the Taylor & Francis Group, an informa business

© 2007 Bart Kamp

Typeset in Garamond by
Newgen Imaging Systems (P) Ltd, Chennai, India
Printed and bound in Great Britain by
Biddles Ltd, King's Lynn

British Library Cataloguing in Publication Data
A catalogue record for this book is available from the British Library

Library of Congress Cataloging in Publication Data
A catalog record for this book has been requested

ISBN10: 0–415–39962–9 (hbk)
ISBN10: 0–203–96828–X (ebk)

ISBN13: 978–0–415–39962–3 (hbk)
ISBN13: 978–0–203–96828–4 (ebk)

To Xavier and Axel

Contents

Figures

Tables

Preface

This study on the formation and evolution of international business networks is not about determining 'under what circumstances a network arrangement is to be preferred to market governance or internalization?' Neither does it aim to find out 'which foreign entry mode strategies do business actors follow to position themselves in international business networks?' as a static observation of a 'one-moment-in-time act'. Instead, the study is aimed at answering the following twofold research question. Once subsidiaries of multinational companies outsource business activities: how do buyer–supplier relationships develop over time from a geographical angle and from an actor composition point of view? Are such relationships characterized by stability in terms of the involved suppliers and the locations from where they deliver, or can a significant turnover in suppliers and supply sites be observed?

The research questions that we address emerged from confronting the outcomes of interviews with executives of car manufacturing companies on change and continuity of buyer–supplier relationships, on the one hand, and the emphasis on network stability that is encountered in most literature on business-to-business relationships and business networks, on the other.

In fact, many existing studies point at longevity as a basic characteristic of business-to-business relationships and business networks constellations. In addition, many contemporary studies point at location determinism as a consequence of lean logistics practices and modular production methods, which should ultimately also lead to a stable and deterministic (one-best-way) situation. The present study calls these claims into question. For that purpose, it taps first of all into lessons derived from three different conceptual frameworks of reference, i.e. the Network and Interaction approach to business-to-business relationships, the Network view on the Internationalization Process Model and the Flagship/Five Partners Model. Parallelly, it builds on insights derived from, among others, change theories and theories with respect to organizational learning and competitive behaviour. As a consequence, the study comes up with interesting conceptual insights and empirical findings.

The combination of the Scandinavia-based Network and Interaction approach to business-to-business relationships and the Network view on the Internationalization Process Model, on the one hand, and the North

America-based Flagship/Five Partners Model, on the other, turns out to be a curious one. For most of the publications in the tradition of either the Scandinavia-based or the North America-based network school do not source from or refer to publications that are produced by their respective 'counterparts'. Also the highly renowned work by Nohria and Eccles (1992), with contributions from North American network scholars, dedicates hardly any attention to Europe-based network research and theorizing. In fact, very few publications (e.g. McKiernan, 1992; Melin, 1992; Fina and Rugman, 1996) form a bridge between the two worlds.

The present work aims to combine conceptual lessons from network research on either side of the Atlantic Ocean into an integrated framework for network analysis, and to contribute to connecting both research environments.

The conceptual framework that is developed in this book and the operationalization of the underlying key concepts follow from a critical review of the three conceptual frameworks of reference, and of other theories that contribute to understanding international business network dynamics (e.g. change theories and theories with respect to organizational learning and competitive behaviour).

To test a number of conceptual propositions, we build on empirical research with respect to two cases of buyer–suppliers networks surrounding foreign-owned car manufacturing plants in Spain. The geographical and actor composition evolutions with respect to the business networks in question are followed over a long period of time. The accompanying analyses are not merely founded on verbal statements expressed in interviews with sources 'close to the horse's mouth', but on revealed and reconstructed facts based on company reports; some of them meant for a wide audience (e.g. annual reports), others to inform a select group of actors (internal publications). Certainly the disclosure of the latter data was a labourious task, as it meant finding and gaining access to them. In certain cases it also implied a great deal of detective work and diplomacy. Finally, the fact that empirical data was consulted in no fewer than seven languages further helped to conduct a broadly founded, rich and multiform empirical research. As a consequence, the final conclusions of the study are supported by a thorough analysis of a wide array of sources.

Bart Kamp
Brussels, Belgium

Abbreviations

AT	agency theory
B	Belgium
b2b	business-to-business
CZ	Czech Republic
D	Germany
E	Spain
EAQF	Evaluation Aptitude Qualité Fournisseur
F	France
FASA	Fabricacion de Automoviles Sociedad Anonima de Valladolid
FDI	Foreign direct investment
FSA	firm-specific advantage
F/5P	flagship/five partners
I	Italy
IB	international business
IPM	internationalization process model
J	Japan
JIT	just-in-time
MNE	multinational enterprise
MPTAS	million pesetas
N&I	network and interaction
NO	Norway
OLI	Ownership-specific advantages, Location-specific advantages and Internalization incentive advantages
P	Portugal
PRA	property rights approach
RBV	resource-based view
R&D	research and development
SME	small and medium-sized enterprise
TCE	transaction cost economics
UK	United Kingdom
USA	United States of America
VW	Volkswagen

1 Introduction

1.1 Background and positioning of the study

From the perspective of a host region, the value of hosting a gatekeeping company to a consumers market, like for instance a car manufacturing plant, is first of all related to the success of the company's end products on the world markets.[1] For it is market success that determines the annual output and own industrial activity of such a company. Moreover, in a time of intensified outsourcing, its value depends strongly on the employment, added value and general wealth such a company generates through spillover effects to the wider economy and its embeddedness within the region in question.[2]

Especially in the case of regions that are peripheral to the home base of a gatekeeping company, such regional spillover effects and embeddedness are not all that self-evident.

Why are certain peripheral regions, some of which may not even be very active in terms of targeted policy actions and public investments with regard to a specific sector, the (long-term) host to satellite business networks with many geographically concentrated backward and forward links within a specific production chain?

This is a general preoccupation in peripheral regions that (want to) host large foreign investments, especially when the investments are in mature industries that are inclined to become footloose.[3] Increasingly, these regions want to host more than just the production activities of a gatekeeping company within their territory. They also want to host the network of suppliers to whom the former company outsources large part of its activities, as well as the business functions that are vital to further development of the products in question, like research and development activities (R&D) and design functions.

We define a satellite business network in a region that is peripheral to the home base of the main network members as follows: 'networks largely made up of subsidiaries of multinationals in regions that do not host the decision-making centres, i.e. the headquarters of the most influential private actors involved in the business networks in question'. This implies that peripheral does not have to refer to a region in a developing country.

The game of attracting and maintaining industries within a locality is usually played through incentives on investments, soil, labour, access to consumer markets and other production factors (see for example, Richardson, 1972, 1973, 1978; Scott, 1988). We posit that these *traditional* factors for explaining location behaviour are especially relevant to the explanation of location choices of largely integrated companies or for companies that form the hub of a network of firms. In addition, we argue that for the firms that form the surrounding network of such a hub company – especially in cases where many of these firms are from abroad as well – the situation is somewhat different. Here, we argue that it is, *ceteris paribus*, the location of a focal buyer company itself and the relative value it represents to the surrounding network of firms (see for example, Nooteboom, 1996; Nooteboom *et al.*, 1997; De Jong and Nooteboom, 2000, pp. 28, 35), which influences suppliers in their 'location behaviour'.

From our viewpoint, therefore, this question is largely an international business-to-business matter. Consequently, in order to shed light on these matters we will focus on those intra-firm and inter-firm parameters, decisions and dynamics that determine the appreciation of location and value characteristics of focal buyers in networks. From there on, we will analyse the impact this has on the geographical articulation of supplier networks around peripherally located subsidiaries of multinational enterprises (MNEs) over time. For this two-step analysis we will make use of context-specific operationalizations of the concepts 'intra-firm network position' and 'inter-firm network positioning'.

Simultaneously, we want to expose a second business-to-business matter, that is, the fact that network theorists perceive and conceive evolutions in the actor composition of business networks as relatively stable, based on long-lasting inter-firm relationships (see for example, Ford, 1980, 1997; Johanson and Mattsson, 1987; Easton, 1989; Johanson and Vahlne, 1990; Håkansson, 1993; Forsgren *et al.*, 1995; Håkansson and Shehota, 1995; Rugman and D'Cruz, 2000). We argue that, for example, competitive and learning behaviour of firms, both on behalf of buyers and suppliers, may well make the composition of business networks prone to changes. As such, we want to explore the tenability of this *stability thesis*. This will be analysed via a context-specific operationalization of the concept of 'buyer–supplier relationship longevity'.

Consequently, we want to concentrate on the following two research problems:

- What determines the (non-)practicing of *co-location* around buyer establishments on behalf of suppliers? What determines the degree to which suppliers are geographically concentrated around focal buyer organizations of international business networks?
- What determines supplier continuity and discontinuity – for example through substitutions or exit – in buyer–supplier networks?

We will deal with these research problems through a longitudinal analysis of the composition and location of the respective groups of suppliers surrounding two long-established car manufacturing plants in Spain. The car manufacturing plants are subsidiaries of different foreign-owned MNEs.

We intend to demonstrate that network theory can be applied or extended in such a way that the location dimension of business-to-business (b2b) processes can also be explained. Through this, we aim to achieve a first form of conceptual progress regarding network theory.

Subsequently, we argue that the phenomena of bonding and trust, which – according to network theory – are supposed to make inter-firm relationships a lasting experience, are unable to explain sufficiently the outcome of business network formation processes over time. Therefore, we propose the inclusion of concepts from other theoretical schools to explain the outcomes of business network formation processes. Through this, we also aim to provide conceptual progress with respect to network theory.

1.1.1 Research context

Over 15 years of research has demonstrated that nowadays a large share of business transactions take place via b2b relationships (Laage-Hellman, 1997).[4] These relationships render network characteristics to the aggregated structure of the companies involved (Axelsson and Easton, 1992; Nohria and Eccles, 1992; Grabher, 1993) and a less pronounced vertical integration in value systems (Child, 1987; Jarillo, 1988; Johnston and Lawrence, 1988). Consequently, business networks can be identified as empirical entities (Håkansson, 1993). Moreover, the explosion in alliances at the end of the twentieth century suggests that a pair or network of firms is an increasingly important unit of analysis and deserves more study (Anderson, 1990; Gomes-Casseres, 1994; Smith *et al.*, 1995). Finally, the fact that inter-firm cooperation can be an important source of rent generation has long been recognized in studies (Alchian and Demsetz, 1972; Cook and Emerson, 1978, 1984; Perry, 1989; Oliver, 1990).

We argue that satellite business networks in peripheral regions can be interpreted as special cases of b2b relationships, that is, as a collection of dyadic b2b relationships in a core–periphery context.[5]

Similarly, due to the satellite and peripheral characteristics involved, these networks can be understood as special cases of internationalization.

Consequently, we will focus primarily on literature regarding business-to-business relationships and business network and on literature on internationalization of firms.

We will also pay attention to business network research that departs from an MNE management angle, as the networks under investigation are to a large extent subjected to intra-firm headquarters–subsidiary relationship aspects.

We focus on the formation and evolution of international business networks as *organizational sets* (Evan, 1966, 1972, 1974), that is, the supplier relations with which the focal buyer of a network chooses to organize the business activities of a peripherally located subsidiary.

We do not look at networks as an alternative governance arrangement to markets and hierarchies (Williamson, 1975, 1985). Neither do we view these networks as if their existence can be called into question and substituted by other governance structures at certain moments in time (Langlois, 1988; Langlois and Robertson, 1989, 1995). Instead, we look at inter-firm networks that are 'a constant' over time.[6] From there, we analyse the way these networks evolve in terms of geographical articulation and actor composition.

We choose not to depart either from a regional economy and economic geography perspective, due to its usual lack of focus on the embeddedness of network nodes in exterior MNE power structures. In the regional economy tradition, the past decades have witnessed a large interest in attempts to explain the relationships between the functioning of business networks and local or regional economic growth (e.g. Porter, 1990; Krugman, 1991; Pyke *et al.*, 1992; Saxenian, 1994). However, most of these explanations are based on empirical data obtained through the study of spatially concentrated networks made up of sovereign business actors.[7] They are not based on the exploration of business networks with a more pronounced international dimension, in terms of the actors that form part of such networks and the locations from where they operate. Neither are they based on analyses of business networks in peripheral localities that largely depend on MNE headquarters located abroad. Therefore, the lessons derived from these studies are not fully appropriate for understanding the networks of our concern, where the decision-making power to a large extent lies outside the regions in question. Moreover, in general they fall short in revealing inter-firm relationships on a microeconomic level.

In view of ongoing economic integration processes on global and on Triad region level, for our focus on business network formation processes we will take into account the ongoing homogenization of economic space. Whereas previously local content rules and other kinds of state regulations determined cross-border investment and trade activities (see for example, Stopford *et al.*, 1991), today these regimes are more and more dismantled and the world is becoming increasingly homogeneous (Melin, 1992). First of all at the level of integrated trading blocks, like the European Union and the North American Free Trade Association, but also at a global level through institutions such as the World Trade Organization. This means that our research will provide insights that are especially valid from an integrated trading block viewpoint.

1.2 Research aim

The central research aim is to explore and conceptualize, from an international b2b research angle, the formation and evolution of satellite business networks in peripheral regions in particular and international business networks in general. In short, to find out how these networks are shaped and how they evolve over time. Especially with respect to:

- Their geographical articulation: the (non-)practicing of co-location by suppliers and the degree to which a conjoint of suppliers is geographically concentrated around the focal buyer of an international business network.
- Their actor composition: continuity and discontinuity (e.g. through substitutions or exit) of suppliers in international business networks.

The reason to focus on the first matter is the following. Although the study of geographical articulation of inter-firm networks appears to be a captive market for economic geographers or location analysts with its own particular limitations (see Section 1.1.1), we argue that for most firms in the networks we examine, it is more a b2b issue than anything else. Moreover, the cross-border aspect of the networks in question and the involvement of MNEs requiring attention for headquarters–subsidiaries relationships, make it an international business matter as well. Consequently, we argue that an international b2b perspective on the networks under consideration should yield new, adequate and comprehensive insights into the matter. Furthermore, we posit that investigating satellite business networks form a useful stepping stone for learning to understand geographical and actor composition dynamics with respect to international business networks in general. In fact, it is our strongly held belief that this is far more useful than studying business networks in the home bases of the focal buyer firms. Taking the latter approach exposes one to the risk of getting bogged down in the kind of biased settings described in Section 1.1.1 with respect to research from an economic geography angle, or getting confronted with excessively weighing local heritage factors or certain political pressures (see also note 3). Consequently, we argue that satellite business networks provide the better setting for studying business network evolutions.

Likewise, we argue that sectoral trends such as modular production methods and the introduction of lean logistics can not be held fully responsible for the location behaviour of suppliers, in spite of what is alleged by many scholars today (e.g. Estall, 1985; Mair, 1991a,b; Wells and Rawlinson, 1992; Marx *et al.*, 1997; Aláez *et al.*, 1999; Adam-Ledunois and Renault, 2001). We reason that if modular production methods and lean logistics were to determine location behaviour of suppliers, the establishment patterns of suppliers vis-à-vis car constructor plants would show strong similarities, as all car constructors evolve towards the adoption of modularity and lean logistics. This is not the case, however, as becomes clear when we consider the fact that supplier parks only arise selectively (Automotive News Europe, 2000, 2005; Ludvigsen Associates, 2000). We therefore reason that additional explanations must exist.

The reason to focus on the second matter is the following. It is generally advocated that inter-firm collaborations are long-standing. Considerations like: 'it takes time to develop trust and trust is important for the well-functioning of relationships and the benefits they can render to the partners involved' (Granovetter, 1985; Helper, 1987; Johanson and Mattsson, 1987; Easton, 1989; Becattini, 1992; Harrison, 1992; Sako, 1992; Nooteboom, 1996), are often forwarded as explanations for the longevity of b2b relationships. Nevertheless, organizational learning on behalf of companies involved in b2b relationships with respect to the management of such relationships (Cyert and March, 1963; Levitt and March, 1988; Lane and Lubatkin, 1998), as well as competitive behaviour on behalf of third parties (Montgomery, 1995) may periodically call into question the continuity of inter-firm relationships. Moreover, change theories teach us that periodically, longer periods of stability are punctuated by sudden and revolutionary changes (Gersick, 1991; Van de Ven, 1992; Van de Ven and Poole, 1995).

Our central research aim to explore and conceptualize the formation and evolution of international business networks will be pursued in a threefold way: (1) the exploration of evolutionary patterns within satellite business networks in peripheral regions in particular and international business networks in general; (2) the testing of hypotheses in order to support the exploration and theory development with respect to the formation and evolution of these networks; and (3) the design of a conceptual model to capture the formation and evolution of these networks.

1.3 Conceptual engineering steps and applied research methods

On the basis of a review of relevant theoretical and empirical research literature with respect to b2b relationships and internationalization of business, a conceptual framework will be developed in order to analyse two research cases.

The frameworks of reference to ground this conceptual framework are the 'Network and Interaction' approach to b2b relationships (Håkansson, 1982, 1987, 1989, 1993; Johanson and Mattsson, 1984, 1987; Laage-Hellman, 1997), the Network view on the Internationalization Process Model (Forsgren, 1989; Forsgren and Johanson, 1992; Andersson and Forsgren, 2000), and the Flagship/Five Partners Model (Rugman and D'Cruz, 2000).

We forward our own view on three central axioms of the frameworks of reference. Subsequently, we will present a conceptual framework that enables us to examine the formation and evolution of satellite business networks in peripheral regions.

The three axioms in question are:

- firms' motivation to improve their network positions;
- the fact that organizational learning with respect to specific activities reduces firms' fear of, for example, repeating, extending or intensifying these activities;
- the emphasis on continuity and longevity of b2b relationships.

The reason we elaborate an own standpoint on these axioms is that the respective frameworks do not share a common view on them, and overall they seem to neglect certain evolutions in relation to the structuring of industries, learning processes, competitive dynamics and triggers of radical change in general.

Due to the fact that the frameworks of reference largely neglect the supramentioned phenomena and processes, it appears that the respective analytical apparatuses have trouble explaining and foreseeing developments in the composition of business networks. As this is one of our two research problems, we need to obtain theoretical help from elsewhere.

In this regard, we argue that in order to construct a conceptual framework that is theoretically and terminologically coherent, manageable and able to produce clear insights, it is necessary to combine theories that coincide on central claims (Groenewegen and Vromen, 1996, p. 371). In addition, one needs to link those parts of such theories that are consistent with one another and which jointly contribute to the comprehension and explanation of the research object (see for example, Noorderhaven, 1995; De Brucker *et al.*, 1998, pp. 58, 476). Therefore, we choose to align b2b approaches with those international business approaches that provide a theoretical and terminological fit. For the sake of theoretical and conceptual 'hygiene', we reject a broad eclectic combination of theories in a single conceptual framework. For example, a combination of theories that are all applicable to a given phenomenon but which may not provide consistency in terms of their central claims and how to explain the phenomenon at stake. For instance, a combination of insights from theories with respect to economic geography, administrative sciences and boundaries of firms would make it more complicated to obtain integrated and consistent insights on the formation and evolution of international business networks. Instead, it could easily lead to contradictory insights, as the different approaches may suggest different explanations for the same events and processes. Consequently, one would have a conceptual framework that is 'all over the place', but which, rather than providing clarity, would lead to 'confusion'.

Therefore, we opt for the alignment of a small number of theories that agree to a large extent on crucial issues such as, for example, underlying assumptions, units of analysis, and respective viewpoints.

The way we deal conceptually with the previously indicated axioms can be underpinned by referring to (competitive) behavioural theories, organizational learning and change theories. Each of these three theoretical bodies coincide with our three frameworks on a number of crucial issues and are thus legitimate sounding boards for the elaboration of an integrated conceptual framework. In concrete terms, competitive behavioural theories share the viewpoint that firms try to improve their network position. Like network theories, several branches of organizational learning theories posit that b2b relationships and collaborations benefit the learning experiences of individual organizations. Change theories confirm network theories' stability thesis, adding that longer periods of stability are alternated with short periods of changes.

In part, our own standpoints with regard to the three axioms in question can also be obtained through the extrapolation of postulations of the proper reference frameworks. Notably with respect to the possible substitution and evolution of partnerships in buyer–supplier relations. On the one hand, through the acknowledgement of the open system setting in which buyer–supplier relationships operate, the competitive bidding by competitors of the involved actors and oligopolizations in the industry. On the other hand, through the exposure of firms to new potential partners due to their own b2b and internationalization activities, the international business and b2b experience they obtain through that and through the integration of economies.

In addition, the literature discussion and comparisons of the postulations on central axioms on behalf of the respective frameworks of reference also lead us to make certain conceptual choices with respect to two other issues:

- the way the reference frameworks deal with the question of power (a)symmetry between buyers and suppliers;
- the way they are able to deal with subsidiaries as parts of MNEs instead of MNEs as such.

To cement these conceptual choices further, we also use insights obtained through empirical research literature with respect to the automotive industry. Part of the empirical literature we consulted for the present research project can be placed in the tradition of internationalization of business and inter-firm relationships. Another part stems from other academic approaches, including location theory and management of the multinational. The latter approaches were scrutinized to gain insights into location behaviour that can help elaborate a network perspective on the geographical articulation or dimension of the formation and evolution of business networks. Simultaneously, it serves to avoid the development of a subjective and 'blinkered' conceptual framework (cf. Einstein, who allegedly stated that the instrument determines what one will see).

The integrated conceptual framework that follows from the conceptual engineering steps outlined before, as seen in Figure 1.1, serves as the basis for the formulation of hypotheses. These hypotheses are tested by investigating two cases of satellite business networks located in peripheral regions from a longitudinal perspective. These empirical cases consist of the supplier networks and headquarters–subsidiary relationships surrounding two car manufacturing plants located in Spain.

The reason for using a longitudinal approach to the research cases is the following.

Evidently, it is impossible to study the changes and dynamics in business networks without taking a time element into account. Therefore, achieving

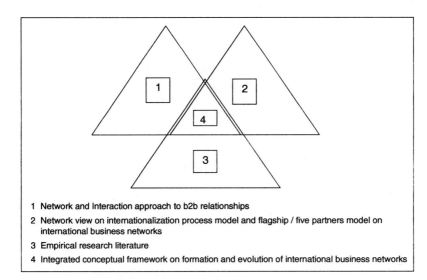

1 Network and Interaction approach to b2b relationships
2 Network view on internationalization process model and flagship / five partners model on international business networks
3 Empirical research literature
4 Integrated conceptual framework on formation and evolution of international business networks

Figure 1.1 Building blocks of conceptual framework for analysis.
Source: Author's elaboration.

our research aim requires the application of a longitudinal research approach. Only when we analyse the networks in question over a longer period of time we will be able to comprehend the '... sequence of events or activities that describes how things change over time' (Van de Ven, 1992, p. 170) and to identify critical events, activities and factors behind those evolutions. Moreover, closer examination of the hows and whys of these changes over a longer period, will better enable us to foresee future changes with respect to the cases in question (case-specific predictive validity over time) or in cases where similar events, activities and factors play a role (cross-case validity). For they will be the result of processing rich and deep information flows, that at the same time provide sufficient input for the required nuances and differentiations. In this respect, Pettigrew (1990, p. 272) posits that longitudinal research '... allows the present to be explored in relation to the past and the future.'

The reason for applying a case study method is the following.

The present research has a highly explorative and theory-developing character. We aim to test own-developed adaptations to existing theories in the form of an integrated conceptual framework in field situations. Therefore, a multiple-case study is applied, followed by a cross-case analysis, as this forms the most adequate way to gain a detailed insight into the variables and dynamics around a phenomenon to be explored (Brinberg and McGrath, 1985; King *et al.*, 1994; Yin, 1994). The particular strength of the case study method for our research purposes is that it allows a detailed analysis of the phenomenon under investigation as such. In addition, it enables an in-depth exposure of the complex factors, events and processes that are interrelated with and determine its shape and evolution (Kerlinger, 1977). Also the under-developed state of literature on the causal structures around suppliers' location behaviour from a network perspective and the phenomenon of substitutions of actors in networks suggests that case studies are an appropriate research method (Kerlinger, 1977; Schoenberger, 1991; Markusen, 1994). Moreover, the fact that several of the data that will have to be processed neither exist in an easily codifiable or numerical form, nor can be found in databases containing uniform and standardized data regarding multiple firms, makes case studies highly appropriate. Especially as the required data will be available under widely diverging forms, it will require much of the analyst's capacities to process and interpret these non-uniform data to be able to draw sound comparisons and arrive at valid conclusions. As our research covers a longer period, it is also likely that – even from an intra-firm perspective – there are discontinuities with respect to the ways the relevant data are presented. Under such circumstances, it is obvious that one cannot simply use straightforward statistical trend analysis (Albinski, 1981, p. 69).

The reason for choosing the automotive industry is twofold.

The automotive industry is a prominent example of a sector where one encounters inter-firm networks on a large scale, for example through all kinds of production and R&D outsourcing and simultaneous engineering practices. This is manifested by many sources (e.g. Hodges and Van Tulder, 1994; Rey del Castillo, 1994; Dyer, 1996; Fine and Whitney, 1996; Chanaron, 1997). According to Castells (1996, p. 191) the automotive industry – together with the electronics industry – is the most advanced industry in the diffusion of global networking patterns. Additionally, for a long time this industry has known an international spread of assets and actors, also in developing countries and backward regions within the more prosperous Triad regions (Ohmae, 1985; Dicken, 1998). Therefore, the automotive industry offers many examples of satellite networks in peripheral regions. This industry thus contains representative cases for determining the explanatory variables and determinants behind the formation and evolution of satellite networks in peripheral regions and arrive at representative and 'generalizable' conclusions.

The reason that the cases to be examined are located in Spain can be legitimized as follows.

Although Spain is a country without autochtonous car constructors that at present enjoy sovereignty, it houses a significant automotive industry. Most of the firms active in Spain are based on foreign capital (Lagendijk, 1994, 1995). This holds true for the complete ensemble of car constructors, but also to a large extent for the suppliers that are located in Spain. As such, it provides an adequate setting for analysing formation processes surrounding satellite business networks in peripheral regions. Moreover, due to its (late) adhesion to an integrated trading block, that is the European Union, it allows us to follow such formation processes as a function of the homogenization of economic space from a dynamic perspective. Therefore, Spain forms the ideal setting to analyse internationalization and b2b formation trajectories surrounding satellite business networks in peripheral regions.

The two car manufacturing plants that were selected for longitudinal case study analysis are FASA-Renault in Valladolid, Castilla y Leon and Volkswagen Navarra in Landaben, Navarra. Both plants are located in regions that saw their first attempts to attract car assembly activities frustrated due to different location preferences on behalf of the 'invited' automobile producer (FIAT in the case of Castilla y Leon, who finally settled in Barcelona, Catalonia and Citroën in the case of Navarra, who finally settled in Vigo, Galicia). Ultimately both regions succeeded in becoming the cradle of foreign-owned car manufacturing plants (Renault in the case of Castilla y Leon and Volkswagen in the case of Navarra). Both also have in common that the owners of the assembly operations are European multinational companies; French in the case of FASA-Renault in Castilla y Leon and German in the case of Volkswagen Navarra in Navarra (unlike the GM and Ford operations in Aragon and Valencia[8] respectively). The involvement of Renault in FASA is from an earlier date (1950s) than Volkswagen's involvement in Volkswagen Navarra (from the 1980s onwards, through its stake in SEAT). The FASA-Renault plants in Castilla y Leon have always been partly or completely under Renault's control, whereas the Landaben plant has switched ownership several times during its existence (from AUTHI to SEAT (in 1976) to Volkswagen (in 1986)).

The insights that follow from the empirical cases will be used to discuss the integrated conceptual framework. They also will be used to reflect on the formulated hypotheses. In addition, they serve to enhance the understanding and conceptualization of the formation and evolution of satellite business networks in specific and, as far as possible, of international business networks in general.

1.4   Structure of the study

After the current introductory part (Chapter 1), relevant theories with respect to b2b relationships and internationalization of business will be discussed in Chapter 2. Chapter 2 is completed by reviewing empirical research literature on b2b relationship practices and internationalization of business in the automotive industry. On the basis of the theoretical and empirical literature review, in Chapter 3 a conceptual framework for the analysis of satellite business networks in peripheral regions is designed. Similarly, certain research hypotheses are formulated.

These hypotheses are then tested through two empirical case studies of, largely foreign-controlled, satellite business networks in peripheral regions. The presentation of the empirical research methodology, operationalizations of the key concepts underlying the conceptual framework and a description of the reporting structure of the case studies are the subject of Chapter 4. The empirical results of the two case studies are presented in Chapter 5 and Chapter 6 respectively.

In Chapter 7, reflections on and a discussion of the results of our own empirical research are presented. In addition, conceptual lessons that can be derived from the conducted research is formulated. Finally, an assessment of the extent to which the conclusions from our own research findings can be generalized, is forwarded.

2 Theoretical and empirical research literature review

2.1 Introduction

In this study we interpret satellite business networks in regions that are peripheral to the home base of the main network members as special cases of inter-firm or b2b relationships, that is, as collections of dyadic (MNE) b2b relationships.

Likewise, due to the satellite and peripheral characteristics which give the networks under consideration a cross-border and a headquarters–subsidiaries dimension, they are also considered as special cases of international(ization of) business.

2.1.1 Structure of the chapter

In this chapter, existing literature with respect to b2b relationships and internationalization of business is discussed. The literature review consists of four parts.

In the first part, attention will be paid to those approaches that focus on the analysis and comprehension of individual and multiple b2b relationships and of business networks. This part is concluded with the lessons most relevant to our research aims and objects of study.

In the second part, the conclusions of the first part on the formation and functioning of business networks will be complemented by a review of theoretical literature on internationalization of business. There, we will focus on those approaches that provide alignment possibilities with the concepts on b2b relationships that are discussed before. The choice for internationalization of business approaches that 'fit' methodologically with the b2b approaches discussed previously is aimed at providing theoretical and terminological coherency to the conceptual framework that will follow afterwards. This part is also concluded with a presentation of the most relevant lessons for the present research project.

In the third part, a review is presented of empirical research literature on the automotive industry and contemporary networking and internationalization practices in this sector. The most relevant lessons of the empirical literature review, in view of the present research project's aim, are then formulated as well.

After the literature review we draw up conclusions and summarize the implications for understanding the formation and evolution of satellite business networks in peripheral regions. This will then allow us to design a conceptual framework for our empirical research and to formulate certain hypotheses in Chapter 3.

2.2   B2b relationships and business networks as scientific research objects

An extensive body of research has proved the richness and diversity of b2b relationships (Turnbull and Valla, 1986; Gadde and Håkansson, 1993, Håkansson and Shehota, 1995; Laage-Hellman, 1997). The relevance of studying b2b relationships is further emphasized by the fact that large shares of business transactions nowadays take place through stable b2b relationships. The latter is enhanced by a continuous increase in outsourcing of all sorts of business tasks and the large number of corporate alliances that have taken place between members of specific value systems in the business community (Contractor and Lorange, 1988; Nohria and Eccles, 1992; Fine and Whitney, 1996; Doz and Hamel, 1998; Fine, 1998). This leads to a less pronounced vertical integration in value systems (Child, 1987; Jarillo, 1988; Johnston and Lawrence, 1988). Instead, many industrial relationships and structures take on appearances, which can be considered networks (Williamson, 1991; Håkansson, 1993).

2.2.1   *Central premises with respect to theories on b2b relationships and business networks*

B2b relationships can be viewed as inter-firm exchange relationships or as interactions between autonomous business units, either initiated by the supplier or the buyer, whereby both parties recognize their mutual dependence and interest in each other's resources (Cunningham, 1980). In a similar vein, industrial networks can be described as sets of exchange relations between heterogeneous actors performing activities and handling and exchanging heterogeneous resources, with as a result, adaptation and interdependence occurring over time (Hood and Vahlne, 1988).

Implicit in these characterizations is the assumption that b2b relationships and business networks shelter advantages for both buyers and suppliers. Consequently, it follows that the firms involved engage willingly in such relationships and networks. Likewise, firms are able to exit b2b relationships and industrial networks out of their own free will. Or they can look for other partners when they consider the current constellation to be no longer profitable.

With respect to the issue of 'free participation' and (a)symmetric dependence in b2b relationships and inter-firm networks – and why organizations enter into, maintain or dissolve these relationships and networks, two opposite academic viewpoints exist.

On the one hand, there is the power and resources dependency approach. This approach argues that inter-firm interactions stem from power relationships (Yuchtman and Seashore, 1967; Aldrich, 1972, 1976, 1979; Kochan, 1975; Pfeffer and Salancik, 1978). Inter-firm power inequality leads powerful firms to entice less powerful firms to interact with them. Less powerful firms accept this interaction to safeguard their own interests and existence.

On the other hand, there is the organizational exchange approach. This approach reasons that firms interact to their mutual benefit (Levine and White, 1961; Tuite, 1972; White, 1974; Bish, 1978). According to this approach, inter-firm exchanges are undertaken voluntarily for the realization of the mutual goals the involved actors share.

It is our strongly held view that dynamism is a key feature of networks and b2b relationships and that both power (in)equality and (un)equal goals can lead to changes. Moreover, that both dominant, dependent and independent partners will use voice or exit (Hirschman, 1970; Helper, 1987) to force changes in or of existing b2b relationships. Finally, that loyalty between incumbent partners of b2b relationships or networks depends on the perceived optimality of the situation.

Networks, in terms of organizational sets (Evan, 1966, 1974), can be conceived and analysed in two ways. First, being a conjoint of various relations between organizations. Second, as a *Gestalt*, meaning as a unit of analysis of its own. The second viewpoint argues that inter-organizational networks can be viewed as acting or evolving entities in themselves and that networks have their own logic (Nohria, 1992). This implies that the analysis of organizations should take into account the dynamics and the specific character of a network of which organizations are part. As a consequence, one should use the right variables and measures that reveal the overall patterns, structure and dynamics of networks, rather than those of the underlying (dyadic) relationships that make up the overall network.

We argue that the second viewpoint holds various risks and limitations. First of all, it only seems likely that a network can be considered as a coherent unit if the network is conceived as it is presupposed in the power and resources dependency approach. That is, with a dominant actor that can seduce the other network partners to behave according to its own will. Or if there is another (external) force which imposes a certain behavioural logic on the network members. In all other circumstances, the usefulness of this viewpoint seems limited. Moreover, even under the previously mentioned circumstances, one should not confuse a network's own logic with the logic of a dominant actor or force. Therefore, it is our view that interpreting networks as consciously acting entities of their own implies a 'reification' risk and may rather follow from a lack of understanding of the relationships and organizations that constitute the network. Therefore, we propose to view and explain network dynamics through the moves of the organizations that make up networks and which function as the acting entities, whereby their network linkages form explanatory factors for individual moves and decisions. Consequently, we propose that the basis for conceiving and analysing networks should be formed by 'bottom-up' research into the relationships and actors that make up a network.

Likewise, we state that the following premises, derived from contemporary research on business networks and b2b relationships are valuable tools to understand the functioning of inter-firm networks:

- Individual organizations are networks:

  - Organizations can be seen as social networks of recurring relationships and linkages among the different components that in their aggregated form make up the initial organization (Nohria, 1992).

- The environment(s) of individual organizations are networks:

  - The environment of an organization can also be viewed as a network of organizations. Proponents of a network perspective on organizations argue that the most important elements of an organization's environment are other organizations with which the initial organization maintains exchange processes. To understand individual organizational behaviour it is necessary to understand the environment and the inter-organizational relationships of an individual organization.

  - Not only the conjoint of organizations, which form the environment of a specific individual organization, are relevant in understanding an organization's environment. It is equally important to know the exact patterns and nature of relationships, resource complementarities and exchange processes through which organizations are related. This is a necessary condition to detect 'overarching structures' and structural patterns in networks or systems of organizations.[9] Similarly, this enables understanding the investments in and the added value[10] of inter-organizational relationships. Such structures and patterns would remain invisible from the standpoint of a single organization.

- An organization's network position is important:

  - Actions of actors are conditioned by their position within networks of relationships. For example, the dependence or sovereignty structures in which a certain actor is embedded may at times be a better indicator of its behaviour than its intrinsic attributes, size and competences (Turnbull and Valla, 1986).

  - 'The structure of relations among actors and the location of individual actors in the network have important behavioural, perceptual, and attidunial consequences both for the individual units and or the system as a whole' (Knoke and Kuklinski, 1982, p. 13). In this regard, the correlation between the concept of centrality and that of power in a network is indicative.

- The position of an organization in a network is a determinant for its power to create and influence networks. The network position of an organization can be measured by means of the roles an organization plays, via the authority and value it extracts from its role and relationships in other networks than the primary one under consideration, and by means of the power an organization controls vis-à-vis other members of the network under consideration. Furthermore, power and positions in networks can both be based on economy (e.g. purchasing power), technology, expertise, trust and authority (Thorelli, 1986).

- Mind the evolutionary character of inter-organizational networks:

  - Networks form both constraints and enablers of organizational action. Inter-organizational networks are, at the same time, actions and products of actions of organizations, that are tied into networks. As a consequence, although network relationships tend to be relatively stable and recurring, new network ties can also be formed.[11] Over time these new ties can change old network patterns considerably. As such, networks are as much process as structure, being continually shaped and reshaped by the actions of actors who are in turn constrained by their structural or network position (Nohria, 1992, p. 7).

2.2.2 Relevant scientific frameworks with respect to b2b relationships and business networks

Within the body of research on b2b relationships and business networks, one can broadly distinguish between work adopting a static or a dynamic approach to the matter.

The static approach views networks as a form of organization through which assets are allocated and transactions are governed. As alternatives to networks, markets and hierarchies can be used as organizational forms for governing exchanges. The static approach compares the appropriateness of each organizational form or governance structure for a given resource or transaction at a certain point in time. Subsequently, it tries to determine the optimal governance or ownership structure. This is, broadly speaking, either done from a transaction cost and control perspective or from a resource-based view. Prominent schools of thought in this respect are transaction cost economics (Williamson, 1975, 1985, 1991; Williamson and Ouchi, 1981; Powell, 1990; Powel and Smith-Doerr, 1994), agency theory (Jensen and Meckling, 1976; Fama, 1980; Fama and Jensen, 1983), property rights approach (Grossman and Hart, 1986; Hart and Moore, 1990; Holmström and Roberts, 1998), and the resource-based view (Wernerfelt, 1984; Barney, 1991).

The dynamic approach to b2b relationships and business networks treats the collection of firms that make up inter-firm networks and inter-firm relationships as a unit of analysis as such (see for example Evan, 1966, 1972, 1974). Furthermore, this approach does not view networks as (temporary) alternatives to market and hierarchy governance structures (Melin, 1992). The main difference with the static approach is that the dynamic approach focuses primarily on stable inter-firm relationships as such. From there on, it is concerned with: 'how do interactions between firms take place?', 'which allocation choices are made?' and 'in which environmental contexts and processes are inter-firm relationships and interactions embedded?'.

The dynamic approach reasons that stable inter-firm relationships and business networks can be seen as cooperative interactions. Firms are first of all viewed as interdependent – in spite of their legal autonomy. They share certain common goals, which link up the firms, their resources and their strategies amidst a broader environment and set of relationships, in which firms and their relationships are embedded.

Contrary to the static approach, the dynamic approach to b2b relationships and business networks is not so much concerned with determining the most appropriate boundaries of firms. Neither does it pay a great deal of attention to the inter-firm governance structures and ditto allocations and divisions of separate assets, resources and activities between firms at a given point in time. Instead, it focuses on the exchange relationship and the inter-firm dynamics and interactions over time between firms, that together function as an interdependent business network through the alignment of complementary assets, resources and activities.

Almost synonymous with the dynamic approach to b2b relationships is the 'network and interaction' approach (Håkansson, 1982, 1987, 1989; Johanson and Mattsson, 1987, 1991; Håkansson and Johanson, 1988; Håkansson and Shehota, 1995; Laage-Hellman, 1997).

In this research project, we focus on business networks and how they evolve over time. That is, we take the conjoint of firms that work together on a specific set of tasks as our primary unit of analysis. Consequently, we do not look at networks as an alternative to markets and hierarchies (Williamson, 1975, 1985). Neither do we treat these networks as if their existence should be called into question and substituted by other governance structures at certain moments in time (Langlois, 1988; Langlois and Robertson, 1989, 1995). Instead, we look at groups of firms that have repeatedly chosen to work as a network to carry out certain business activities together. From that point onwards, we want to analyse the way these networks evolve in terms of geographical articulation and actor composition.

As a consequence, the analytical apparatus of the static approach does not seem suitable for truly dynamic process analysis. At the same time, choosing the dynamic approach for this purpose seems highly logical.

This choice if further backed up by the fact that, among the static approaches, the assumption seems to prevail that individuals and firms tend not to comply with agreements and act opportunistically. This is certainly the case as far as transaction cost economics (TCE), agency theory (AT) and the property rights approach (PRA) are concerned. In addition, TCE, AT and PRA tend to see inter-firm relationships as a result of market failure. This demonstrates the basically negative perception of the network phenomenon held by these schools of thought. Moreover, they often deny the possibility for b2b relationships to survive a long time, arguing that hybrid governance structures are temporary organizational forms that will eventually be replaced by a hierarchy or market relationship.

The former points would represent severe shortcomings for our research aims. It also contradicts the conclusion that in recent times many industries have seen the rise of stable business networks and cooperative arrangements (see for example, Contractor and Lorange, 1988; Ohmae, 1989; Alter and Hage, 1993; Jarillo, 1993; Mitchell and Singh, 1996).

On the whole, the outsourcing and alliances phenomenon we have witnessed since the end of the 1980s cannot be explained solely through power or cost aspects on behalf of the outsourcing parties (Jarillo, 1988). Instead, there are also benefits for the contracted or supplying partner (Kalawani and Narayandas, 1995; Pilorusso, 1997; Dyer and Singh, 1998).

As a consequence, due to the win-win character that b2b relationships can have for the parties involved, network theories should be able to explain lasting inter-firm relationships from a (positive) systemic viewpoint.

The resource-based view (RBV) does take long-lasting b2b relationships and alliances seriously. Moreover, it focuses substantially on the network governance option in order to obtain competitive advantage for firms. Therefore, RBV holds a more positive view with regard to b2b relationships and business networks. However, the primary unit of analysis of the RBV is the individual firm and its focus is on those resources that the firm itself possesses (Dyer and Singh, 1998, p. 660).

Elaborating on this shortcoming, Dyer and Singh (1998) develop a relational view on resources, in which the exchange relationship in dyad or network form between firms is the unit of analysis. This relational view is elaborated to explain the competitive advantage of individual firms due to resources that span the boundaries of individual firms or are embedded in inter-firm routines and processes (Dyer and Singh, 1998, p. 661). As such, it takes the exchange relationship between firms (dyad or network) as the primary unit of analysis. This view does not focus on the sequential inter-firm dynamics surrounding such exchange relationships and inter-firm resources, routines and processes. Instead, it focuses on their impact on competitive advantages at a given moment in time. Consequently, in its present form it is not a dynamic approach.

In view of the previous arguments, for the present research aim we hold on to the superior appropriateness of the dynamic approach to b2b relationships and business networks, that is, the network and interaction approach. We will now present a more detailed discussion of this approach.

2.3   Dynamic approach to b2b relationships and business networks

The dynamic approach with respect to b2b and business network research is dedicated to the formation, functioning and evolution of sets of organizations that are inter-related through exchange processes. This research angle can be traced back to network studies, as initiated by Evan (1966, 1972) and Aldrich (1979).

The dynamic approach aims at describing and explaining evolutionary aspects of industrial systems and strategies pursued by firms in such systems. Similarly, the aim is to analyse the functional activities of the firms involved that are subjected to inter-firm exchange and adaptation processes, like purchasing, R&D and production (Johanson and Mattsson, 1987).

A coherent paradigm around the dynamic perspective on inter-organizational arrangements, has been developed by scholars from the Uppsala University of Sweden (see for example, Håkansson, 1982, 1987, 1989; Johanson and Mattsson, 1987, 1991; Håkansson and Johanson, 1988; Håkansson and Shehota, 1995; Laage-Hellman, 1997). It was Håkansson *et al.* (1977) who put in place the conceptual foundations of this paradigm. This paradigm can be termed as the network and interaction approach (N&I approach) to business-to-business relationships.

Also British scholars like Ford (1980) and Cunningham (1980) were early contributors to the N&I framework. In this regard, Ford (1980, 1997) stresses the longevity and 'tightness' of relationships between buyers and suppliers as a variable for formalization of relationships and for the inter-dependence and mutual adaptation of firms. In his view, these issues co-determine choices regarding exchange arrangements and geographical locations, as well as the creation of barriers for competitors.[12]

The N&I approach can be considered a truly dynamic approach to the evolution of network formation and governance, as it attempts to explain dynamic aspects of industrial systems and strategies pursued by firms in such systems (Johanson and Mattsson, 1987). As such, the N&I approach takes the inter-firm relationship, rather than firm boundaries, as the central point of reference to reveal and analyse the systemic dynamics behind it.

All things considered, in terms of providing a formal framework for the analysis of b2b relationships that is, providing conceptual tools for the analysis of the environmental contexts, and the inter and intra-firm organizational and assignment structures behind it, the N&I approach seems to offer sufficient *grip*.

As regards the applicability of this framework, it can be stated that, due to the vast quantity of empirical analyses, the N&I approach can claim that its theoretical foundations have sufficient empirical employability as well (Meeus and Oerlemans, 1993). Thus, it offers a formal body of operational concepts and terminology for applied network analysis.

2.3.1 Network and interaction approach to buyer–supplier relationships

This N&I approach is built upon elements of industrial marketing theory (Kotler, 1980), firm heterogeneity concepts (Macaulay, 1963; Alderson, 1965; Richardson, 1972), social exchange theory (Emerson, 1962; Blau, 1964; Cook and Emerson, 1978, 1984), institutionally oriented economics (Alchian and Demsetz, 1972; Williamson, 1975, 1979, 1980), behavioural theories of organizations (Cyert and March, 1963; Thompson, 1967), and resource dependence theory (Pfeffer and Salancik, 1978).

After the initial foundations of this approach were put in place in the 1970s (Håkansson *et al.*, 1977), subsequent further elaborations (e.g. Johanson and Mattsson, 1987; Håkansson, 1989; Håkansson and Shehota, 1989, 1995; Forsgren and Johanson, 1992; Håkansson, 1993; Laage-Hellman, 1997) led to an interaction model. This model consists of three main parts: the exchange process, the actors and the environment. The relationship between two or more actors is the result of an exchange process (i.e. the interaction), which in itself is influenced by the characteristics of the actors and the environment.

In the N&I approach, the process of interactions and exchanges between industrial buyers and suppliers is the central object of study.

According to the N&I approach, the interaction process between buyer and supplier can be characterized using the following 'physical' aspects:

- The frequency with which exchanges take place between a specific set of firms[13]
- The characteristics of the product or service being exchanged
- The degree of formalization of the exchange process[14]
- The characteristics of the parties involved.

In addition, the N&I approach argues that interactions are characterized by social exchange and learning experiences between the representatives of the respective firms involved and by mutual adaptation processes on behalf of the implied firms. Consequently, over time bonds of various kinds are developed between firms (Forsgren *et al.*, 1995).

Furthermore, the N&I approach assumes that mutual interest and interdependence exists among the b2b parties involved in inter-firm relationships (Johanson and Mattsson, 1987; Forsgren *et al.*, 1995; Laage-Hellman, 1997).

As regards the network theory premises forwarded at the end of Section 2.2.1, the following elements from the N&I approach to b2b relationships should be highlighted.

- With respect to Individual organizations as networks:

  - According to the N&I approach, interaction processes between organizations are not only a matter of the separate organizations involved in or of the characteristics of specific exchange processes. They also depend on the intra-organizational structures and actors (individuals, departments) involved in specific exchange processes. Organizations as units of analysis can be divided into a number of actors like departments (Jüttner and Schlange, 1996).

– Similarly, interaction processes depend on wider overarching structures responsible for intra-organizational assignment and control of resources, competences and activities.

– The N&I approach distinguishes internal characteristics of b2b actors. This refers among others to the resources possessed or controlled by an actor and to the production and other resource-transforming activities (other 'business functions') they carry out.

– As regards the way resources and activities are organized and governed, the degree of centralization and specialization is considered relevant. Also the formalization and institutionalization of routines and relationships they are subjected to is of importance. Such organizational design parameters influence the internal functioning of the b2b actors involved. For instance, in case a b2b actor is a subsidiary of an MNE, the intra-firm position, the intra-firm assignment practices and other subsidiary management essentials with regard to this subsidiary matter.

– Organizational design parameters also influence the way actors can interact with external parties. For instance, due to the degree of autonomy and sovereignty actors have regarding the initiation and management of b2b relationships and the content and depth they can give to such relationships.

– The fact that the N&I approach sees actors as being heterogeneous (non-uniform) entities – in terms of their needs, demands and 'competential mandates', offers possibilities to analyse interacting actors at different organizational levels. For example, at the level of individuals, departments, firms, holdings and branch locations. Each of these actors is embedded in a network of relationships that provide access to resources. At the same time, such networks can constrain, condition or influence the actors they relate to and the interactions they embark upon. Actors are therefore surrounded by a unique combination of demands and opportunities, which affect how they act and react in specific interactions.

• With respect to the environment(s) of individual organizations as networks:

– The environment of organizations can be interpreted as the conjoint of relationships in which they are embedded. These can be relationships with the multitude of clients or suppliers they are related to, with daughter, mother or 'sister' plants of the same firm and with, for instance, governmental, university or other (semi-)public institutes.

– The N&I approach focuses on b2b relationships from a positive viewpoint. The issue of asset complementarity among network partners is one of its central themes:

> The logic behind the establishment of such [b2b] relationships is the need for utilizing and handling complementarities between the supplier's and the customer's production systems.
>
> (Laage-Hellman, 1997, p. 14)

– Similarly, resources are not viewed as a given and their usage is not isolated or exclusive to its owner. Instead, resources can be linked up or developed by joint efforts of b2b parties. Consequently, b2b relationships are seen as positive and as value adding (Håkansson, 1993), through which complementary resources and competences are combined (Håkansson, 1987; Forsgren *et al.*, 1995).[15] To illustrate this point further:

> All over the network there are strong incentives to cooperate.
>
> (Forsgren *et al.*, 1995, p. 21)

– The N&I approach focuses strongly on the potential positive externalities of collaborating in business networks and the collective advantages stemming from such collaborations (see for example, Håkansson, 1993, p. 214).

– It is stressed that the value of resources should be seen from a network perspective, as their value may depend upon the resources with which they are combined, and, thus, to which interaction they are allocated. Consequently, the value of resources '. . . is determined by the activity in which they are used' (Håkansson, 1989, p. 17).

– The same can be said about a firm's activities. The added value of such activities may also depend on the comparative complementarity obtained from possible interactions with other actors, that is to say, through a bundling of separately controlled activities.

– The interconnectedness of b2b relationships at the level of specific actors provides a legitimization for using the network metaphor. If one would presuppose that interactions between two parties would take place in a kind of vacuum, multiple interactions would only consist of a bundle of independent dyads (Laage-Hellman, 1997, p. 16). Instead, the embeddedness of interactions in a broader network structure implies that particular interactions can only be understood when taking into account the bundle or network of b2b relationships through which actors operate (Håkansson and Shehota, 1989).

– Legal systems, as part of firms' environments, may also have an effect on the interaction between firms, for instance by prohibiting certain types of contacts and cooperation. For instance policy measures on behalf of governments can influence the possibilities and ways in which actors can interact with each other. Trade policies and economic integration policies are but two of the policy examples that can have a pervasive effect on the way inter-firm relationships are shaped.

- With respect to an organization's network position:

    - The network position of an organization can be interpreted by means of the following parameters. The roles it plays for other organizations that it is related to, directly or indirectly; its identity or that of an overarching structure to which it belongs; the power or dependence relationship it entertains with other organizations in the network under consideration; and its relative importance to the network under study (Mattsson, 1985).

    - The N&I approach recognizes that relationships in industrial markets, in addition to dominance or leadership by one of the involved firms – usually the buyer, can be characterized by a symmetrical distribution of resources and capabilities (Laage-Hellman, 1997).

    - Inter-firm exchange processes depend, first of all, on the resources and activities of each party. This distribution of resources and capabilities forms an important source for the possible (a)symmetry between the actors interacting in the b2b relationship. These resources can be controlled in a direct way by actors (either by owning or by having the right to use them) or in an indirect way (by having close relationships with other actors who possess the formal control).

    - The objectives and strategies pursued by the actors taking part in the exchange process can vary on a scale from 'mutuality' to 'inequality'. That is, between a strong complementarity (shared objectives and strategies), to an exploitation by one of the interacting actors of the other's resources and capabilities.

    - Firms are moved by the desire to improve their network position (Laage-Hellman, 1997). Either by enhancing their centrality in a network to which they already belong or by entering a network to which they do not belong.

    - It is stressed that network positions are the outcome of an accumulation of interactions over time, and that the network position is therefore prone to evolutions.

    - The outcome of an exchange process in a specific interaction depends upon the specific constellation of relationships actors entertain. Thus, the exchange that takes place in a specific interaction, conditions and is conditioned by other relationships in which the interaction-specific actors are involved.

    - In this way, actors' embeddedness in relationships may also co-determine, for example, its investment, internationalization and settlement choices (Johanson and Mattsson, 1987; Forsgren, 1989).

- Therefore, the linkages or the position that each of the interacting actors holds with respect to their surrounding relationships and networks can be seen as relevant for each specific interaction.

- With respect to mind the evolutionary character of inter-organizational networks:

  - The N&I approach takes the past experiences with respect to specific actors, exchanges and environments into account. This makes it possible to explain exchange processes and actor relationships from a dynamic and longitudinal perspective.
  - Moreover, the N&I approach takes long-lasting b2b relationships and alliances seriously. As a consequence, more or less solid business networks can exist. In this respect, the N&I approach views continuity in relationships both as an indicator and as a prerequisite for symmetry between and mutual respect within inter-firm relations. It is also the result of mutual adaptations of the actors involved along the way. The time perspective on relationships makes this kind of reasoning further possible.
  - The N&I approach acknowledges that certain relationships – even those that are vital to the parties involved – may be disrupted, that their content may be changed or that entire relationships may be traded in for others over time. In concrete terms, Gadde and Mattsson (1987) found – through analyses of individual dyadic relationships and of *'one buyer'* – *'several suppliers' relations* – that apparently stable relationships are subject to clear changes in the long run. Also Hertz (1992) and Lundgren (1993) report on radical changes in industrial networks. Nevertheless, experience suggests that change is mainly incremental with radical change being rare (Easton *et al.*, 1997, p. 275). Consequently, the N&I approach argues that most b2b relationships tend to show a striking continuity. In addition, it posits that drastic changes in a network structure are counteracted by the durability and stability of many of the network's business relationships (Hägg and Johanson, 1982). Consequently, business networks are relatively stable (Johanson and Mattsson, 1987; Forsgren *et al.*, 1995; Håkansson and Shehota, 1995).
  - The time perspective used in the N&I approach enables it to view b2b relationships from a dynamic perspective. One can argue, therefore, that adaptations in inter-firm relationships can take place over time (Håkansson, 1987; Johanson and Mattsson, 1991).[16]

A comparison of static and dynamic approach to b2b relationships and business networks on a selection of essential parameters is given in Table 2.1.

Table 2.1 Comparison of static and dynamic approach to b2b relationships and business networks on a selection of essential parameters

	Static approach		Dynamic approach
	Transaction perspectives	Resource-based perspectives	Network and Interaction approach
Network actors as (in)dependent units	Independent units	Interdependent	Interdependent
Power distribution	Relatively asymmetrical	Relatively symmetrical	Relatively symmetrical
Supposed longevity of network arrangements	Temporary due to the fact that risks of opportunism, guile and deceit induce shifts towards superior governance arrangement	From temporary to long-term	Long-term
Motivation for network governance	Market failure	Inter-firm complementarities	Inter-firm complementarities
Time perspective	Focus on arrangements around individual transactions (choices at specific moments in time)	Focus on arrangements around individual ventures (choices at specific moments in time)	Focus on sequences, coherencies and backward and forward linkages between subsequent exchanges and collaboration (process-oriented)
Continuity of partners	Unspecified	Continuity due to trust and interdependence	Continuity due to trust and interdependence, in case superior partners present themselves; bonding enables b2b partners to achieve new performance standards in order to go on together
Aggregated level/unit of analysis	Boundaries of individual firm	Boundaries of individual firm	Pair or network of firms or pair or network of relationships
Representative scholars and publications	Williamson, 1975, 1985, 1991; Williamson and Ouchi, 1981; Powell, 1990; Powel and Smith-Doerr, 1994	Wernerfelt, 1984; Barney, 1991; Mahoney and Pandian, 1992; Amit and Shoemaker, 1993; Dyer and Singh, 1998	Håkansson, 1982, 1987, 1989; Johanson and Mattsson, 1987, 1991; Håkansson and Johanson, 1988; Håkansson and Shehota, 1995; Laage-Hellman, 1997

Source: Author's elaboration.

2.4 Apparent shortcomings of the network and interaction approach

Concerning the network theory premise that advocates the evolutionary character of networks, the N&I approach is indeed able to reason that adaptations in inter-firm relationships can take place over time. However, the N&I approach emphasizes above all, adaptations of already initiated and existing relationships within networks. Adaptations of networks through the inclusion of new relationships or the substitution of current relationships by others, is emphasized to a far lesser degree. It is argued that the appearance of high-performance actors as potential substitutes for incumbent network partners principally serve as a benchmark to upgrade the performance of the current partners.

Håkansson (1987), Johanson and Mattsson (1987, 1991), Mattsson and Hultén (1994), Håkansson and Henders (1995) and Håkansson and Shehota (1995) argue that there is room for adaptations within relationships and that actors are able to cope with changes in their relative network positions. As such, they acknowledge that networks are both structure and process and that networks can be changed within certain limits.

Moreover, they argue that from time to time new relationships are formed. At the same time, they emphasize that most exchanges take place within earlier existing relationships and that it is these existing relationships that change over time.

As a consequence of the fact that the N&I approach stresses a relatively high continuity and stability of relationships, one deducts that '[although] actors in network models are not seen as atoms locked in a crystalline grid, their every action [is] determined by their structural position' (adapted from Nohria, 1992, p. 7). As such, it seems that the N&I approach views *actors in networks to a large extent as a fixed group of pieces on a chess board that can change their positions and mutual strategies, but where few or no new chess pieces enter the game.* Therefore, the N&I approach considers above all the evolutionary character of existing relationships. It is less concerned with an open system perspective on relationships in which actors enter and exit.

It appears, therefore, that, for example, competitive processes between rival buyers and suppliers are underestimated (Montgomery, 1995). Moreover, it also appears that voice, trust and commitment are viewed as a panacea for longevity.

Instead of following this position, we argue that business network and b2b relationship analysis should not depart from the somewhat naïve assumption that companies, buyers and suppliers, operate in a sort of competitive vacuum. That is, an environment in which competitors are presumed to be passive players that have no desire to occupy the network position currently under control of others. Moreover, we argue that the practice of benchmarking does not only serve for further bonding of current b2b relationships or voice (Hirschman, 1970; Helper, 1987), but can also lead companies to switch partners.

Halinen *et al.* (1999) have also observed the former. They argue that network research is principally concerned with incremental changes within existing relationships. Instead, little attention is paid to changes of relationships, including the substitution of relationships or partners. Easton *et al.* (1997) express similar objections.

Also from literature on embeddedness it can be reasoned that firms may consciously choose to substitute business partners. From Grabher's (1993, p. 24) and Uzzi's (1997) observation that firms risk 'lock in' if they become too embedded in their alliances with other firms, it follows that entrepreneurial instincts make firms consider partner substitutions in order to regulate 'lock in' effects or path dependences on long-standing relations.

Moreover, organizational learning theories (Levitt and March, 1988) lead us to think that whilst companies gather experience and knowledge regarding inter-firm collaborations, they may become less 'aversive' to enter into wholly new relationships. Thus, it can be argued that the willingness of firms to change b2b or network partners from time to time is enhanced by the accumulation of b2b experience.

This kind of reasoning can also be derived from Carlson (1966) and Johanson and Vahlne (1990) who argue that learning how to enter unknown markets enhances the willingness of companies to proceed on other markets. Similarly, b2b experiences help firms to learn how to obtain knowledge on unknown partners and how to manage relationships with them. In addition to Nooteboom's (2002) observation that learning is an important goal of inter-firm collaboration, we stress that through working together, firms also learn how to relate and manage inter-firm relationships. Consequently, it helps firms to cope with starting new inter-firm relationships. This also reduces fear of establishing new or replacing old relationships.

It can of course be argued that the former can implicitly be derived from the N&I approach's interpretation of 'environment'; which can include competitors that may aim at increasing their control of and within the network, and thus try to get access to and position themselves inside a network if they are currently outside it. Nevertheless, it is important that this issue is made more explicit. Moreover, with 'environment' the N&I approach refers to the environment of a certain multi-party exchange relationship. Whereas the main argument forwarded here is that a relationship itself may be substituted or disappear over time if a different set of two or more parties succeeds in improving or imitating the activity links or resource combinations and ties provided by the current set of two or more parties.

To counter the lack of attention to the dynamics of competition and other change factors, we propose the incorporation of and a stronger emphasis on an open system perspective and of competition dynamics than the N&I approach does. This should enhance the explanation of business network formation and evolution processes.

A second shortcoming, or rather, ambiguity, in the N&I approach is the view on power symmetry or asymmetry and authority issues between organizations involved in an exchange relationship. On the one hand, Johanson and Mattsson (1991) argue that there tends to be a certain asymmetry between firms, for example with one firm being more dependent on the other than vice versa. Grabher (1993, p. 11) forwards a similar suggestion: 'mutuality...must not be confused with symmetry'. Similarly, Morris and Imrie (1992) argue that even co-operative b2b relationships are frequently based on considerable power differences. On the other hand, Johanson and Mattsson (1987) and Håkansson and Shehota (1995) argue that relationships between firms are characterized by symmetry with respect to the relevant production factors due to the interdependence involved between firms. As a matter of fact, according to the symmetry lecture, buyers can even be considered to be indirectly dependent on suppliers' other clients (if a supplier is not selling exclusively to a specific buyer), as the strategies of suppliers will also depend on their multiple client relationships. The latter is consistent with the proposed open system perspective on b2b relationships that argues that these relationships do not operate in a vacuum.

In this research project, we argue that the former ambiguity and seeming contradiction can be reconciled through the assumption of mutual adaptation, whereby decisions and moves made by one of the firms involved in a network should have an impact on the decisions and moves of the other firms belonging to the network under consideration. Within this process the most obvious sequence would be that mutual adaptation processes are initiated through considerations and actions on behalf of the principal buyer of a given network. For, ultimately, the principal buyer forms the gatekeeper to the final market and as such arranges, manages and sets out the basic principles of organization and functioning of a network. Take note that, whereas this points at asymmetry in terms of the action–reaction sequence, this need not be reflected in the inter-firm division of production factors or resources and their respective importance for the relationship or network itself. As such, it provides an elegant and workable solution for the analysis of network dynamics.

2.5   Conclusions

From the discussion of the static and dynamic approach to b2b relationships and business networks, the following lessons are retained:

1   Inter-firm networks are usually conceived through a common interest to reap mutual complementarities between firms. They tend to be the result of b2b relationships that have been built up and have become stabilized over a longer period.

2   During such periods, mutual inter-firm adaptation processes and strategies lead to adjustments of the fundamental structure of the network.

3   Contrary to consumer market situations, adaptation processes and strategy formations take place in an interdependent and interactive way among buyers and suppliers. The most obvious sequence in this process is that mutual adaptation processes are initiated through considerations

and actions on behalf of the principal buyer of a given network upon which the suppliers (inter)act.

4   While network and inter-firm patterns are to a large extent fairly stable and recurring, the structure of networks can certainly undergo changes as a consequence of specific events.

5   Changes in business networks can be interpreted as a desire on the part of firms to improve their network position.

2.6   Internationalization of b2b relationships and business networks

2.6.1   Introduction

After discussing the N&I approach to b2b relationships and business networks, in the following paragraphs we review conceptual applications or '*extensions*' of the dynamic approach to b2b relationships, that is, regarding the internationalization of business and or international business networks.

2.6.2   Relevant scientific frameworks with respect to the internationalization of b2b relationships and business networks

For the explanation of internationalization patterns, various concepts have been developed.

The phenomenon of internationalization of business life has been studied from various angles. Roughly speaking, a distinction can be drawn between theories of international trade and theories of international business (IB).

Among the international trade theories notably the theories developed by Smith (1776), Ricardo (1817), J.S. Mill (1848), Hecksher (1919), Ohlin (1933) and Samuelson (1948) should be mentioned. The central issue in these theories is to determine how comparative and country-specific advantages can explain international trade patterns.

IB theories aim also at explaining internationalization choices and trajectories of firms. IB theories can be divided into *static* theories and *dynamic* theories (Melin, 1992). Static theories aim at comparing different (governance) choices with respect to a firm's internationalization options at every stage in the process and at determining the best choice at every 'multiple option point'. Dynamic theories are more focused on the explanation of the dynamics involved in a firm's or product's internationalization process as a whole. While taking into account possible backward and forward implications of internationalization choices, they attempt to explain and predict a firm's behaviour and choices in an international setting over time.

Among the static IB explanations we find the structural market imperfections theory (Hymer, 1960 – later published in 1976; Kindleberger, 1969;

Caves, 1971), the internalization theory (Buckley and Casson, 1976; Rugman, 1981), and Dunning's eclectic *OLI* paradigm (1979, 1981, 1988).[17,18]

The static approaches provide explanations for the existence of MNEs and for their structural form, but not for the process dimensions, that is, the formation and continuance of firms' internationalization trajectories (Toyne, 1989; Melin, 1992).

The dynamic IB approaches, on the other hand, view internationalization not as the product or outcome of separate choices at different points in time. Instead, they look at it as a sequential process with interdependence between the subsequent stages, whereby future decisions are embedded in choices and processes of the past.

Prominent examples of the dynamic IB approaches are the international product life cycle model (Vernon, 1966), the Uppsala internationalization process model in its 'starting' form (Johanson and Wiedersheim-Paul, 1975; Johanson and Vahlne, 1977, 1990; Luostarinen, 1979; Welch and Luostarinen, 1988; Luostarinen and Welch, 1990), the Network view on the Internationalization Process Model (Forsgren, 1989; Forsgren and Johanson, 1992; Andersson and Forsgren, 2000) and the Flagship/Five Partners Model (Rugman, 1999; Rugman and D'Cruz 2000; Rugman and Verbeke, 2003).

The focus of this study is on the process dimension of inter-firm relationships and b2b interactions in view of the formation and evolution of business networks. Therefore, we will focus on conceptual frameworks explaining internationalization processes through inter-firm relationships dynamics over time. Hence, static approaches are excluded as they merely explain the existence of MNEs from a firm-level perspective whereas they are less concerned with internationalization processes as such, let alone from an inter-firm network perspective.

Vernon's international product life cycle theory is left aside as well, as it focuses on and analyses the level of product (line)s and countries (perhaps as a heritage of international trade theories) rather than at the level of firms (Melin, 1992). As a consequence, this results in an underexposure of the organizational structure of firms (Rugman and D'Cruz, 2000). On top of that, Vernon's theory does not explicitly refer to inter-firm dynamics within internationalization processes.

Finally, the value of the international product life cycle theory has proved to be limited for internationalization processes surrounding goods with rapid innovations, for goods where cost minimization is not the most important issue, for goods with high transport costs (like cars and certain automotive components) and for goods with high brand loyalty. Its validity in explaining internationalization processes has also proved to be limited, due to the fact that nowadays MNEs already consider foreign direct investment at a very early stage (McKiernan, 1992; Melin, 1992).

Consequently, we will build upon the insights provided by the (Network view on the) Internationalization Process Model (Johanson and Wiedersheim-Paul, 1975; Johanson and Vahlne, 1977, 1990;

Luostarinen, 1979; Welch and Luostarinen, 1988; Forsgren, 1989, 1995; Luostarinen and Welch, 1990; Forsgren and Johanson, 1992; Andersson and Forsgren, 2000) and the Flagship/Five Partners Model (Rugman, 1999; Rugman and D'Cruz, 2000, Rugman and Verbeke, 2003).

Subsequently, a comparative analysis of the two selected conceptual frameworks will serve to establish their (joint) usefulness in explaining the formation and evolution of international business networks.

2.7   Selected dynamic approaches to international business

2.7.1   *Network view on the internationalization process model*

Several scholars have contributed to the development of the internationalization process model (IPM) (e.g. Johanson and Wiedersheim-Paul, 1975; Johanson and Vahlne, 1977, 1990; Luostarinen, 1979; Welch and Luostarinen, 1988; Luostarinen and Welch, 1990). Much of the empirical research conducted in the tradition of this model came from work on industrial marketing and b2b relationships in an international context (Håkansson, 1982, Mattson, 1986, Cunningham and Culligan, 1988; Easton and Lundgren, 1992).

According to the IPM, firms go through a sequential process of international operations. This process is based on a gradual acquisition, integration and use of knowledge about foreign markets and operations, and on a successively increasing commitment on behalf of firms to foreign markets (Johanson and Vahlne, 1977).

A basic assumption of the IPM is that a lack of knowledge with regard to foreign markets forms a major obstacle to foreign market entry and to international operations.

In the same line of thought, the IPM argues that decisions concerning market commitment and foreign direct investment (FDI) depend on two factors: on the one hand, unfamiliarity with and knowledge of foreign markets, and, on the other hand, the perceived psychological distance to foreign markets.

The IPM argues that the required knowledge to even out these barriers can be acquired (Johanson and Vahlne, 1977). By incorporating organizational experience and learning with respect to internationalization through international operations, it is reasoned that the willingness of firms to continue internationalizing is enhanced (Carlson, 1966; Johanson and Vahlne, 1990; Forsgren, 2000). Notably, as it helps firms to learn how to obtain the required knowledge with regard to unfamiliar markets and how to use it. Similarly, it helps firms overcome or learn to cope with the psychological distance to such markets in terms of, for example, language, business culture and practices, and legislation. As such, the IPM is firmly rooted in the behavioural theory of the firm (Cyert and March, 1963) and in organizational learning theories (Levitt and March, 1988). 'Once the firm has passed the cultural barriers and had its first experience of foreign operations, it is generally willing to conquer one market after another' (Carlson, 1966, p. 15).

Based on risk aversion and organizational learning logics, the IPM consequently assumes that firms start their internationalization on markets with the lowest perceived uncertainty (notably neighbouring countries) and first via export and later via local production in a foreign market (Melin, 1992).

The 'groundwork' of the IPM has received certain critics over time. For example, of being too deterministic in presupposing firm-related IB sequence patterns, whereby the internationalization of firms is not seen as the outcome of a deliberately planned and executed strategy. As a consequence, it is said to play down the possibilities for managers and firms to make voluntary choices as regards strategic management and foreign market entry-mode (Melin, 1992). The inability on the part of the IPM to explain acquisitions as an early foreign entry mode, rather than FDI or export, is claimed to be another shortcoming (Forsgren, 1989, p. 3). Moreover, it has been argued that the significance of the IPM is limited to the early stages of internationalization. Additionally, critics claim that the explanatory value of the psychological distance parameter tends to decrease while the world is becoming more homogeneous and as trade barriers disappear. Finally, it does not take into account the possibility that over time the foreign-based operations of companies may become '... so extensive and so dominant that the idea of centre and periphery must be modified' (Forsgren, 1989, p. 2).

These criticisms led to the elaboration of a series of theoretical elements regarding the internationalization of firms by scholars that can be placed in a tradition of a 'network view on the IPM', such as Forsgren (1989) and Johanson and Mattsson (1988).

Forsgren's (1989) contributions in this respect can be centred around two points:

1   IB decisions are embedded in intra-firm relationships and power balances,
2   IB decisions are embedded in inter-firm relationships and power balances.

These two points to a large extent make sure that there is compatibility between the network view on internationalization and the premises of network theory we subscribed to in Section 2.2.1.

The first point has to do especially with the 'individual organizations are networks' premise. The second point concerns the following premises: 'the environment(s) of individual organizations are networks', 'an organization's network position is important' and 'mind the evolutionary character of inter-organizational networks'.

We will now address these points in greater detail.

Ad 1. Several scholars (e.g. Forsgren, 1989; Ghoshal and Nohria, 1989; Ghoshal and Bartlett, 1990, 1993; Forsgren and Johanson, 1992; Andersson, 1997; Andersson and Forsgren, 2000) argue that an MNE can be seen as a network in itself. As a consequence, IB and especially FDI may be the

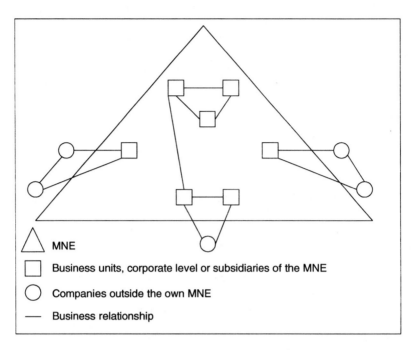

Figure 2.1 Intra- and inter-firm relationships of MNE subsidiaries.

Source: Author's elaboration based on Forsgren, 1989.

outcome of headquarters–subsidiary dynamics. Similarly, b2b relationships can be sustained at various levels of an MNE. Thus, subsidiaries are engaged in business relationships with other units both within and outside the MNE (Holm *et al.*, 1995, p. 102). This is also the case for units within individual organizations, such as subsidiaries: 'A specific feature of business relationships in an international context … is that relationships exist at different levels' (Hadjikhani and Håkansson, 1996, p. 443). Figure 2.1 illustrates this in a powerful way.

In relation to the intra-firm relationships and power balances, Forsgren (1989) and Andersson and Forsgren (2000) point at: (1) the role a subsidiary plays within its mother MNE over time; (2) the value of a subsidiary's capabilities and the external network principally tied to a subsidiary for the whole MNE; (3) the experiences a subsidiary builds up over time in negotiating mandates and budgets and (4) the subsidiary's emancipation over time. They argue that these factors serve as additional driving forces behind repeated investments in foreign markets in which a firm is active and where a firm-specific advantage (FSA) or inter-firm relationships are not needed (anymore) to overcome initial market fears.

A further, and related, characteristic of the network view on the IPM is that it does not adopt an (implicit) centre–periphery perspective on organizations (Forsgren, 1989, p. 2, 58; Andersson and Forsgren, 2000). In many companies it will still be the headquarters that has an exclusive say about the (inter)national activities and resources of foreign subsidiaries. Nonetheless, according to the network view on the IPM, current MNE structures are more multiform than that and they may even vary within the same MNE from one headquarters–subsidiary relationship to another (Forsgren, 1989; Forsgren and Johanson, 1992; Andersson and Forsgren, 2000).

The extent to which subsidiaries can obtain company-wide roles and can compete for strategic responsibilities has to do with the points (1) to (4) mentioned after Figure 2.1 and with the level of integration of the geographical markets where the various parts of an MNE's business apparatus are located. Integration of these markets enhances both the needs and the possibilities for MNEs to build on the specific strengths of their subsidiaries and for strong subsidiaries to claim leading roles within the company.

Integration of markets also enhances the need for MNEs to rationalize their aggregated business apparatus and to co-ordinate business functions across national subsidiaries. This leads to a variety of organizational solutions, such as matrix structures (Stopford and Wells, 1972; Bartlett, 1981) or MNE structures that have been termed 'heterarchic' (Hedlund, 1986), 'polycentric' (Perlmutter, 1965) or 'decentralized federations' (Bartlett and Ghoshal, 1986, 1989). In such structures, the distinction between core and periphery becomes less clear (Sölvell and Zander, 1995, p. 3).

The former can translate into situations whereby decisions on IB are no longer made exclusively at the top, but are (also) prepared by foreign subsidiaries (Forsgren, 1989; Forsgren and Johanson, 1992; Forsgren *et al.* 1992; Andersson and Forsgren, 2000). As a result, the added value of subsidiaries within MNE structures is acknowledged and ways to foster their contributions are provided. Similarly, it is recognized that subsidiaries take initiatives and build competences and power within the organization (Forsgren and Holm, 1993). In this regard, Andersson and Pahlberg (1997, p. 320) add that strategic behaviour inside an MNE can be seen as a consequence of the '... struggle between actors promoting their own interests at different levels and with different functional roles', that is, subsidiaries will try to obtain company-wide strategic roles (Forsgren, 1989, pp. 59, 67; Holm, 1994), reflecting the desire to improve their intra-MNE network position.

Ad 2. The network view on the IPM does not view internationalization processes as the exclusive domain of a single company's headquarters. It stresses that it is important '... to complement the hierarchical [intra-firm] view of the subsidiary by identifying the industrial [inter-firm] network to which every subsidiary or unit belongs' (Forsgren, 1989, p. 71). Therefore, as firms are inter-related with other organizations (suppliers, customers, etc.), the behaviour of individual organizations regarding international business is related to the behaviour and strategic significance of other organizations to which they are related (Forsgren, 1989, p. 69).

The inter-organizational perspective, in which internationalization is seen as a way to manage strategic interdependences within the business network to which a company belongs, works two ways. To begin with, it explains the behaviour of a focal buyer firm. Its subsidiaries may form the pivots of branch location–own networks that can be important to the focal buyer firm as a whole, and therefore the focal buyer firm may decide to dedicate resources to its foreign subsidiaries. Second, it is able to explain the location behaviour of partners of focal organizations in business networks. It is argued that such partners may go abroad to follow an organization that functions as a focal buyer or at the instigation of a focal organization to which they are (asset-related or dependent in another way).

Thus, parallell to the N&I approach's argument that b2b relationships are often long-standing ones, internationalization processes may be embedded in familiar relationships as well. Such relationships seriously lower the barrier to the foreign markets a firm wants to enter. As such, the desire to capitalize on long-standing b2b relationships not only explains the willingness of firms to go abroad (Johanson and Vahlne, 1977, 1990; Forsgren, 1989; McKiernan, 1992). Additionally, it also implies that a firm can gain easy access to the knowledge a business partner may have with respect to a foreign market (Levitt and March, 1988; Lane and Lubatkin, 1998). Consequently, the bond with a certain firm that internationalizes, forms a *vehicle* for other firms to internationalize as well.

As such, the network view on the IPM distances itself from the assumption that organizations invest abroad to build upon and exploit an FSA. Instead, it argues that the embeddedness of firms in specific b2b relationships in one location may induce firms to follow their relationships abroad. Consequently, what is important for the internationalization choices of individual firms is the inter-firm relationships they maintain.

Moreover, in line with the N&I approach, the network view on the IPM argues that FSAs are highly conditioned by the connections of their 'owners'. Also in line with the N&I approach to b2b relationships, the network view on the IPM presupposes that long-standing b2b relationships form the fundament for subsequent and interdependent internationalization processes. Consequently, the network view on the IPM postulates that a similar degree of power symmetry between parties can exist, as is assumed in the N&I approach to b2b relationships (Forsgren, 1989, pp. 75–78).

The network view on the IPM also explains international activities of companies by assessing the impacts of internationalization in terms of competitive advantage or network position (Forsgren, 1989, p. 36; McKiernan, 1992, p. 108). That is, the position or advantage companies will obtain vis-à-vis or within a certain network through its internationalization operations. The strategic intent is to influence (change or preserve) their position(s) in network(s) (Turnbull and Valla, 1986; Forsgren, 1989, p. 36; Jüttner and Schlange, 1996, p. 482). If an organization is already involved in a foreign or cross-border network, its (additional) FDI will be aimed at defending or developing its position. If it is not yet involved in such a network, its FDI will be aimed at obtaining a position in it. Similarly, if a firm is not pulled into an internationalization venture due to existing b2b relations, its internationalization steps can be interpreted as a strategic action to establish relationships with firms in other national networks (Johanson and Mattsson, 1988, 1997).

This way, although emphasis is placed on long-standing relationships and mutual adaptations, the network view on the IPM provides starting points to reason possible member changes in international business networks.

Also sudden acquisitions on foreign markets as the chosen foreign entry mode, rather than exports or FDI, can be explained this way (Forsgren, 1989, pp. 36–38; McKiernan, 1992, pp. 108–109). If a targeted b2b relationship demands a swift presence of a firm on a certain market, acquisition is the 'bridging' strategy to get there (Pfeffer and Salancik, 1978; Forsgren, 1989, pp. 37, 115). Of course, acquisitions may also serve to penetrate foreign markets and gain new customers (Johanson and Mattsson, 1988), or to horizontally acquire rival companies' FSAs (Johanson and Mattsson, 1988; McKiernan, 1992).

2.7.2 Flagship/Five Partners Model

Rugman and D'Cruz' (2000) Flagship/Five Partners Model (F/5P model) can be seen as an alternative model to the internationalization of business from a network perspective. It is built on elements similar to those that can be found in the N&I approach to inter-firm relationships and in the network view on internationalization processes of firms. In addition, it contains elements from more static approaches on inter-firm relationships and internationalization, notably RBV, TCE, internalization theories and Dunning's eclectic *OLI* paradigm.[19]

The F/5P model is based on the assumption that sustainable international competitiveness can best be achieved through co-operative relationships in a business network structure. It argues that MNEs are depending less on internalization as the sole means to leverage their FSAs and to gain competitive advantage (Rugman and D'Cruz, 2000, p. 57; Rugman and Verbeke, 2003). Instead of depending on internalization, the F/5P model posits that a flagship firm focuses on sharing knowledge among partners in order to facilitate inter-organizational learning. The F/5P model thus reduces the importance of individual FSAs and views them from a network perspective. Long-term collaboration is therefore seen as a promising mode of internationalization.

According to the F/5P model networks with which international activities and investments are developed on a Triad region basis, have an international character and are not geographically bound. They are made up of inter-industry relationships, include partnerships across national borders, and aim to serve an ongoing strategic purpose. As such they are distinct from industrial districts (e.g. Becattini, 1979; Harrison, 1992), and from strategic clusters as in Porter (1990) and Krugman (1991). In the latter concepts, the emphasis is on one nation or on locality-based networks and clusters, on intra-industry links, and on path-dependent evolutions of networks and clusters through historical and local peculiarities. Instead, Rugman and D'Cruz (2000) draw a comparison with Lorenzoni and Baden-Fuller's strategic network framework (1993 – later published in 1995). Lorenzoni and Baden-Fuller speak of a central firm or a strategic centre instead of a flagship firm, and they also stress asymmetry between the central firm and the partners.

The term 'flagship firm' refers to an MNE operating at the core of an extensive business network or a cluster. Usually the flagship has long-term relational contracts with a set of five partners. The additional partners themselves are not conceived as networks. They are conceived as homogeneous actors, abstracting from, for instance, intra-Triad region headquarters–subsidiary and centre–periphery questions. This means that network and partner dynamics are (conceived as) the outcome of top management strategies and decisions (see for example, Rugman and D'Cruz, 2000, p. 9).

The model distinguishes five partners of which the flagship firm (usually a leading MNE in its field) is the first. The other partners are: key suppliers, key customers, competitors, and the non-business infrastructure. In addition to the key suppliers and key customers there are also non-key suppliers and non-key customers that are treated at arm's length. The status of a supplier and its incorporation into the F/5P network depends on the vitality of the input it delivers for the competitiveness of the network. From Rugman (1999) and Rugman and D'Cruz (2000) it can be understood that the difference between key and non-key suppliers in an automotive industry setting, is the difference between first tier and lower tier suppliers (see for example, Rugman and D'Cruz, 2000, pp. 36–37, 86, 94 and notably pp. 166–170). They argue that the first tier suppliers provide a key input to the network whereas the other suppliers do not. Among those first tier suppliers, all are treated in the same way. As a result, a paint manufacturer (Rugman and D'Cruz, 2000, p. 94) or a supplier of parts, seals and devices (Rugman and D'Cruz, 2000, p. 169) are also considered key suppliers to a car constructor.

The distinction between key and non-key status is roughly similar to the network centrality concept suggested by the N&I approach and the network view on internationalization. The F/5P model argues that the internationalization behaviour of key suppliers can be explained through their asymmetrical dependence on the flagship firm's strategy and their exclusive dedication to a certain flagship from a single industry perspective (Rugman and D'Cruz, 2000; Rugman and Verbeke, 2003). The implication of this position is that the focal flagship MNEs in an international business network are able to provide the Triad-based strategic perspective for the partners and that each true partner does not need a separate international strategy except to be a 'key' partner of the flagship MNE. At the same time, the view is that there is less coherence between the behaviour of non-key suppliers and that of a flagship, precisely because they occupy a less important network position.

In the F/5P model, the strategic network partners are supposed to share a common global strategy and purpose, and the flagship has the resources and perspective to lead the network and strategically manage its activities. The partners yield the strategic leadership to the flagship because it is the flagship's product and global strategies that makes the partners join the network. The partners' acceptance of the strategic leadership and autonomy of the focal MNE in the network is, however, selectively complemented by strategic leadership and responsibilities on behalf of the partners themselves. Nonetheless, key suppliers are expected to give near or total exclusivity to the flagship firm i.e. with regard to internationalization issues (Rugman and D'Cruz, 2000, pp. 2, 9, 31, 41, 65, 84–86, 96).

As such, the model presupposes an asymmetry of power between the flagship and the other partners within a specific network setting. The following statement emphasizes this: 'The relationship is asymmetric in that the four other network partners have no reciprocal influence over the flagship's strategy' (Rugman and D'Cruz, 2000, p. 9 and p. 41–bullet 1).

Nevertheless, on the whole the F/5P model is also somewhat ambiguous or contradictory on the issue of inter-firm dependence/asymmetry, as it also hints at interdependence. For instance, Rugman (1999, p. 11) argues that '(t)he key supplier relationship is built on both performance and trust. The key suppliers and flagship MNEs are mutually dependent and exhibit more trust in their long-term managerial relationships than would be normal between suppliers and MNEs'. Similarly, Rugman and D'Cruz (2000, p. 37) claim that '(t)he role of key suppliers in the crafting of strategy for the network is critical, and requires a two-way process'.

Implicitly, this indicates that the key suppliers, due to their excellence in certain fields, dispose of certain countervailing powers and voice and exit options, including options to shift to other networks. In this respect, Rugman and D'Cruz (2000, p. 56) state that '... partners may compete in business systems not related to that of the business network, [and therefore] it should be emphasized that the flagship firm's asymmetric strategic control extends only to those aspects of its partners' business systems committed to the network'.

This emphasis on partners' excellences, on partners' relationships outside the F/5P network and on inter-industry relations, means that it may be problematic to argue that asymmetry and exclusive dedication generally govern key b2b relationships within a F/5P model.

The F/5P model stresses the longevity of the collaborative relationships. It also argues that the parties involved operate under the assumption that they will continue collaborating indefinitely (Rugman and D'Cruz, 2000, p. 86). As a result, joint internationalization moves and co-location activities are developed. For instance, through setting up dedicated and site-specific assets.

Like the bonding thesis in the N&I approach, the F/5P model argues that through collaborative relationships and long-term associations, trust is developed among the members. Additionally, this explains why a hybrid governance arrangement can continue to last without evolving over time into a market relationship or hierarchy.

2.8   Comparison of selected approaches on internationalization of b2b relationships and business networks

Conceptually speaking, the network view on the IPM and the F/5P model have a lot in common. Nevertheless, they also display several remarkable differences in viewpoints on specific issues. Their discussion will be the subject of the present paragraph. Where different viewpoints are hard to reconcile or exclude one another, we will argue our own position.

Networks: vehicle towards internationalization or targeted institutional arrangement when planning IB? The network view on the IPM (e.g. Forsgren, 1989) argues that inter-firm collaboration forms a *vehicle* for and can lead to mutual adaptations and joint activities surrounding internationalization ('internationalizing existing collaboration patterns'). Instead, Rugman and D'Cruz (2000), stress that when internationalization is considered, networks rather than markets or hierarchies are a promising governance structure. This indicates that networks are more a means to internationalization in the network view on the IPM, whereas they are seen as an institutional option for the sake of (international) competitiveness in the F/5P model.

Focus on different stages in life cycle of international business networks: The F/5P model argues that networks constructed around partners from different nations can mark the start of indefinite operations. The network view on the IPM suggests that it is typical for internationalized business networks to grow out of long-standing national b2b relationships that in time can get a more pronounced multinational character, that is, with the possibility of including foreign partners into the network. The former suggests that both models may focus on different stages of the life cycle of international business networks. The network view on the IPM would then focus on pre-F/5P business networks.

Furthermore, whereas the groundwork of the F/5P model is based on networks *ipso facto* formed around partners from various countries, the network view on the IPM is more locked into a nationalities or country '*bias*'. The emphasis of the latter framework appears to be on the way in which firms, jointly or separately, organize internationalization actions into foreign markets from a single home base, or on the way in which firms, jointly or separately, intend to obtain positions in networks in other nations.

Relevant (business) context for strategy formation in international business networks: In the F/5P model, internationalization is seen as the outcome of deliberately planned and executed strategic intents on the level of the network or – even more limited – by the flagship firm. That way, the model stresses the possibilities for managers and firms to make voluntary choices regarding strategic management and modes to enter foreign markets. The network view on the IPM agrees on the latter, but with respect to strategic planning it emphasizes that strategic choices will be guided by the embeddedness of b2b relationships and network positions of partners in both the network under consideration and the broader business environment of the partners. That is, also in business systems that are *not* related to that of the business network under consideration in the eyes of the F/5P model. In fact, in the network view on the IPM, 'not related' does not exist at all or at least covers a lot less than in the F/5P model. The network view on the IPM emphasizes the interrelatedness of specific b2b relationships to a very broad business context through its thesis of embeddedness.

Power (a)symmetry and strategic (in)dependence in b2b relationships in international business networks: Whereas the network view on the IPM suggests interdependence and joint planning, the F/5P model argues that asymmetry and supplier dependence (including 'exclusivity' and 'indefinite' dedication) are the dominant elements in the b2b relationships of a business network.

The network view on the IPM (like the N&I approach) argues – as it were from a cybernetic or open system viewpoint – that asymmetry and sheer exclusivity are only thinkable if a specific b2b relationship would exist in a vacuum. But as b2b relationships are embedded in overarching structures and environments, and as they are linked to other b2b relationships, these structures and environments condition the b2b relationships and vice versa. Consequently, *'no business is an island'* (cf. Håkansson and Shehota, 1989). Additionally, the network view on the IPM stresses the mutual interdependence of resources between buyers and suppliers, which keeps asymmetries in check.

The F/5P model, instead, bases its dependence argument on a resource-based viewpoint, arguing that the flagship is superior in terms of means and leading capabilities. Therefore, suppliers are conditioned by asymmetrical dependencies on flagship firms. Subsequently, the F/5P model dedicates relatively little attention to other, for example, (inter-firm) relationships and issues in organizations' environments that may co-determine the relationships between the flagship and its partners.

Nevertheless, due to its acknowledgement of the activities of partners in other business systems and their own excellences, claims concerning exclusivity, asymmetry and indefiniteness seem somewhat hard to sustain.

Moreover, the (unconditional) strategic asymmetry thesis is challenged by the existence of industry-wide suppliers (O hUallachain and Wasserman, 1999) and practices like reverse, simultaneous and black box engineering (Liebermann and Montgomery, 1988). These phenomena indicate that certain suppliers can have a strategic influence on a flagship firm. If on top of this, such suppliers are also active in other sectors (Hodges and Van Tulder, 1994), their dependence on the flagship firm of a certain business network may be questioned even more. Furthermore, in such situations it is hard to sustain that a flagship firm can determine the activities of such key suppliers and that a flagship firm is the exclusive user of the services of such key suppliers.

Since it is possible that several firms of the F/5P networks operate multiple divisions, each playing different roles in complex business networks, a straight-forward assumption of exclusivity and even asymmetry seems to lose its meaning. In any complex network there are likely to be asymmetries in strategic leadership, particularly where firms possess different complementary assets. However, this need not necessarily be reflected in asymmetric dependence relationships between the flagship firm and the partners in terms of, for instance, internationalization moves or even product development. Both due to the resources held by the partners and by other relationships next to the relationship with the flagship firm of a specific network.

Moreover, it is hard to maintain that suppliers would freely render themselves completely at the mercy of one client. Instead, it is more logical to expect that they will try to become key suppliers for different clients, participating in various networks. Possibly, a key supplier might be willing to decompose its apparatus of assets and resources in such a way that each of them turn into 'dedicated assets' vis-à-vis certain networks or key clients. Then, there may be exclusivity on a plant basis, but this is very different from exclusivity at a corporate level and/or at the level of a specific industry in which a certain F/5P network operates.

In agreement with the viewpoint that both b2b relationships as such and (a)symmetry and (in)dependence between firms can not be explained at the level of a specific network as it does not operate in a relational vacuum, in this research project a sequence perspective is proposed to examine the internationalization moves in international business networks, that is, a sequence in which the internationalization moves of a buyer precede those of the supplier(s). This is also in line with similar arguments forwarded in our discussion of the N&I approach. (see Section 2.4).

Longevity of b2b relationships and continuity of partners in international business networks: Both the network view on the IPM and the F/5P model agree that longevity is of vital significance to b2b relationships. In this respect, the F/5P model is the firmest one, suggesting that relationships in F/5P business networks are entered into on an indefinite basis. The network view on the IPM does provide starting points to reason possible member changes in international business networks, but also emphasizes voice, rather than exit or substitution. As was suggested in the discussion of the N&I approach to b2b relationships, the network view on the IPM and the F/5P model also appear to neglect or underestimate competitive processes between rival buyers and suppliers and other factors of substantial change.

As this does not seem to be a realistic postulation, we suggest that rivals do try to obtain improved network positions, and network positions currently held by competitors. Similarly, we argue that also other events in the relevant environment of firms and inter-firm relationships can provoke considerable changes to business networks. This should enable the explanation of possible substitutions of members of international business networks. For a more detailed exposé on this issue, we refer to the discussion of the N&I approach in Section 2.4.

Segmentation among suppliers: Whereas the network view on the IPM draws no explicit distinction between suppliers, the F/5P model distinguishes between key and non-key suppliers. As a result, the network view on the IPM presumes there can be coherence between internationalization dynamics with regard to all b2b relationships. The F/5P model, on the contrary, argues that the asymmetry between buyers and suppliers and the subsequent internationalization dynamics between them, are only applicable to buyer–key supplier relationships. This implies that the key suppliers depend stronger on the flagship firm and that they should show a more pronounced and correlated (co-)location behaviour with respect to the flagship firm's internationalization moves.

Perception of the MNE as a network or as a homogeneously acting single, unitary entity: The network view on the IPM adopts a network perspective on individual MNEs engaged in international business networks, arguing that MNE subsidiaries can interfere in the internationalization moves of the MNE itself. Similarly, it holds that the competence assignment and resource allocation to a certain MNE subsidiary may be the outcome of headquarters–subsidiary dynamics. Additionally, it offers space for the development of alternatives to a top–down led centre–periphery perspective on MNEs. It also enables the analysis of subsidiary–b2b relationship dynamics. The F/5P model does not pay explicit attention to this issue. From its leadership thesis, it suggests a more top–down approach, with the flagship's subsidiaries being strategically dependent on the firm's headquarters, much like its suppliers are.

2.9 Conclusions

From the discussion of the selected approaches related to internationalization of business networks, we can draw the following conclusions:

1   Literature recognizes the link between b2b relationships and international (ization of) business. The discussed approaches support the view that b2b relationships are a *vehicle* to international business and that IB leads to a setting up of b2b relationships and business networks. They acknowledge that mutual or sequential internationalization moves are intertwined with b2b relationships, either because they have been built up and have become stabilized over a longer period of time or because they are set to mark the start of a cooperative relation for an undefined period.

2   Due to interdependences between buyers and suppliers in b2b relationships and business networks, IB choices on behalf of one party have repercussions for choices the others make. The approaches diverge when it comes to the intensity, the one-way-direction or both-ways-character of dependence in such b2b relationships. They also differ with respect to the extent to which the embeddedness of actors and relationships in the broader business environment are of influence, and the group of suppliers affected by IB moves on the part of the buyer (whether this only affects on key

suppliers or on all suppliers). After discussing the various viewpoints on this topic, we propose a sequence perspective to examine the internationalization moves in international business networks, that is, a sequence in which the internationalization moves of a buyer precede those of the supplier(s).

3   Regarding the continuity of b2b relationships the frameworks of reference emphasize longevity. A critical review of the underlying postulations suggests that international(ized) networks are prone to adaptations over time in terms of relationship contents and possibly also in terms of composition of partners. In concrete terms, as a consequence of: (a) learning effects on behalf of the partners involved (either with respect to IB or b2b relationships), (b) competitive pressures on behalf of rivals of the partners involved, and (c) the general open system characteristics (including the exposure of actors to new environments and actors due to their mere internationalization) in which such relationships operate.

4   From a network perspective on MNEs it can be argued that MNEs are not homogeneous entities. Headquarters, subsidiaries and other MNE units form a network of their own. The members of such networks are out to improve their intra-firm network position for the sake of resources and influence. As subsidiaries may vary in terms of their assets and negotiating skills, the intra-firm network position and business function profile of subsidiaries of MNEs need not be the same.

2.10   Review of empirical research literature on b2b relationships and internationalization in the automotive industry

As regards empirical research literature on b2b and international business practices in the automotive industry, in addition to articles with respect to the automotive industry from many refereed journals we consulted publications of the two most important academic automotive research groups in the Western world: *Groupe d'Etudes et de Recherche Permanent sur l'Industrie et les Salariés de l'Automobile* (GERPISA) and International Motor Vehicle Programme (IMVP).

The relevant literature in this respect can be divided into two segments. A first segment that studies the internalization–externalization choices involved in b2b relationships. The second segment studies the management and structuring of the international business apparatus of automotive companies, that is, internationalization operations and centralization–decentralization choices within automotive firm hierarchies.

2.10.1   *Internalization–externalization in the automotive industry*

By the end of the 1970s increased global competition, the development of new information technologies and consumer demands with regard to the automotive industry put a stronger emphasis on cost competitiveness, on quality standards, on short delays of delivery to the final client and on minimal product development delays. The former led to an increased out-sourcing and relying on b2b relationships in the automotive industry. This trend started among Japanese car manufacturers, who had already established a high level of supplier involvement in product development, production and logistics (Womack *et al.*, 1990). The same practices and intensified reliance on b2b relationships in the automotive sector were subsequently observed in the United States of America (USA) and in Europe (Helper, 1991). Today, all over the world, assembly firms have devolved considerable responsibility to selected component suppliers for the design and development of whole systems (Sadler, 1999, p. 110).

Moreover, many studies indicate that currently more than half of the total value of a car is developed and produced under the responsibility of the suppliers and that this share is still growing (Vickery, 1996; Chanaron, 1997; CEC, 1999; European Monitoring Centre on Change, 2004).

Hodges and Van Tulder (1994) demonstrate that in today's car industry the making of an automobile requires the input from a wide range of industries. Among these industries, non-automotive branches – or branches not dedicated exclusively to the automotive business – such as the electronics and chemical industries, have become two of the most crucial suppliers. In addition, Hodges and Van Tulder suggest that the conceptualization, design and manufacturing of electronics and chemicals was never one of the core activities of the car constructors and that this will probably not change. This is due to the knowledge gap that exists between current providers of such components and the investments that would be necessary on behalf of car constructors to be able to master the technologies and production techniques in question in a competitive way. The authors conclude that even the largest car manufacturers will encounter difficulties in keeping up with technological progress in all relevant areas, that is, due to the high R&D costs involved in developing each single technology. As a consequence, they argue that the penetration of 'new' technologies and materials on the car conceptualization and manufacturing scene will oblige car manufacturers to continue to outsource certain components and capabilities which they themselves can not secure in a competitive way.

The former emphasizes the dependence of assemblers on certain specialized input providers for the conception and production of cars. There is another aspect, which adds to the relative power or independence of, for example, chemical and electronics companies vis-à-vis the car industry. This is the fact that most chemical and electronics companies are large companies that do not depend exclusively on the automotive business for their client base. Although the 'dependence' relationships between the chemical and electronics supply companies, on the one hand, and car manufacturers, on the other, is a somewhat special case, it does illustrate what kind of power shifts occur when car assemblers start depending more and more on (first tier) suppliers for necessary inputs. This in(ter)dependence can also be observed with regard to highly sophisticated supply companies with a long automotive tradition. Like companies who supply high-tech elements and who at the same time have a diversified package of activities spread over several industries, like Bosch, Siemens and TRW. The rise of large, broadly diversified suppliers – in terms both of client base and of the industries to which they sell – has led to suggestions that a change is underway in the power balance within automotive value systems in favour of leading component manufacturers (Sadler, 1999; Kamp, 2000; Trends, 2002).

With respect to the size and critical mass of suppliers from the automotive sector, several studies report on evolutions of consolidation (Amin and Smith, 1991; Boston Consulting Group, 1993; Sadler and Amin, 1995; CEC, 1996; Freyssenet and Lung, 1996; Aláez et al., 1999; Sadler, 1999; Shimokawa, 1999).

O hUallachain (1996, 1997) argues that the disintegration of the stages of production at car constructors has also given way to a parallel vertical integration among supplier production stages.

Freyssenet and Lung (1996), Boston Consulting Group (1993), Shimokawa (1999), Amin and Smith (1991), Anderson and Holmes (1995), and Sadler and Amin (1995), attribute the process of supplier consolidation to the demands for vast financial, technological and managerial capacity, economies of scale, global supply coverage, capabilities to respond to the latest logistics demands and for integrated system and module design. They argue that only larger groups can comply with such demands.

Several studies witness that car assemblers' outsourcing and externalization policies are usually conceived around a set of common cornerstones, like: platform sharing, modular construction, communality of pieces and global and or single sourcing. Through this, they aim to reduce the supplier base and co-ordination costs (Womack et al., 1990; Lamming, 1993; Nishiguchi, 1993; Pallarès-Barbera, 1996; Sako and Warburton, 1999).

This process is not only a product of car constructors' attempts to reduce their supplier base. The aim to centralize the purchasing competences within car manufacturing companies also contributes to it. Consequently, the practice of subsidiary–specific supplier bases disappears more and more.

While concentration is less pronounced in the suppliers segment than in the car constructor segment of the automotive industry, Wells and Rawlinson (1994) and O hUallachain and Wasserman (1999) observe that in certain product ranges a small number of leading system suppliers currently hold dominant positions. Ultimately, oligopolization trends among suppliers also cause a concentration of power among them, leading to the creation of industry-wide suppliers.

Regarding the involvement of suppliers in the development of new car models – as an indicator for early reliance of car constructors on b2b relationships, several scholars testify that these increasingly begin at the embryonic stage of the conceptualization of the car. Features of this early involvement of suppliers in the product development process are the 'black' or 'grey box' development practices (Fujimoto, 1995; Kesseler, 1997).

A survey among car constructors, held by Ellison *et al.* (1995) in the first half of the nineties, revealed a considerable supplier participation in the development of parts in the automotive industry of the USA, Japan and Europe. In Europe, supplier participation in parts development was just below 30%, whereas this was 44% in Japan and 33% in the USA. With respect to the highest added value segment of parts development for suppliers, the share of suppliers was 24% in Europe, 30% in the USA and 55% in Japan. Additionally, the survey revealed that European car manufacturing companies planned to increase their reliance on suppliers during the development process in the future. Current forecasts are that suppliers will be responsible for nearly 60% of the industry's research and development work by the year 2010.

Whether or not single sourcing leads to exclusive relationships between assemblers and suppliers appears to co-depend on the willingness of car manufacturing firms to allow suppliers to start other relationships in the automotive business. Dyer *et al.* (1998) report on the different attitudes car assemblers adopt in this respect: from prohibiting suppliers to work for other car constructors (South Korea), to a laissez-faire stance (USA). Pries (1999) and Florence (1996) report on the practice among German and French assemblers to stimulate multiple client operations. The already discussed oligopolization trends and the critical mass of a certain supplier should also influence a supplier's relationships with other car constructors.

Finally, several scholars demonstrate that the restructuring of the automotive industry is not just limited to a redistribution of competences and activities between assemblers and suppliers alone. Simultaneously, a segmentation of the supplier base can be observed (Amin and Smith, 1991; Lamming, 1993; Beije, 1994; Sadler and Amin, 1995; Pilorusso, 1997; Dyer *et al.* 1998) with notably first and second tier suppliers. The first tier suppliers, whose number is limited and diminishing, are responsible for the design, production and assembly of complete (sub)systems. The second and lower tier suppliers provide more elementary parts to the first tier suppliers who integrate them into (sub)systems.

2.10.2 *Management and structuring of international business in the automotive industry*

Homogenization of economic space, enlarged (information) technological possibilities and harmonization of basic consumer taste and demands enables firms to adopt an integrated management approach towards a unified market and business apparatus.

In relation to the former, Sleuwaeghen (1991) and Dudley (1989) argue that improved co-ordination possibilities and a drive for a better exploitation of scale economies within Europe change the configuration of activities. They foresee a reallocation of strategic competences towards recognized centres of excellence within the integrated economic space, while tactical and operational competences move to lower cost zones.

In a comparative analysis on internationalization models by automotive assemblers, Bélis-Bergouignan *et al.*, (1994, p. 747) effectively demonstrate that '(t)he more homogeneous a firm's space is, the more it tends to co-ordinate its activities in a centralized manner' (our translation). Internationally integrated production apparatuses require a higher level of control on industrial processes, product quality, sourcing and trade flows by an MNE (Bélis-Bergouignan *et al.*, 2000). This leads to the creation of a hierarchical order between a firm's establishments in terms of the allocation of more or less strategic business functions at different places.

In the automotive industry, such rationalization processes and geographical reshufflings have been reported in various publications (e.g. Boston Consulting Group, 1993; Hudson and Schamp, 1995; Bordenave and Lung, 1996). A stronger segmentation between strategic competences (strategic co-ordination, design and purchasing functions) at the headquarters of car manufacturing firms and tactical and operational competences at subsidiaries is observed. Miller (1994) calculated that approximately 30% of the production of the larger automotive companies is carried out abroad, while only 12% of R&D costs is the product of activities outside the home country.

A similar segmentation process can be observed between suppliers' subsidiaries and headquarters. This is induced by an increased centralization by car constructors of vehicle design and of purchasing decision making, and the shift towards working with first tier suppliers of complete systems or modules (Boston Consulting Group, 1993).

As a result, one sees that, whereas before many companies – both car manufacturing firms and suppliers – conducted business on a nation-per-nation basis and assigned and allocated responsibilities and assets correspondingly, today the redundancies in resources and competences that were previously built up are gradually eliminated.

Several scholars report on the ways in which automotive companies currently plan and carry out their business in an integrated and geographically coherent way per Triad region, and how they allocate their business functions in a corresponding way. In the case of Europe, this phenomenon has been coined 'Europeanization' (Hudson and Schamp, 1995; Bordenave and Lung, 1996).

From the side of suppliers, a trend towards '*co-location*' of their R&D and design facilities in the vicinity of the design centres of car manufacturing companies is also observed (Boston Consulting Group, 1993; Bélis-Bergouignan *et al.*, 1994, 2000; Sadler, 1999). Boston Consulting Group (1993) also suggests that the increased introduction of black box design and simultaneous engineering reinforces the trend towards co-location.

Several studies demonstrate that the current allocation of assets and business functions of automotive networks in different localities reveals core–periphery patterns, as understood by Wallerstein (1974), Lipietz (1977, 1985), Leborgne and Lipietz (1988) and Scott and Storper (1986). In concrete terms, the global strategies of automotive actors with a presence in several countries translate into a network-related way of organizing separate business functions in different regions (Bordenave and Lung, 1993; Cabus, 1997; Caniëls, 1997; Carrincazeaux and Lung, 1997). In general, it is observed that the assignment of business functions over space in networks leads to a spatial reproduction of the intra-firm hierarchy between automotive headquarters and branch locations (Bordenave and Lung, 1993; Cabus, 1997; Caniëls, 1997; Carrincazeaux and Lung, 1997).

The outcome of this process is a distribution of responsibilities between so-called home base (central) and peripheral regions (Carrincazeaux and Lung, 1997). Ultimately, the spatio-functional outcome of the way in which automotive activities are co-ordinated on the continent is a hierarchical collection of interdependent regions (Chanaron and Lung, 1995). These findings are consistent with those of Bordenave and Lung (1993), which indicate that the location-related logics in the European automotive industry show clear spatio-distributive features.

Carrincazeaux and Lung (1997) report on the localization of conceptual and R&D activities in the European automobile industry. The geographical distribution of these centres reveals a banana-shaped zone between London and Milano, with a strong concentration in the South of Germany. The authors establish that in many cases the centre of decision-making and the historic production nucleus, on the one hand, and the main R&D centre of a firm, on the other, tend to coincide.

Cabus (1997) has detected similar patterns regarding the production of components for Belgian car manufacturing plants by Europe-based suppliers. He demonstrates that there are certain important industrial core areas. These are concentrated along the Rhein and the Ruhr, the Ile-de-France basin near Paris and the border regions between France and Germany continuing South until Lyon.

Further findings by Cabus (1997) on the basis of analyses of the links between car manufacturing plant establishments in Belgium and their suppliers provide empirical evidence to support the existence of a national bias on behalf of car manufacturing firms in their choice of suppliers. He observes how the most important components and subsystems come in their majority from the country where the car constructor has its home base, that is, Germany for Ford-Europe, Opel and Volkswagen, France for Renault and Sweden for Volvo.

In a similar vein, Lagendijk (1994, p. 323) observed that, in spite of efforts to unlock this situation, the European automobile industry is still dominated by a small number of national champions with their own nationally focused supply chains.

Nonetheless, Larsson (2000) posits that alliances and takeovers among car constructors, such as the incorporation of Volvo by Ford, will probably have an impact on the origin of capital and location of supplier networks with which the respective car manufacturing plants work. He especially foresees changes for the domestic suppliers of the entity that is taken over, as in the Volvo case.

Balcet and Enrietti (2001), show how the origin of supplies and the capital behind them evolves as a function of intra-firm integration and centralization of decision-making powers. They comment upon a case of increased integration of a FIAT branch plant from Türkiye. Before the consolidation of this branch plant into FIAT's international purchasing hierarchy, supplies of inputs from independent Turkish companies dominated. Afterwards, a steady reduction in the number of independent Turkish suppliers took place. At the same time, there was an important increase in supplies from Turkish affiliates to foreign MNEs. Their study also indicates that the integration of the Turkish branch plant into FIAT's international business scheme led to increased imports from FIAT sites outside Türkiye. Additionally, imports from foreign companies – mostly based in Italy – also grew considerably.

Carillo and Gonzalez Lopez (1999) studied b2b relationships surrounding car manufacturing plants of German car constructors in Mexico (VW, Mercedes-Benz and BMW) and reveal the following. Many of the Mexico-based suppliers were German companies, which had followed the car constructors from the home base where they already had been working together for a long period. Moreover, their study reveals a convergence between buyers and suppliers with respect to their globalization and international investment strategies. The study demonstrates that the establishment of German suppliers in Mexico was fundamentally the result of corporate negotiations between VW Germany and the respective suppliers' headquarters in Germany in order to secure a smooth functioning of operations abroad. As a consequence, Carillo and Gonzalez Lopez (1999) argue that b2b relationships in an international context are often strongly embedded in a mutual business culture and nationality. In addition, they argue that the origins of the capital of interrelated buyers and suppliers tend to show similarities outside their nations of origin. Their study also reveals that the suppliers, once established *in situ*, diversify their client base and start selling to various assemblers.

In a study on Japanese, American and German automotive companies in Mexico, Gonzalez Lopez (2000) found additional proof that buyers and suppliers – notably the first tier suppliers – are often from the same country.

Aláez *et al.* (1999) also report on suppliers' recognition that cultural and organizational proximity helps to obtain contracts from car manufacturing companies. Consequently, they argue that this is a driving factor for local firms to become part of (foreign) MNEs.

On the basis of an analysis of the internationalization of the German automotive industry, Pries (1999) reports that globalization processes of assemblers and suppliers are deeply interlaced. He observes how establishments of German car constructors in North, Central and South America are accompanied by a pull of German suppliers. In addition, Pries (1999) testifies how assemblers urge their German suppliers, both large and medium-sized, to build up facilities wherever they go. Simultaneously, his research reveals that assemblers stimulate their suppliers to engage in other buyer–assembler relationships as well. The same argument is forwarded by

Florence (1996), discussing supplier management practices at Renault. With respect to the activities of overseas networks developed around German car manufacturing plants, Pries (1999) describes how VW made its Mexican branch location 'leading plant' for the overall and worldwide management of the Beetle production. Subsequently, he describes how more than 50 suppliers (mainly German system integrators and first tier suppliers) came to Mexico or made additional large investments over there. These observations also show how supposedly core–periphery task segmentations can be broken by the assignment of superior added value activities to branch locations that are situated in peripheral areas.

In a similar way, Shimokawa (1999) observes how Nippon Denso became an international component supplier through its privileged supplier relationship with Toyota. Volpato (1997) and Sadler (1999) observe the same phenomenon at Magneti Marelli due to its preferential contacts with FIAT.

Sadler (1999) also reports on car constructor firm-led internationalization patterns on behalf of automotive suppliers. He documents how, for instance, TRW, Allied Signal and Tenneco internationalized their automotive activities via following Ford and General Motors abroad.

As an alternative to these (early) co-internationalization signs between assemblers and suppliers from the same country, Laigle (1997) reports on cross-border alliances between suppliers in order to establish relationships with car manufacturing companies outside their home continent. Similarly, she reports on moves by individual companies whose internationalization path is not guided (anymore) by privileged assembly contacts with fellow-nation car constructors. As an example, she presents the case of Valeo. Valeo actively tries to compete overseas for buyer relationships with assemblers from outside its home base, through acquisitions and the creation of establishments *sur place*. Sadler's (1999) description of the LucasVarity case and the Bosch Bendix case are comparable to the internationalization moves of Valeo. In addition, Sadler (1999) describes how many British automotive component suppliers attempted to internationalize their client base in the early 1980s, due to the collapse of the UK auto industry in that period (Sadler, 1999, p. 114).

In terms of production locus, Sadler (1999) observes that a substantial spread of production and employment outside the country of origin of automotive companies took place between 1990 and 1995. This was, for example, the case for FIAT, Renault and VW, and for component manufacturers like BBA, GKN, Lucas, T&N and Valeo. He observes that, comparatively speaking, component manufacturers showed a higher intensity of investing abroad in this period than car manufacturing firms. Subsequently he argues that component manufacturers are increasingly less dependent on their home markets. Implicitly, the former points either at a rupture of suppliers' dependence on co-home market car constructors for internationalization, or at a catching up with these and other car assembly firms' investments abroad. It also indicates that internationally oriented companies forge new ties in a rather path-independent way.

Dicken and Oberg (1996) provide additional arguments in favour of more multinationally organized business networks in the automotive industry. They draw on tendencies that encourage firms to set up organizational networks focused on Europe as a whole, rather than at individual national markets.

Phelps and Fuller (2000) report on how subsidiaries of automotive companies located in various countries push for improved intra-corporate positions. Moreover, they describe how headquarters of automotive MNEs use the wish on the part of subsidiaries to improve their status within the hierarchy to organize inter-plant competitions prior to investment allocations. They argue that the organization of such competitive processes depends on the organizational structure of MNEs (see for example, Bartlett and Ghoshal, 1989), and the integration of the markets where MNEs have their different business units (Phelps and Fuller, 2000, p. 228).

Dyer (1996) observes how car manufacturing units that persuade their suppliers to invest in on-site establishments and highly dedicated production facilities outperform those car manufacturing units that do not dispose of such inter-firm infrastructures. Consequently, if car manufacturing units were to be engaged in intra-corporate competitions (Phelps and Fuller, 2000) the former would have a greater chance to win the race, that is, to be allotted a specific investment or the maintenance of a product mandate.

In a study on Japanese investments in Canada and the USA, Rutherford (2000) reveals the following. The difference in value of end products, allocation of R&D activities and length of production runs carried out by overseas subsidiaries of identical automobile manufacturing companies leads to a corresponding segmentation in, on the one hand, the densification of localized supplier networks around these subsidiaries and, on the other hand, the degree of sophistication of the outsourced components and operations these networks house and supply. Moreover, the suppliers involved in the networks localized around the most strategically valued car manufacturing subsidiaries also tend to supply sophisticated components to strategically less important car manufacturing subsidiaries, despite a potential distance-related disadvantage. He shows how dense and localized supplier networks are more likely to arise around strategically important automobile manufacturing subsidiaries. Similarly, his work reveals how co-location *in situ* is fostered by the site-specific value of production tasks and other business assignments. Consequently, Rutherford (2000, pp. 743, 746–747) shows that suppliers choose to set up establishments that serve more than one client rather than setting up sites for every customer they serve, as an expression of the relative importance of the respective b2b relationships a supplier entertains. Rutherford (2000, pp. 743, 747) also demonstrates just-in-time requirements do not necessarily determine location choices of suppliers. In addition, Rutherford states that selecting locations from where to serve multiple clients appears to become more detached from pure logistics factors when integration of economic space takes place (2000, p. 743). His study also found proof of supplier substitutions (Rutherford, 2000, p. 746). Finally, his study demonstrates the importance of a car constructor's home base as a significant origin of high-end components such as electronics and propulsion parts (p. 746).

Further to the location and logistics logics signaled by Rutherford (2000), Frigant and Lung (2002) indicate that fulfilling just-in-time (JIT) schemes allows for more logistics solutions than co-location alone. They argue that also possibilities for scale economies *in situ* need to be fulfilled. Finally, they reason that co-location is a way for suppliers to demonstrate their willingness and commitment to long-term mutual agreements with customers.

A final empirical observation is the following. Regarding the intra-firm and geographical distribution of suppliers' manufacturing activities, sector surveys demonstrate that the following location logics appear to be dominant (Altersohn, 1992; Boston Consulting Group, 1993):

- Final assembly activities for high volume bulk components and systems are located near car manufacturing plants. These require, on the one hand, frequent loading and unloading and, on the other, delivery in the order in which cars are produced (unit-specific supplies).
- Production of low volume and or basic components and production-cost intensive components are concentrated in a limited amount of – or in one – plant(s) from which several clients are serviced. These need not be delivered in sequence with car assembly order production (no need for unit-specific supplies).

The latter principle is the most universally followed, whereas the former shows a larger variety. In relation to the first principle, certain suppliers, for example, Valeo (2000), Lingotes Especiales (Muruzabal, 2000) and Grupo Antolín (2000), argue that by improving their logistics from the plants they already possess, suppliers are also able to fulfill their contracts, in terms of lead times, costs, and so on. Moreover, to achieve economies of scale, a concentration of production and sub-assembly under one roof is more attractive to suppliers (Rhys, 2000).

As such, it is voiced by the industry that 'on-site' location of suppliers at a supplier park near a car manufacturing plant or in the near vicinity is not a *conditio sine qua non* to be able to comply with JIT and sequenced logistics.

2.11 Conclusions

1 The empirical research review clearly contributes to the argument that internationalization patterns of firms are embedded in inter-firm relations. The observed geographical reshuffling and co-location of suppliers' activities parallel to buyers' operations provides confirmation for the interdependences in IB and b2b relationships. Similarly, it provides support for the thesis that the car constructors are the actor acting as *point man* in this sequential process.

Empirical literature also provides proof in favour of the argument that suppliers internationalize together with key buyers. This thus corroborates the claim that IB grows out of long-standing relationships or that b2b relationships are a vehicle for IB.

2   Empirical research literature also corroborates the growing importance of b2b relationships and a broadening of the actors and sectors that provide input for the main buyers of the automotive industry; the car manufacturing firms. Consequently, suppliers are playing an increasingly important role within automotive networks.

Similarly, the literature review reveals that reverse, simultaneous and black box engineering, specialization and oligopolization among suppliers and the demand for integrated systems contribute to a relative power or dependence balance between first tier suppliers and car constructors in the industry. Exclusive or 'dedicated' functioning of suppliers for certain car manufacturing firms appears to be less typical, at least, as far as the first tier suppliers or crucial input providers are concerned.

3   The reported intra-firm centralization–decentralization operations also confirm that the concept of MNEs as networks in themselves, especially once they can function as systems in a homogeneous (economic) space, is a useful and correct one.

4   Furthermore, empirical literature demonstrates that the traditional centre–periphery dichotomy, which in general appears to be fortified through economic integration processes, can be broken, that is, through singular intra-MNE assignment decisions and subsequent b2b dynamics. In general, from a sectoral and a geographical perspective a distribution of tasks between core and periphery can be observed. However, at the level of concrete networks surrounding car manufacturing company units, they appear to depend more on car constructor-specific distributions and assignments of competences among its assets, than on a straightforward core–periphery logic. In order to decide about such assignments, it appears that there is a kind of (organized) competition among subsidiaries of specific car manufacturing companies, which push for improved intra-corporate positions.

5   Literature research also provides proof that supplier substitution is an empirical reality. Suppliers trying to seduce car constructors to switch providers, takeovers among car constructors and benchmarking of supplier performance by car constructors are important explanatory factors behind this phenomenon.

Literature indicates that after the initial stages, supplier companies intend to diversify their corporate and subsidiaries' client bases in a multinational way, expanding beyond buyer relationships rooted in their home base.

Moreover, the empirical research review suggests that buyers encourage suppliers to engage in multiple client relationships rather than by exclusivity relationships.

6   Finally, the review reveals that site-specific investments depend – in addition to the relationship with one specific client and the expectation regarding the longevity of a certain relationship – on other b2b relationships, possibilities for economies of scale *in situ*, and component-intrinsic logistics and production considerations.

3 Conceptual framework and hypotheses

3.1 Introduction

In view of the results of the literature review, we argue that the following issues should primarily be kept in mind with regard to the design of a conceptual framework for the formation and evolution of satellite business networks in peripheral regions in particular and of international business networks in general.

Longevity of inter-firm relationships is confirmed as an important factor in explaining joint international operations of firms. Nevertheless, empirical research literature also suggests that competitive behaviour of rival firms and sector oligopolization makes new relationships possible. Consequently, a total path dependence on relationships with a specific buyer does not explain all internationalization moves made by suppliers. Moreover, theoretical literature points at the learning processes firms undergo through their experiences with b2b relationships and internationalization. Both types of experience enhance their courage to internationalize to less familiar places and to enter into b2b relationships with less well-known partners. Other kinds of events can also cause ruptures in b2b relationships or other kinds of profound modifications to business networks. From the empirical literature we learn that geo-economic integration can be such an event.

Empirical studies suggest that the homogeneity of economic space in which an MNE has a series of establishments is an important factor in the intra-firm spread of competences, resources and autonomies. It appears that the more homogeneous the economic space is, the more integrated the management of an MNE apparatus is.

At the same time, both theoretical and empirical studies suggest that intra-MNE assignment and location strategies of business partners take place in a co-ordinated and, possibly, simultaneous way, that is, through interactions between respective network partners. Many moves of suppliers are planned and carried out as a function of moves made by the focal buyer of a network. To a large extent these strategies appear to be co-ordinated at a corporate level between the focal buyer firm and the key supplier firms of a network. Apparently, these processes influence both the presence of actors in a locality and the competences, resources and sovereignty assigned to the establishments *in situ*.

Literature suggests that such 'co-location' decisions are an expression of the degree of willingness on the part of suppliers to commit themselves to a relationship with a certain car constructor or car manufacturing subsidiary.

Empirical studies weaken the argument that key suppliers work exclusively for a certain client and that b2b relationships are characterized by strategic dependence of key suppliers on buyer firms and that the latter aim for relationship-specific investments on the part of (key) suppliers. Instead, it appears that suppliers try to diversify their client base and car manufacturing firms also encourage them to do so. The former argues in favour of the argument brought forward in the N&I approach that a specific b2b relationship should be understood against the background of the other b2b relationships an actor is involved in.

Similarly, the collection of b2b relationships an actor is involved in should be seen as an important explanatory factor behind site-specific investments, rather than supplier status or any single b2b relationship and its history. In addition, component-specific logistics and production factors play a role.

3.2   Presentation of the conceptual framework

The conceptual framework provided in this chapter is based upon three main pillars. First of all, it builds upon Halinen *et al.* (1999) elaboration on change theories with respect to business network research. Second, it takes into account a limited set of theoretical assumptions that can be considered as highly determining for the behaviour of business network actors from a b2b and international business perspective. These assumptions follow from the theoretical and empirical literature review that was presented in Chapter 2. Third, it is based on a limited set of forces and events to which actors in business networks are subjected. Forces and events with an impact on the behaviour of actors in business networks and which jointly determine the evolutionary patterns of the business networks. For the design of the conceptual framework, we will focus on those forces and events that – in line with the previous literature review – are the most relevant for the formation and evolution of business networks from a b2b and international business approach.

3.2.1   *Modelling of changes in business networks*

In line with Halinen *et al.* (1999), who refer to existing change theories and concepts like the punctuated-equilibrium model (Gersick, 1991; Van de Ven, 1992; Van de Ven and Poole, 1995), we suggest a distinction between two types of change. First, incremental change: adjustments within ongoing business relationships and overall stability of the deep structure of a network. Second, radical change: changes of entire relationships including their termination and a substitution of partners, which cause modifications to a network's deep structure. The term 'deep structure' refers to the fundamental choices which sets of business actors have made regarding who they are connected to (Gersick, 1991; Halinen *et al.*, 1999). The concept of 'critical event' is proposed as the term for occurrences that trigger changes. Critical event refers to those events that have a decisive effect on the development of relationships. Halinen *et al.* (1999) mention mergers and acquisitions (pp. 784, 787), changes in a company's business, marketing and purchasing strategies (p. 787) and major geopolitical and macro-economic events (p. 788) as examples of critical events that can trigger radical changes.

Environmental changes such as geopolitical events, for example the creation of trading blocks, are channelled through business relationships with specific parties, rather than operating as a kind of general market force influencing the firm (Håkansson and Johanson, 1993, p. 44). As a consequence, the extent to which a certain force or event leads to an incremental or radical change is to a large degree casuistic and depends, for example, on the idiosyncrasy of firms and the organizational choices companies make in response to such forces or events.

In addition, the extent to which the term 'radical' is completely appropriate, for instance for the substitution of a supplier – possibly combined with a change in the *locus* from where supplies are shipped – is probably debatable. Nevertheless, based on the work of, for example, Van de Ven (1992) and Halinen *et al.* (1999) and thus in order to establish a link with renowned viewpoints and commonly used terminology, it is a sound choice. Moreover, to distinguish it from changes within a given b2b relationship it is very useful.

3.2.2 *Theoretical assumptions behind the behaviour of business network actors*

A first set of assumptions is based on the following rationales. According to the N&I approach on b2b relationships (e.g. Laage-Hellman, 1997) actors are moved by the desire to improve or maintain their network position. This desire can be seen as a basic logic or independent variable. On the one hand, as far as the focal actors of business networks are concerned – like subsidiaries of automobile manufacturing companies – this implies that they push for improved intra-corporate positions (Phelps and Fuller, 2000). The outcomes of such intra-firm competitive processes are specific subsidiary assignment choices. On the other hand, as far as suppliers are concerned it implies that incumbent suppliers will attempt to prolong acquired network positions[20] whereas rival companies will display competitive behaviour in order to conquer network positions currently not under their control (Rutherford, 2000). The former supplier behaviour forms the effect or dependent variable vis-à-vis the previously presented basic logic. As such, we reason that the intra-firm position of buyer plants forms an incentive for suppliers to invest in such relationships. In other words, it increases suppliers' commitment – or readiness to commit themselves – to a relationship in terms of their efforts to maintain and continue the relationship (Helper, 1987; De Jong and Nooteboom, 2000). Consequently, it is notably the buyer's intra-firm position that determines its relative importance or value to their suppliers amidst the conjoint of b2b relationships these suppliers entertain. This conjoint of b2b relationships can include both relationships with plants of the same company to which the buyer in question belongs or plants or enterprises belonging to other legal entities. Subsequently, it is argued that an important means to achieve continuation or improvement of network positions is to have establishments located in the vicinity of premium value buyers (see for example, Frigant and Lung, 2002).

A second set of assumptions results from the following rationales. According to the IPM (e.g. Carlson, 1966; Johanson and Vahlne, 1977, 1990) and according to organizational learning theories (e.g. Cyert and March, 1963; Levitt and March, 1988; Lane and Lubatkin, 1998), actors lose their fear of internationalizing and establishing b2b relationships after they accumulate corresponding learning experiences. We argue that these experiences are a significant factor underpinning the choices of focal buyer firms in networks in their attempts to safeguard sustained competitiveness of their networks as a whole (Rugman and D'Cruz, 2000). Buyer firms' aim to sustain a network's competitiveness forms a second basic logic with regard to conceiving the formation and evolution of international business networks. Consequently, this should have repercussions over time for the choices buyer firms make about which suppliers to include in these networks. The outcomes of these choices, as a dependent variable, follow from the basic logic that focal buyer firms of networks strive for overall network competitiveness. We argue that such buyer firms evaluate on a regular basis, which suppliers contribute most to the competitiveness of the network. Arguably, such evaluations may lead to the conclusion that changes in the composition would benefit the network's competitiveness and thus induce changes in partnerships. See also Grabher (1993) and Rutherford (2000) in this respect. Similarly, it is expected to be a significant factor in the articulation of their supplier relationship policies, for instance in terms of 'practicing' longevity. Additionally, similar b2b and internationalization learning experiences on behalf of suppliers, combined with competitive behaviour of rival supplier firms (e.g. Montgomery, 1995; Laigle, 1997) will also contribute to substitutions in buyer firms' supplier network. For, supposedly, rival firms will also attempt to occupy positions currently not under their control via competitive bidding. Lastly, changes in industry structures, such as oligopolization and consolidation – as an exponent of competitive behaviour to occupy improved inter-firm network positions – will also contribute to ('virtual') substitutions in buyer firms' supplier networks. Certainly, consolidation moves such as takeovers can also include rival firms taking over incumbent suppliers to a focal buyer firm of a network in order for the former to obtain more favourable inter-firm network positions.

Wrapping up, we argue that (a) the focal buyer firm's concern to sustain the competitiveness of the network, (b) learning experiences of b2b partners, (c) consolidation processes, (d) geo-economic integration processes and (e) competition among rival firms in industries, complement and may exceed the forces that should result in a preservation of incumbent b2b relationship and network compositions. Consequently, we argue that considerable changes in the composition of b2b networks can take place.

To conclude with and to establish a bridge with the first set of assumptions, we argue that the substitution of an 'old' supplier for a new one can be accompanied by location behaviour on the part of the new supplier as a function of the relative value and intra-firm network position of the targeted buyer.

3.2.3 Forces and events that act as stability or change agents

The conceptual framework also takes into consideration the forces that determine the formation and evolution of the deep structure of satellite business networks in peripheral regions in particular and international business networks in general. These forces can either be directed at stability or at incremental or radical change.

Forces fostering stability: Forces that foster stability are notably partner-specific bonding and capabilities. Bonding and the building up of relationship-specific qualities stimulate the continuity of b2b relationships (Hägg and Johanson, 1982; Granovetter, 1985; Helper, 1987; Johanson and Mattsson, 1987; Easton, 1989; Becattini, 1992; Harrison, 1992; Sako, 1992; Forsgren *et al.*, 1995; Håkansson and Shehota, 1995; Nooteboom, 1996). This is also true in an international(ization) context (Johanson and Mattsson, 1987; Forsgren, 1989).

Forces fostering incremental changes: In case spatial proximity abroad is desirable, this stimulates co-location behaviour on behalf of suppliers (Altersohn, 1992; Boston Consulting Group, 1993; Frigant and Lung, 2002). Similarly, if the foreign subsidiary of a buyer firm fulfills certain strategic activities, it contributes to a corresponding assignment policy on behalf of suppliers with respect to those branch locations that maintain relationships with the subsidiary of the buyer firm in question (Bordenave and Lung, 1993; Boston Consulting Group, 1993; Bélis-Bergouignan *et al.* 1994, 2000; Cabus, 1997; Caniëls, 1997; Carrincazeaux and Lung, 1997; Sadler, 1999). Both matters lead to adjustments in existing relationships that subsequently can be considered incremental changes.

As observed in the empirical research review, component-specific logistics and production requirements are intervening variables that co-determine the location and assignment choices of suppliers (Altersohn, 1992; Boston Consulting Group, 1993; Frigant and Lung, 2002). The same holds true for other b2b relationships (Rhys, 2000; Rutherford, 2000). They bring about changes that are incremental rather than radical, as they first of all influence the location from where a supplier attends its (multiple) client(s). A priori, then, it does not so much rule out the continuity of an existing b2b relationship. Rather, it conditions the (geographical) adjustment to be made to the b2b relationship in question.

Sector oligopolization can also lead to consolidations of previously separated suppliers (Amin and Smith, 1991; Boston Consulting Group, 1993; Sadler and Amin, 1995; CEC, 1996; Freyssenet and Lung, 1996; Aláez *et al.*, 1999; Sadler, 1999; Shimokawa, 1999). As such, it is a potential source of incremental alterations of incumbent b2b relationships. For it can lead to, legally speaking, the linking up of previously unrelated business partners. If, for example, company A takes over company B and from that moment onwards client C has in name company A instead of company B as its supplier, such a substitution should be seen as a virtual one. Therefore, these substitutions should be interpreted as incremental changes to the deep structure of business networks.

Modified conceptualization of products may also lead to an adjustment of logistics and production schemes (Estall, 1985; Mair, 1991a,b; Wells and Rawlinson, 1992; Marx *et al.*, 1997; Aláez *et al.*, 1999; Adam-Ledunois and Renault, 2001). Subsequently, this leads to incremental changes with respect to component-specific logistics and production requirements.

Finally, homogenization of economic space can bring about incremental changes as well (Dudley, 1989; Sleuwaeghen, 1991; Bélis-Bergouignan *et al.*, 1994, 2000; Hudson and Schamp, 1995; Bordenave and Lung, 1996). That is, if at an intra-firm level – economic integration only alters buyer firms' subsidiary assignment decisions without affecting the actor composition of incumbent b2b relationships, its impact will be limited to correlated competence assignment choices on behalf of incumbent suppliers.

Forces fostering radical changes: Forces that foster radical change are first of all the learning experiences with respect to b2b relationships and internationalization. Both kinds of experience make buyer firms and suppliers lose their fear of entering into new b2b relationships in a cross-border context (Dicken and Oberg, 1996; Laigle, 1997; Sadler, 1999; Rutherford, 2000). Therefore, they contribute to possible substitutions of partners and facilitate entry to networks of new actors.

Competitive behaviour of rival firms has a similar effect (see for example, Montgomery, 1995; Laigle, 1997), making it possible that incumbent b2b partners are replaced and existing b2b relationships are dissolved. If such substitutions occur, one can speak of radical changes as they alter the deep structure of business networks in terms of the business actors to whom b2b partners are connected.

Sectoral consolidation processes may also affect incumbent b2b partners. In those cases where mergers between, and takeovers of, companies lead to a reorientation of a supplier company's core business, this can lead to radical changes to the deep structure of business networks. The result of such consolidations may eventually be a withdrawal from b2b relationships that are 'situated' in sectors the company no longer considers to be its core business. This would force focal buyer firms to look for substitute suppliers.

Sector oligopolization can thus lead to incremental and to radical changes to the deep structure of business networks.

Another factor that can trigger radical changes is homogenization of economic space. Economic integration can alter the intra-firm distribution of

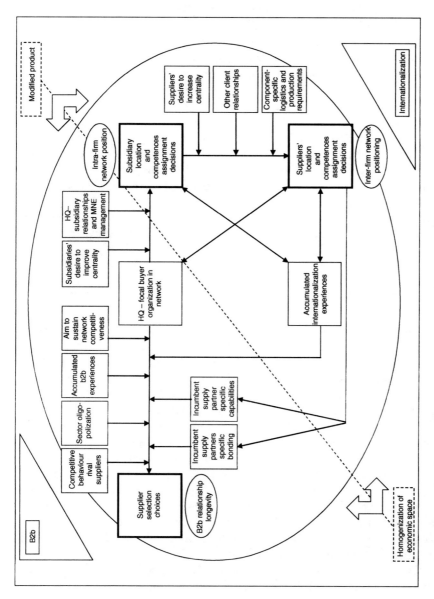

Figure 3.1 Conceptual framework for analysis.

Source: Author's elaboration.

competences (Dudley, 1989; Sleuwaeghen, 1991; Bélis-Bergouignan *et al.*, 1994, 2000; Hudson and Schamp, 1995; Bordenave and Lung, 1996). If this leads to a reallocation (i.e. centralization) of decisions taken with respect to the selection of suppliers, it can result in the effective replacement of incumbent suppliers of subsidiaries. This can also lead to a termination of existing b2b relationships as a trade-off between redundant b2b relationships formerly held by various subsidiaries that are now managed as a single business apparatus.

Economic integration can thus lead to incremental and to radical changes to the deep structure of business networks as well.

Radical changes can also take place when a modified conceptualization of the end product of a network leads to a change in the structure of the production chain behind such products (Amin and Smith, 1991; Lamming, 1993; Beije, 1994; Sadler and Amin, 1995; Pilorusso, 1997; Dyer *et al.*, 1998). For instance, when modularization of an end product leads to a 'tiering' of the suppliers conjoint, it means that several b2b relationships can be ended and replaced by alternative b2b channels.

Based on the previous considerations, in Figure 3.1 we present our conceptual framework for analysis, accompanied by a concise and explanatory legend.

Legend:

Central part and surroundings: The 'ellipse-shaped bubble' contains the reviewed elements of international business networks' deep structure, the assumptions underlying international business network actors' behaviour and the relevant forces and events they are exposed to.

'Homogenization of economic space' and 'modified product conceptualization' are presented as contextual forces as their impacts are principally channelled through the above-mentioned elements, that is, through behavioural assumptions and forces and events that are pictured inside the ellipse-shaped bubble, rather than operating as a kind of general market force influencing companies (Håkansson and Johanson, 1993, p. 44).

In the upper half of the ellipse the elements are situated that are especially derived from b2b research literature. The bottom half contains the elements that follow largely from concepts derived from international business research literature.

Basic logics, (in)dependent and intervening variables: A subsidiary's activities and responsibilities 'palette' as an indicator for its intra-firm network position (dependent variable) is the outcome of its desire and efforts of subsidiaries to improve or maintain their intra-firm network position (basic logic) and of headquarters decisions on the part of the focal buyer firm of a network regarding allocation and assignment of responsibilities to subsidiaries (independent variable).

As suppliers are moved by the desire to improve or maintain network positions too (basic logic), the intra-firm network position of a focal buyer plant in a network also determines the decisions that suppliers make regarding the location and empowerment of their assets (dependent variable). These decisions are also subject to accumulated internationalization experiences on the part of suppliers, the logistics and production peculiarities of the components and the relative importance of a certain b2b relationship amidst other relevant ones for a specific supplier (intervening variables).

The suppliers chosen by a network's focal buyer firm, and therefore the stability and longevity of b2b relationships (dependent variable), follow from the focal buyer firm's aim to achieve sustained competitiveness for the network as a whole (basic logic) and from the competitive behaviour displayed by candidate suppliers in order to improve or maintain network positions (basic logic).

These choices are also subject to b2b and internationalization experiences on the part of the respective parties, to the oligopolization degree of the respective component niches concerned, to specific bonds between the respective partner combinations and to specific capabilities (like FSAs) on behalf of the respective suppliers (intervening variables).

Nota Bene: the dependent variables are placed in bold squares.

3.3 Hypotheses and research methodology

Following the conclusions of the theoretical and empirical literature review and the conceptual framework that was subsequently designed, in this paragraph a set of research hypotheses is presented. These will be tested in order to explore and conceive the formation and evolution of international business networks.

3.3.1 *First hypothesis*

Hypothesis 1: The degree of co-location on the part of suppliers pertaining to a satellite network in a peripheral region is the result of intra-firm assignment decisions taken by the focal buyer firm of the network, followed by inter-firm network dynamics with the relevant b2b relationships.

This hypothesis applies the following network view on the IPM argument to satellite networks in peripheral regions. That is that internationalization moves and subsidiary assignment decisions on the part of suppliers are interdependent with the intra-MNE competence and resource assignments of buyers vis-à-vis their respective subsidiaries.

The network view on the IPM suggests that the internationalization of suppliers can be seen as a process that depends on intra-buyer MNEs' competence and resources assignment policies.

In line with the former, a subsidiary has possibilities to develop itself and acquire certain mandates. First of all, because organizations themselves can be seen as networks in which business units compete for resources (Phelps and Fuller, 2000) and push for improved (intra-firm) network positions. Second, the obtainence of all kinds of company-wide responsibilities and premium business functions on behalf of a certain subsidiary within an MNE co-depends on the value a subsidiary's internal capabilities and its b2b relationships represent to the whole company (Andersson and Forsgren, 2000). As a consequence, developing both themselves and their suppliers forms a stimulus for subsidiaries as it helps to improve their centrality and status within the mother concern and thus to acquire mandates.

Consequently, the interaction thesis with regard to b2b relationships suggests that the outcome of assignment processes with regard to MNE branch locations, as focal buyers in business networks, should have an effect on the activities and presence of suppliers around such branch locations.

Differences in buyer–supplier co-location patterns are thus believed to depend both on intra-firm and on inter-firm b2b dynamics. First, they depend on investment and location decisions made by buyer firms with respect to physical equipment and facilities of subsidiaries and the assignment of business functions to subsidiaries. Second, on the b2b relationships that exist between such subsidiaries and their suppliers. It is thus suggested that there is an interaction between subsidiary assignment choices and investment decisions by buyer firms, on the one hand, and the decisions made by suppliers aiming to occupy a network position vis-à-vis buyer firm's subsidiaries, on the other hand. It is argued that the value buyer firms subsidiaries acquire through intra-firm competition and assignment processes influences assignment and location decisions by suppliers with respect to supplier subsidiaries. Together, this is expected to determine the co-location degree of satellite business networks.

Empirical research method to test this hypothesis: Two independent variables serve as points of departure here: (1) the status of a buyer subsidiary with respect to the final engineering, mass production launch and market introduction of a certain car model and (2) the production share a buyer subsidiary holds in the total production of a certain car model. As a function of these two independent variables, the assignment and location dynamics on the part of suppliers surrounding the car manufacturing subsidiaries that act as focal buyers of the business networks to be investigated will be analysed from a longitudinal perspective.

3.3.2   *Second hypothesis*

Hypothesis 2: The co-location thesis combined with the theoretical and empirical observations that most inter-firm relationships have long-standing traditions, suggests that satellite business networks in peripheral regions should show a strong participation of companies originating from the same country as the focal buyer firm, certainly at the outset.

It appeared that b2b relationships in an international context are strongly embedded in mutual features of business culture and nationality of the actors involved (Carillo and Gonzalez Lopez, 1999; Pries, 1999; Sadler, 1999; Gonzalez Lopez, 2000). Consequently, the origin of the capital of buyers and suppliers tends to show similarities outside their nations of origin as well. The argument that many relationships go back a long time suggests that satellite networks will be embedded – in terms of input supply – in home-base relations. Similarly, the tendency to keep certain (notably strategic) development tasks and sophisticated component production at the home base or to co-locate such activities near the strategic business apparatus of the focal buyer firm in its home base suggests the likeliness of important import relationships coming from the focal buyer firm's home base.

Empirical research method to test this hypothesis: This hypothesis will be tested through a longitudinal analysis of quantitative data on the origin and value of incoming supplies at the level of the car manufacturing subsidiaries that function as the focal buyers of the networks to be investigated, selectively complemented with relevant qualitative data.

3.3.3 *Third hypothesis*

Hypothesis 3: The actor composition of business networks evolves significantly over time. Homogenization of economic space, competitive behaviour of rival firms, sector oligopolization and learning experiences as regards b2b relationships and internationalization are facilitating factors in this respect.

Internationalization of buyer-MNEs and their subsequent exposure to a broader range of international suppliers (and vice versa) enables the construction of new relationships. These can facilitate the inclusion and broader spread of supplier nationalities involved in business networks over time. Moreover, shifts in b2b relationships can also be explained through pointing at company-specific accumulation of experiences with b2b relationships and internationalization. Consequently, they obtain and internalize capabilities, which make them enter into new relationships more easily, also in unfamiliar environments or with previously unknown partners. Sectoral consolidation, acquisition trends and competitive behaviour on the part of rival suppliers trying to break into current buyer–supplier relationships contribute to changes in b2b partnerships as they shape a stimulating context for it.

In this regard, the reported wave of mergers among automotive suppliers and car constructors (see Section 2.10.1) illustrates the fundamental reshuffling of the supplier and assembler landscape. It also implies that the start of wholly new relationships has become more plausible. This refers to a situation where the nationalities of firms are less 'fixed' and holding on to relationships with companies from the same country is not a strategic long-term option or a realistic prospect anymore. It also points at the current, fundamentally international character and spirit of firms. Consequently, it can be argued that their search for b2b partners is no longer predominantly guided by national sentiments or by positive past experiences with a certain partner, but by rent seeking and establishing b2b relationships with partners that operate internationally, irrespective of (the nationalities behind) their capital structure.

Getting acquainted with internationalization (Carlson, 1966; Johanson and Vahlne, 1977, 1990; Forsgren, 2000), also contributes to new internationalization moves through ventures with new partners. Similarly, entering into inter-firm relationships as such and obtaining positive experiences with new relationships is also a catalyst for firms to interact with other companies. All together this lays the foundation for multinational inter-firm relationships. Also, it would explain the occurrence of changing business partner relationships over time.

Empirical research method to test this hypothesis: This hypothesis will be tested through a dynamic 'actor analysis' with respect to the partners involved in the satellite business networks in peripheral regions to be investigated. By identifying the respective suppliers involved in the research cases over time, as well as their capital structure and nationalities, possible shifts in this respect can be presented. The launching of new product versions will be used as the main point of reference to monitor the developments in question through time.

3.3.4   *Fourth hypothesis*

Hypothesis 4: Other b2b relationships and component-intrinsic logistics and production requirements determine to a larger extent whether or not a supplier will make site-specific investments than a (mutual) aim for exclusive relationships and or supplier status.

It is suggested that site-specific investments depend on a sort of 'network rationality' on the part of buyers and suppliers, that is, on determining the most economic way of manufacturing (among others based on possibilities to achieve economies of scale) for delivery of products to a set of specific assembly sites, and on the logistics requirements the assembly process imposes on the various component inputs. We argue that a buyer–supplier exclusivity thesis should be questioned. Among other things, based on the observation that buyers encourage suppliers to work for multiple clients (Florence, 1996; Pries, 1999)[21] and on suppliers' intention to optimize their production and delivery structures (Rhys, 2000; Rutherford, 2000). Consequently, it is suggested that if site-specific investments appear to be relation-specific – irrespective of the supplier's status, this should rather be understood as network–rational behaviour in terms of cost-efficient production and logistics with respect to the component in question. In addition, it is posited that such investments are made in view of a specific buyer's value to the supplier in terms of, for instance, the quantities this buyer purchases annually. If co-located investments are not only used to serve the nearest buyer plant but also other buyers, then it can be deduced that the nearest buyer plant represents superior value to the supplier in question compared to its other clients. If no or few site-specific investments are found in a region where a buyer plant houses, this is arguably caused by the relative lack of importance this buyer represents to its suppliers compared to their other clients. Such suppliers will then try to service the buyer plant in question from sites from where they can simultaneously attend all the clients they wish to service.

Empirical research method to test this hypothesis: The testing of the first hypothesis, combined with selective information on the client bases of the suppliers from our business network research cases, as well as the production and logistics characteristics of the components they provide, will allow us to test this hypothesis.

3.4   Summarizing the conceptual mission of the empirical case studies

Having outlined the various hypotheses, we can summarize the conceptual mission for our empirical case studies as follows.

First of all, we want to determine whether empirical proof can be found that the intra-firm network position of an MNE subsidiary that acts as the focal buyer of a business network influences the inter-firm network positioning behaviour on the part of its suppliers. In other words, do suppliers – when the relationship with a specific buyer plant gains importance through improvement of the latter's intra-firm network position – set up, expand or acquire (dedicated) facilities near such a client and empower these, so as to secure or establish a more competitive inter-firm network position vis-à-vis the plant in question?

Second, we mean to find out whether empirical proof can be found that the composition of a satellite business network in a peripheral region in particular and international business networks in general changes substantially over time.

We want to make it clear that, contrary to the research methods we will apply with respect to the first mission, for the second conceptual mission we do not attempt to meticulously determine the whys behind possible changes in the actor composition of business networks. Instead, our research with respect to the second mission is of a more exploratory nature. If we succeed in confirming the argument that the composition of business networks may change substantially over time, it is up to future research to explain the logics behind such changes.

4 Empirical research methodology and reporting structure

4.1 Introduction

After presenting the conceptual framework and research hypotheses in Chapter 3, this chapter serves to connect the conceptual framework with the empirical research cases and to describe more thoroughly how the formulated hypotheses will be tested in practice. On the one hand, this chapter contains an operationalization of the key concepts underlying the framework plus the way they will be monitored and measured. On the other hand, it contains a description of the case study reporting structure, which also provides an in-depth account of how the longitudinal case studies has been carried out. Together, it offers a description of the way the collection, processing and analysis of our primary data has been executed.

4.1.1 Critical note on the applied research methods

For the empirical research a multiple case study method is applied followed by a cross-case analysis. Although the appropriateness of case studies for our research purposes has been legitimized in Section 1.3, we should also point out the drawbacks of this method. These should be overcome in order to arrive at conclusions that truly have an explanatory and predictive value (Yin, 1994).

One of the main concerns is that the selected cases be representative (Albinski, 1981, p. 26). We dealt extensively with this issue in Section 1.3, when we indicated from which industry (automotive) and host regions (Navarra and Castilla y Leon, both in Spain) we would select our research cases. Therefore, we consider we have taken the necessary precautions to ensure that our research cases are sufficiently representative to warrant the conclusions at which we arrive. Generally speaking there is doubt as to the extent to which conclusions based on case studies are valid and can be generalized, especially due to the limited number of observations carried out (King *et al.*, 1994; Yin, 1994). On the one hand, we address this aspect via a thorough analysis and breakdown of the cases at hand and a large number of observations at various levels of analysis, as recommended by King *et al.* (1994, p. 209). These include observations at the levels of firms, inter-firm and business networks. This should both lead to in-depth insights and to the necessary nuances and differentiations with respect to our research object. On the other hand, we include a critical review of our findings in Chapter 7, where we will assess the predictive validity of our conclusions for similar cases of business networks.

With respect to validity, we argue that construct validity is secured in Sections 3.2 and 4.2 via the establishment of proper operationalizations of and plausible causal relations between the key variables underlying the conceptual framework presented in Chapter 3. Especially via extensive cross-referencing of theoretical assumptions with relevant publications of other scholars (see Section 3.2), substantial support for the construct validity of our conceptual framework, its key variables and the underlying relations is obtained. In addition, where this is expedient we also make suggestions (notably in Section 4.2) concerning extensions and refinements that can be made to the operationalizations we use. Extensions and refinements that are beyond the reach of the present research project, given the data and research means at our disposal. Finally, content validity is assured through the fact that the design of the data collection activities (see Section 4.3) follows seamless from our central research objectives, the various hypotheses and the constructed operationalizations of the respective key concepts. It should thus provide adequate coverage for the various research questions we have set out (Emory, 1985).

One of the other questions usually associated with case studies is whether they are reliable and can be replicated (Yin, 1994). In the present chapter, we offer a highly transparent presentation of the methods we have used in our research. We do acknowledge that, since a great deal of the required data is neither disseminated widely nor publicly (e.g. internal publications), it may not always be easy to obtain the data in question. Specifically in Section 4.3 we will explain how we went about obtaining the necessary information for our research. Evidently, when limitedly circulated data are needed, it goes without saying that researchers should not only be able to master scientific methodologies, tools and techniques for research and analysis. They also need 'navigation' skills to find out which data exist and to get access to the information they require.

4.2 Definition and measurement of key concepts

4.2.1 Operationalization and measurement of the intra-firm network position

In line with Nooteboom (1996) we argue that the relative value of buyer firms can be measured in terms of growth parameters such as: turnover, profit, learning and innovation possibilities. Consequently, the intra-firm network position of a car assembly subsidiary can be defined as follows: 'the role the subsidiary plays within the various stages of the life cycle of the car model(s) it produces, relative to the conjoint of activities carried out within the firm–hierarchy it pertains to, in relation to these stages'.

By life cycle stages or activities, we refer to the development, design, engineering and production activities surrounding product and manufacturing techniques and technologies involved in the conception and mass production of a car model. These do not include commercial and logistics activities such as sales and marketing of the final product and dealership deliveries.

Based on Nooteboom (1996), Nooteboom, Berger and Noorderhaven (1997) and Rutherford (2000), the following operational parameters are considered indicative of the intra-firm network position of a car assembly subsidiary within a large corporation.

- the managerial and production competences assigned to the plant in question;
- the character and strategic content of the relationships it maintains with suppliers;
- the production share of the plant vis-à-vis the total production of the model(s) it produces.

Furthermore, it is argued that a subsidiary's intra-firm network positioning is guided by its desire to increase its centrality and role in and share of corporate, notably strategic, business functions, competences and resources (Forsgren, 1989; Forsgren and Holm, 1993; Holm, 1994; Andersson and Pahlberg, 1997; Forsgren *et al.*, 1999; Phelps and Fuller, 2000; Nooteboom, 2002). To comprehend the basic logic behind this desire, the following statement by Nooteboom (2002, p. 10) is indicated: 'A characteristic of network position is centrality...One's centrality in a network increases the dependence of partners, since one offers them more opportunities for indirect access to competence, knowledge, or markets'.

For our case studies, we will analyse the evolution of the car manufacturing subsidiaries' intra-firm network position by means of the following two proxies (see also Hofer and Schendel, 1978; Grant, 1991; Andersson and Pahlberg, 1997).

1   The assignment of business functions and responsibilities to the car manufacturing subsidiaries in question over time, analogous to the first two parameters outlined earlier.
2   The model-specific production shares assigned to the respective car manufacturing subsidiaries compared to the entire model-specific production totals, through time analogous to the third parameter outlined earlier.

The first proxy requires further elaboration before it can be applied. When we take a look at the tasks involved in a car model's production life cycle, we get the following breakdown.

First of all, at the start of a car model's production life cycle a conceptual, design and product engineering part takes place. Second, a small set of pre-series is built together with the suppliers of production equipment and components. Third, final production engineering takes place. Finally, industrial mass manufacturing of the product in question takes off.

The degree to which a subsidiary plays a role in each of these stages – as the outcome of internal assignment policies and choices within the firm–hierarchy – determines its score on the first intra-firm network position proxy.

Obviously, it is especially the role a plant plays in the upstream stages of the production life cycle that accentuates the status and intra-firm network position of a plant, as it signifies the responsibility to (co-)prepare and manage the global production of a (new) car model. At the same time, it also increases its value to third parties, like suppliers. Furthermore, it helps obtain a number of tasks with higher added value than is offered by pure assembly activities. Finally, it also provides a certain degree of autonomy in the final engineering of production activities and the tightening of b2b relationships with suppliers in the pioneering phases of production for the whole corporation.

For, whereas in the development phases of a new model, the b2b relationships have a conceptual and strategic character, when production routines and engineering are being put into place the relationships take on a tactical and fine-tuning character. Once serial production commences, the b2b relationships become more operational in nature.

The attempts by subsidiaries of car manufacturing firms to play a role in the upstream stages of the production life cycle can be seen as a way for them to improve their intra-firm network position. Once a plant has managed to do that, it can then prove that it can carry out the accompanying managerial tasks satisfactorily. Consequently, the chances on repeating and confirming its upstream role become bigger. As a consequence, also the chances on the dedication of new resources to the plant in question increase. It is the prospect of such resources assignment that fuels MNE subsidiaries' desire to improve their intra-firm network position (Birkinshaw, 1996, p. 491; Forsgren *et al.*, 1999, p. 183; Phelps and Fuller, 2000).

Another factor that determines a subsidiary's intra-firm network position is the share it is allotted in the production of a specific model. The logic behind this parameter is as follows. Given that each plant has a limited absolute manufacturing capacity, there is a correlation between, on the one hand, model-specific production share and, on the other hand, the amount of different models a plant manufactures. We reason that it is in the interest of a plant to be involved in the production of only a few models, as this will increase efficiency and returns on investments (see also Skinner, 1974; Stalk and Hout, 1990; Dyer, 1996). At the same time, it enhances the plant's centrality with regard to the model(s) in question and it implies less changing and reprogramming of manufacturing devices, maintaining less distinct supplier relationships and delivery patterns and more possibilities of investing in highly dedicated material. All this will have a positive effect on the plant's productivity rates and its relative value to internal and external parties.

The attempts by subsidiaries of car manufacturing firms to obtain a product mandate, 'product exclusivity' or, to produce large batches of only a few models, as possible, can thus be seen as a way to improve their intra-firm network position (see for example, Laage-Hellman, 1997; Phelps and Fuller, 2000). Once either of these objectives is achieved, a plant can demonstrate it can deliver high productivity rates and corporate value in general. Consequently, the chances of confirming or achieving centrality with regard to specific product(s) increase, as does the chance of dedication of new resources to the plant in question. As stated above, these objectives fuel subsidiaries' desires to improve their intra-firm network position.

4.2.2   Operationalization and measurement of inter-firm network positioning

With inter-firm network positioning we refer to the spatial and assignment choices that independent suppliers make with regard to servicing specific car manufacturing subsidiaries in order to improve or maintain their network positions. This reasoning follows from the previously forwarded position that a supplier's inter-firm network positioning is guided by the relative importance or value (Nooteboom, 1996) a certain buyer represents in terms of growth parameters and that these growth possibilities are correlated to the buying entity's intra-firm network position, as described in Section 4.2.1.

With 'relative' we refer to the fact that a buyer plant's value to a supplier is compared to the value other client relationships represent to the supplier in question. These other clients can include both plants of the same organization to which a specific buying entity belongs. They can likewise be plants or enterprises belonging to other legal entities.

It is argued that also suppliers' location behaviour is driven by the postulation that actors strive to improve or maintain their network positions (Forsgren *et al.*, 1999; Phelps and Fuller, 2000; Nooteboom, 2002) and an important means to do that is to set up establishments near buyer plants that occupy important intra-firm network positions (Frigant and Lung, 2002).

The decision by suppliers to locate in the vicinity of a major client and thus boost their inter-firm network position is also in the interest of buyer plants themselves. Because such behaviour on the part of suppliers has a positive impact on their own intra-firm network position, it increases its chances of maintaining that position, leading as it does to agglomeration economies and comparative advantages vis-à-vis 'rival' factories of the same corporation (Sölvell *et al.*, 1990; Dyer, 1996; Forsgren *et al.*, 1999, p. 193; Andersson and Forsgren, 2000, p. 334).

The following indicators reflect the inter-firm network positioning behaviour of a supplier with regard to buyer firms.

- The geographical location of supplier sites, that is, near a specific client ('co-location') or at a distance;
- The assignment of specific business functions or responsibilities to supplier sites.

In our case studies we will analyse the evolution of the inter-firm network positioning of suppliers with regard to car manufacturing subsidiaries by means of the following three proxies.

1   The identity and nationality of the suppliers involved in the business network of a car manufacturing subsidiary (composition of its supplier networks) over time;
2   The origin of the conjoint of inputs the subsidiaries receive for their assembly activities over time;
3   The location of a sample of individual suppliers relative to the car manufacturing subsidiaries in question measured at a number of occasions through time.

The first proxy serves to measure the continuity and longevity of buyer–supplier relationships.

Proxies two and three allow evaluating the evolution of the overall spatial pattern of supplier networks in reaction to assignment practices with regard to the focal actors of business networks, for example, geographical densification or fragmentation.

We do not analyse the degree to which suppliers' branch locations are dedicated to a single client. It is true thats client-specific assets may indicate a supplier's strong commitment to a certain client. However, it can also be argued that especially when a supplier's branch location serves multiple clients and it is located near one of these respective clients, this ought to be related to the superior value of the client in question. It is this value that leads to a corresponding inter-firm network positioning of the supplier vis-à-vis this specific client. Therefore, location behaviour as such – irrespective of whether or not the assets are dedicated to a single client – is a more valid indicator of inter-firm network positioning than the level of dedication. Nevertheless, where expedient we will comment on this indicator to analyse and interpret further the inter-firm network positioning of the suppliers around the focal buyer plants in our case studies.

We neither include an analysis of the resources and competences assigned to supplier establishments in our case studies. Also here it is fair to state that the mere location of supply sites (and their distance to clients) is the primary indicator of inter-firm network positioning behaviour. Nevertheless, we admit that analysing the business functions and competences of supplier branch locations would help to further refine the measuring of inter-firm network positioning.

Two final observations should be made with respect to the measurement of inter-firm network positioning.

Our research attempts to control for any geographical behaviour that is primarily due to component-specific logistics requirements. For example, the delivery of certain components may be subject to such tight time schedules that irrespective of a car manufacturing subsidiary's intra-firm network position, the components in question will always be supplied from a more or less nearby-located site. The sample of components on which we base our inter-firm network positioning analyses contains but one example of such a component, that is, car seats. We will filter out its 'interference' when we discuss the empirical results regarding inter-firm network positioning, by clarifying the way in which the component-specific logistics requirements acted as an intervening variable in the inter-firm network positioning behaviour around this component. The remainder of the sample of components leaves more room for variation in terms of location behaviour. Consequently, we argue that analysing the geographical and assignment behaviour on the part of our sample's suppliers is a valid method for shedding light on the hypothesized correlation between 'buyer's intra-firm network position' and 'supplier's inter-firm network positioning'. The reason that the one component that requires supply from a site located nearby is not excluded from the sample, is because it contributes to the analysis of the actor composition of business networks over time.

As a second observation, we argue that buyer-specific purchasing and supplier selection practices can also be considered intervening variables in the location behaviour of suppliers. For instance, when a buyer practices a local-for-local purchasing and supplier selection policy, the constellation of suppliers will always reveal an intense co-location character. To avoid this 'error', we focus on buyers who practise centrally managed global sourcing. This way, one is able to reveal the inter-firm network positioning of suppliers as a function of the intra-firm network positions of car manufacturing subsidiaries.

4.2.3   Operationalization and measurement of b2b relationship longevity

Hub firms of networks are motivated by the objective to preserve or improve the competitiveness of the network they lead (Rugman and D'Cruz, 2000). Consequently, this implies that over time, choices as to which suppliers they will include in these networks can be revised. An outcome of reconsidering previously made supplier selections can be supplier substitutions. Likewise, from network and competitive behaviour theories it follows that suppliers are motivated by a desire to improve their network position or network centrality (Laage-Hellman, 1997; Nooteboom, 2002). As far as inter-firm network positioning is concerned, this implies that incumbent suppliers will try to maintain network positions they acquired in the past, whereas rival firms will show competitive behaviour in order to conquer network positions currently not under their control. Also consolidation moves, such as takeovers and mergers are then exponents of competitive behaviour by suppliers aiming to obtain improved network positions. It is in this field of forces that (dis)continuity of the actor composition of business networks takes shape.

To assess the stability and continuity of business networks, we make use of the concept of longevity. Longevity refers to the time during which a buyer firm maintains relationships with its various suppliers. Alternatively, it refers to the degree of substitution that can be observed with regard to the subsequent suppliers for a specific part or component.

In practice, this can be measured via the (average) amount of years or subsequent product generations during which a buyer firm maintains the same component-specific suppliers. Alternatively, it can be measured as a quotient of the (average or respective) amount of component-specific suppliers a buyer firm engages for the number of product generations or updates that fall into a specific period of analysis.

In our case studies, we measure the longevity of b2b relationships by dividing the amount of supplier substitutions by the amount of change possibilities for the conjoint of components under consideration in a given time period. This proxy can serve as a preliminary indicator for stability and continuity in business networks. For this we make use of the following formula.

Degree of longevity of b2b relationships

$$
L_{T_0-T_n} = 100\% * \left(1 - \frac{\Sigma \text{supplier substitutions } T_0 - T_n}{\Sigma(\text{N product generations}*\text{N components}) T_0 - T_n}\right)
$$

Source: Author's elaboration.

Obviously, the presented formula can only serve as a relatively 'clinical' proxy for assessing a network characteristic like stability. Therefore, in order to obtain a less sterile assessment of (in)stability of business networks' supplier involvement, when analysing supplier substitutions we will distinguish between (a) virtual or oligopoly-related substitutions (takeovers and alliances); (b) competitiveness-related substitutions (involvement of wholly new suppliers); (c) externalization-related substitutions (first time outsourcing of a component) and (d) internalization-related substitutions (re-internalization of the production of a component). Through dividing the changes and substitutions to be perceived into four different categories, it will be possible to get a broader sight on what are the dominant forms of change and substitution in a given buyer–supplier network. Whether they are more radical changes through substitutions of incumbent suppliers by entirely new supplier relationships. Or whether they are more incremental changes through the exchange of incumbent suppliers for other, already acquainted suppliers.

With regard to our research cases, the number of change possibilities (the denominator of the formula), is determined by the number of car model changes that take place during the time period under consideration, multiplied by the number of components whose supplier identity is followed.

Concerning the latter, we only focus on those suppliers whose components and parts are delivered directly to the subsidiaries that function as the focal buyers in our research cases. In other words, we concentrate on first tier supplier relationships.

The numerator of the formula expresses the amount of genuine third party substitutions. That is, the competitiveness-related substitutions and the oligopoly-related substitutions that can be judged as a genuine substitutions.

Take note that a substitution is only valued as a genuine substitution when the (leading entity behind the) 'new' supplier is completely new to the buyer. Similarly, whether a genuine substitution is valued as a whole substitution, half or, for instance, a quarter of a substitution, depends on the fact whether during the time segments considered, the buyer firm practised single sourcing, double or multiple sourcing for the component in question. In addition, whether it sourced in separate parts that make up a component instead of an integrated conjoint. It also depends on the question whether the substitution was in vigour during only part of a specific sub-period. Consequently, it is possible that the numerator of substitutions is expressed in fractions.

The first-time externalizations and re-internalizations do not refer to the substitution of a third party supplier for another. Therefore, these substitutions are not used to determine the value of the numerator. However, they do represent changes to the structure of a network. As a consequence, they are also worthwhile monitoring.

As also the nationality of the capital providers behind the involved suppliers is identified, this serves to further elaborate on the assessment of continuity or discontinuity of business networks.

To round off we make the following observation with regard to the measurement of longevity. Because we focus on buyers that practise centrally managed global sourcing, supplier selection is a corporate issue. Consequently, we argue that the results one will encounter with regard to b2b relationship longevity at the level of car manufacturing subsidiaries are representative for the entire mother corporation.

4.3   Data collection methods and case study reporting structure

Analogous to Berkhofer's (1969) approach, the chronological changes in the geographical and actor composition of the supplier networks surrounding the two car manufacturing branch plants of our research cases are described in terms of particular periods between the mid-1980s and 2001. Data description and analysis is performed in order to detect evolutionary patterns as well as stages and critical events with respect to (ruptures in) deep structures (Van de Ven, 1992; Halinen *et al.*, 1999). Data description and analysis is built up around the previously operationalized key concepts. First, the respective intra-firm network positions of the two car manufacturing subsidiaries that function as focal buyers of the buyer–supplier networks to be investigated.

Second, the inter-firm network positioning of their respective suppliers, and third, the longevity of the respective inter-firm relationships they entertain (see Section 4.2).

The introduction of a new product can be seen as the typical window of opportunity for buyer firms to evaluate current relationships and judge whether actor changes are convenient. It is also a good moment to evaluate the efficiency and quality of its different plants and see which (product-related) distribution of business functions and production shares is convenient from an intra-firm perspective. Finally, it is also the appropriate time for suppliers to consider their inter-firm network positioning in terms of geographical location and competence assignments vis-à-vis buyer plants in function of the latters relative value. As such, product changes serve as excellent points of reference to follow the evolutions of our interest. Therefore, these product changes are useful to determine the particular periods in our empirical case studies. Likewise, they serve to identify and assess (radical) changes in deep structures and detect critical events underlying such changes (Gersick, 1991; Van de Ven, 1992; Halinen *et al.*, 1999).

First, we will address the supplier network surrounding Volkswagen Navarra in Landaben as our first car manufacturing subsidiary. The primary empirical analyses and the field work concerns the period when the Landaben factory produced the Volkswagen Polo, that is, from 1984 onwards.

The analysis of the trajectory of Volkswagen Navarra's intra-firm network position, the inter-firm network positioning of its suppliers and the longevity of the relationships with the respective suppliers involved are broken down into three particular sub-periods to distinguish evolutionary patterns. The first sub-period runs from 1984 until 1994. This is the period during which it manufactured the VW Polo A02 model. A second sub-period runs from 1994 until 2001. This is the period in which the factory produced the VW Polo A03 and its restyled version, the VW Polo GP 99. The third sub-period runs from 2001 until 2003 and captures the VW Polo A04 production period.

Subsequently, we will address the supplier network around the FASA-Renault factory in Valladolid as our second car manufacturing branch plant. The primary empirical analyses and the field work concerns the period when FASA-Renault Valladolid was gradually integrated into the hierarchy of the Renault Group, also from 1984 onwards.

The analysis of the trajectory of the Valladolid plant's intra-firm network position, the inter-firm network positioning of its suppliers and the longevity of the relationships with the respective suppliers involved are broken down into four particular sub-periods to distinguish evolutionary patterns. The first sub-period runs from 1984 until 1990. This is the period when the Valladolid plant was fully integrated into the Renault hierarchy. In this period it shifted from – primarily – producing Renault Supercinqs to producing Renault Clios. A second sub-period runs from 1990 until 1996. This is the period in which the factory produced the Renault Clio first-generation and the restyled second-generation. The third sub-period runs from 1996 to

2001 and includes the Renault Clio II production period. The last sub-period runs from 2001 until 2003, the period in which FASA-Renault Valladolid produced the New Clio.

4.3.1   *Data collection methods and information sources consulted with respect to Volkswagen Navarra*

To analyse the evolution of Volkswagen Navarra's intra-firm network position and the geographical articulation and composition of its supplier network, we proceeded in the following ways.

First of all we made use of annual reports of VW for the years 1980–2002 and of SEAT for the years 1976–1986. The latter was done because the factory in Landaben, which obtained the denomination 'Volkswagen Navarra' in 1995, stayed under SEAT governance until 1994, even though cooperation between VW and SEAT began in 1981 and the Landaben factory exclusively produced VW Polos as of 1984. The fact that from 1984 onwards the Landaben factory was increasingly managed by VW, made a further follow-up of SEAT annual reports for information on the Landaben factory as of 1987 irrelevant.

The focus of the annual report analysis was especially on information and numerical data regarding:

1   car constructor-specific headquarters–subsidiary relationships;
2   the specific roles of the car manufacturing subsidiary in question within the overarching mother company;
3   the intra-firm distribution of competences;
4   the car model-specific production totals of the car manufacturing subsidiary in question;
5   other plants of the same car constructor assembling the same car models as the car manufacturing subsidiary under consideration.

In addition, interviews were held with representatives from Volkswagen Navarra, and with representatives from the headquarters of Volkswagen in Wolfsburg. The persons that were interviewed were involved in logistics, purchasing, sourcing and the organization of the start up of the production cycle for subsequent Polo editions at plant and corporate management level. During the meetings also all kinds of text or otherwise codified data were received. Together, this allowed establishing a clear understanding of both the operational practices at plant level and strategic considerations behind intra-firm competence assignment practices and the logistics, location and procurement aspects with regard to b2b relationships.

All this information served as an important point of departure for a reconstruction of the intra-firm network position of Volkswagen Navarra within the VW concern.

The same can be said about the geographical articulation and actor composition of the supplier network surrounding Volkswagen Navarra between 1984 and 2003. The data extracted from the annual reports analysis and the oral and written information obtained via the interviews held at Volkswagen Navarra and at VW's corporate level served to establish a clear view on:

(i) in-house activities both at the car manufacturing subsidiary in question and at other plants of the same mother company;
(ii) the distribution of internalization and externalization between the car constructor hierarchy and independent suppliers;
(iii) car constructor-specific management of supplier relations;
(iv) the value of the supplies to the car manufacturing subsidiary under consideration, in terms of their geographical origins;
(v) car manufacturing subsidiary-specific overviews of the suppliers for a selection of components, with the respective locations of the sites from where these components are delivered and the nationality of the owners of the suppliers involved over time.

However, due to (a) confidentiality reasons, (b) the overall accent of these data on suppliers that delivered just-in-time, (c) the fact that a complete breakdown of a car model's content would result in an endless list of components and suppliers, (d) the time-consuming character of looking up all those details for people at Volkswagen Navarra or at corporate level, and (e) limited access to company archives for external researchers, the gathered data still needed substantial additions in view of our research problems.

Therefore, interviews were also held with representatives of umbrella institutions in Navarra, such as Sodena (regional development company) and the Ministry of Labour in Navarra (department of labour relations). For decades, these institutions maintained a close relationship with the automotive industry, and tapping into their knowledge allowed gaining additional insights with regard to present and past situations of Volkswagen Navarra itself and of the supplier network around it. In addition, also a number of interviews was conducted with a leading scholar in relation to Navarra's automotive industry: Dr Longas.

Furthermore, interviews were held with a selection of locally established (past and present) suppliers to Volkswagen Navarra. At the same time, information regarding the Navarra-based suppliers of Volkswagen Navarra was gathered through targeted written correspondence with selected companies and through the screening of annual reports and other publications of those suppliers with the longest tradition of working with Volkswagen Navarra.

These companies were traced via information obtained from Volkswagen Navarra and via a set of company *directorios*, published by the *Gobierno Foral de Navarra* and the Regional Development of Navarra 'Sodena' (e.g. CEIN; the automotive index under the *Gobierno Foral de Navarra*'s export.navarra.net and its *Catalogo Industrial de Navarra*; and Sodena's 'Companies with foreign capital').

Finally, secondary analysis and data processing was conducted on a large variety of data provided by Volkswagen Navarra (e.g. the review 'Apunto'; an article written by Volkswagen Navarra staff members Sanchez Jauregui and Royo Vicente, 1997; and statistics with respect to the geographical origin of assembled materials and components) and by the corporate level of VW (e.g. statistics; slide shows; and material from the website of the VW Group related to supply issues: vwgroupsupply), on articles that appeared in the regional press in Navarra (e.g. articles in *'Diario de Navarra'* and *'Diario de Noticias'*, from the Chamber of Commerce and Sodena), on articles that appeared in specialized automotive reviews (e.g. Autorevista, Automotive Sourcing and Automotive News Europe) and on a selection of scientific publications concerning the automotive sector in Navarra (notably works of Aláez *et al.*, 1996, 1999; and Longas, 1998).

4.3.2   Data collection methods and information sources consulted with respect to FASA-Renault Valladolid

To analyse the evolution of FASA-Renault Valladolid's intra-firm network position and the geographical articulation and composition of its supplier network, we made use of the following sources.

First of all, the annual reports of the Renault Group for the years 1985–2001, the *'Renault Atlas économique'* éditions 1990–2001, and the annual reports dedicated exclusively to FASA-Renault for the period 1985–2001 (*'Memoria y Balance/Informe Annual*).

The focus of the annual report and *Atlas économique* analyses was on identical information and numerical data as for Volkwagen Navarra, as shown under items 1 to 5 in Section 4.3.1.

In addition, interviews were held with representatives from FASA-Renault, and with representatives from the headquarters of Renault in Boulogne-Billancourt and from the Technocentre in Guyancourt. The persons that were interviewed were involved in logistics, purchasing, sourcing and the organization of the start up of the production cycle for subsequent Clio editions at plant and corporate management level. During the meetings also all kinds of text or otherwise codified data was received. Together, this allowed establishing a clear understanding of both operational practices at plant level and strategic considerations behind intra-firm competence assignment practices and logistics, location and procurement aspects with regard to b2b relations.

All this information served as an important point of departure for a reconstruction of the intra-firm network position of the Valladolid plant within the Renault concern.

The same can be said with regard to the geographical articulation and actor composition of the supplier network around the plant during the period 1990–2003 (Clio production period). The data obtained via the annual report and *Atlas économique* analysis and the oral and written information obtained in the interviews held at FASA-Renault in Spain and at Renault's corporate level served to establish a clear view on the issues 'i' to 'v' as listed under Section 4.3.1.

Also in this case the gathered data still needed substantial additions in view of our research problems, especially with respect to the changes in the supplier network surrounding the Valladolid subsidiary during the Clio era.

Therefore, interviews were held with academics which had monitored the changes in the automotive sector of Castilla y Leon over a long period of time (Prof. Dr Rosario Pedrosa Sanz, Prof. Dr Fernando Manero Miguel, Prof. Dr José Ramón Perán González), as well as representatives of umbrella institutions in Castilla y Leon such as the regional development company ADE ('Agencia de Desarrollo Economico') and a consultancy company (SOCINTEC), which had carried out research activities, commissioned by ADE, with respect to the automotive sector in Castilla y Leon.

Furthermore, interviews were held with a selection of locally established suppliers to the Valladolid plant. In addition, information regarding the Castilla y Leon-based suppliers of the Valladolid plant was gathered via targeted written correspondence with selected companies and via the screening of annual reports and other publications of those suppliers with the longest tradition of working with the Valladolid plant.

These companies were traced via information obtained from the Valladolid plant and via a set of company *directorios*, published by Excal, the Chamber of Commerce of Valladolid, Telecyl and Cidaut.

Finally, secondary analysis and data processing regarding both FASA-Renault Valladolid itself and its suppliers was conducted on a large variety of data facilitated by the Valladolid plant (e.g. the internal reviews *'Rombo'*; *'Comunicacion Mandos'*; and *'Info Mandos'*) and by the corporate level of Renault (e.g. the internal review *'Global Magazine'*; and material related to supply issues as they appeared on the website of Renault: renault.com), on articles that appeared in the regional press in Castilla y Leon (e.g. articles in *'El Norte de Castilla'*) or from the hand of the *Junta de Castilla y Leon* (i.e. hinter-land.com), on articles that appeared in specialized automotive reviews (e.g. *El Mundo Motor, Finanzas, Boletin ACEA, El País Negocios, Autorevista, La tribuna de automocion, Autoprofesional, Automotive Sourcing* and *Automotive News Europe*), on a selection of scientific publications that deal with the automotive sector in Castilla y Leon (notably works of Pedrosa Sanz, 1983, 1993; Lagendijk, 1994, 1995; Fernandez Arrufe and Pedrosa Sanz, 1997; and Manero Miguel and Pascual Ruiz de Valdepeñas, 1998), and on publications that report on Renault's supplier relation management (e.g. Gorgeu and Mathieu, 1995; Florence, 1996; Layan, 1997; Bonzemba and Okano, 1998).

5 Empirical results with respect to Volkswagen Navarra

This chapter presents the results of the empirical case study with respect to the Volkswagen Navarra car factory – located in Landaben, Navarra – and its supplier network, during the period this plant produced the Volkswagen Polo.

5.1 Empirical study on the Volkswagen Polo era

5.1.1 Introduction: integration of the Landaben plant into the VW hierarchy

The car factory at Landaben near Pamplona, Navarra, was founded as 'Automoviles Hispano Ingleses' (AUTHI) in 1965 in order to subsequently manufacture car models from British Motor Company (BMC) and from British Leyland (BLMC). Eventually, due to managerial and financial problems, the British partner withdrew from the AUTHI project and SEAT took over the Landaben plant in 1976.

By the end of the 1970s the Spanish government, through INI, sought to integrate SEAT into FIAT. This was seen as the best way to ensure the company's survival in an increasingly open and competitive market, especially keeping in mind the already certain integration of Spain in the European Union in 1986. The need for constant investments to keep up with (foreign) competition not only demanded a financially sound partner, a role that had until then been played by INI, but also a technologically powerful partner.

With the objective of securing SEAT's competitiveness through FIAT's care taking, negotiations between INI and FIAT were initiated in 1979 (SEAT, 1980, p. 52). On 11 June 1979, it was agreed that FIAT would be allowed to acquire an ample majority in SEAT's capital on or before the 31 December 1981, provided certain conditions (principally investments and the co-financing of SEAT's capital extension in May 1980) would be met by FIAT.

Nevertheless, FIAT encountered unexpected commercial problems due to an unfavourable development of its business in the international car market in 1980. Consequently, the company decided to concentrate on the problems of its factories in Italy (Gonzalez de la Fé, 2001).

In June 1980, FIAT finally decided not to take over SEAT and its representatives on SEAT's board of directors were replaced in the summer of 1980. By the end of 1980, SEAT was already for 70.8% in the hands of INI. In 1981, when FIAT withdrew completely, INI became the 95% owner of SEAT (SEAT, 1982, p. 61). To safeguard foreign sales, the export relations between SEAT and FIAT remained intact until 1985.

Due to the rupture with FIAT and the absence of sufficient critical mass to seize internal and external growth possibilities to ensure an efficient and independent enterprise, SEAT was obliged to establish a new relationship with another major car manufacturer. A manufacturer that, through its production dimensions and commercial outlets, would be able to sustain the elevated costs of R&D and innovation of new products intrinsic to the contemporary needs of automobile manufacturing (SEAT, 1982, p. 62). Or as stated by VW (1988, p. 73): 'Due to lowering market shares there was a growing lack of means [at SEAT] to cope with necessary investments in production establishments and R&D. Also the fact that there was no own export organization worked counterproductive' (our translation).

With this aim in mind, negotiations were held with principal European carmakers and with Toyota and Nissan (Gonzalez de la Fé, 2001). In the end, SEAT signed an agreement with VW on the 30 September 1982 concerning commercial and technological co-operation. Among other things, this implied production cooperation as from the 1 January of 1983 onwards during 7 years.

VW was interested in this deal, as it would help to increase its presence on the Spanish market and to solve its production capacity problems (VW, 1988, p. 37). Likewise, it offered a way to circumvent the high production costs in Germany, which were especially unfavourable with regard to compact models with fewer technical requirements. VW especially sought to manufacture these models in Spain, where costs would be lower.

Due to the continuous investments in the Landaben plant up to 1982, VW encountered a highly modernized and efficient factory, to which it assigned an important role within its organization and production structure. The SEAT-VW agreement included, among other things, the decision to manufacture 90,000 units of the VW Polo in the Landaben plant as of 1984.[22]

From the moment the Landaben plant started to function as a VW production centre, the factory no longer frequently switched with regard to which model(s) it had in production. This not only meant that the plant could now identify itself much stronger with a single product, but it also implied higher productivity rates and more labour tranquility.

In June 1986 Volkswagen acquired 51% of the shares of SEAT from INI and in December of the same year VW's participation in SEAT reached 75% (SEAT, 1987, p. 29; Sanchez Jauregui and Royo Vicente, 1997). On the 31 December 1986 SEAT was completely consolidated in the VW concern (VW, 1987, p. 8). As a consequence, in 1986 INI transferred the entire SEAT *patrimonium* (including, among other things, its two factories in Barcelona and the one in Landaben) to VW (Seidler, 1991; El País, 1996). The agreement also included the definition of a strategic plan for SEAT for the period 1986–1995 (SEAT, 1986, p. 25).

This strategic plan included large investment plans for the Spanish plants (VW, 1986, p. 13): 'Due to the urgent need for restructuring, our SEAT strategy will entail large investments and considerable reorganization costs will have to be made during a number of years' (our translation). Substantial investments were also made with regard to the Landaben plant (see for example, VW Navarra, 1995; El País, 1997b; De Lloyd, 1998).

In 1990 VW obtained complete ownership of SEAT and further amplifications to the Landaben plant were carried out. The main aim of these works was to prepare it for engine block assembly on the basis of knocked-down engine blocks delivered by VW Salzgitter (VW Navarra, 1995, p. 3).

In 1991 additional factory extensions were carried out in order to internalize the stamping activities of large exterior body parts as of 1994. Also new investments were made to prepare the factory for an extension of its assembly activities from 1994 onwards (VW Navarra, 1995, p. 3).

In September 1992 the complete Polo A02 production was moved to Landaben and the factory acquired the title of 'leading plant' with total responsibility for the model (VW Navarra, 1995, p. 3).

At the end of 1993, the legal entity *Fabrica Navarra de Automoviles S.A.* was created, as a part of SEAT (Longas, 1998). In 1994 VW gained full ownership of the plant. SEAT's critical financial situation made VW buy *Fabrica Navarra de Automoviles S.A.* from SEAT to provide SEAT with a capital injection (El País, 1994; La Vanguardia, 1994). In 1995 its name was changed to Volkswagen Navarra.[23]

5.1.2 Corporate features of VW's headquarters–subsidiary relationships

To interpret the intra-firm network position of the Landaben plant within the VW concern over time, we will now shed light on the hierarchical and intra-firm distribution of competences at VW and, related to this, the assignment of business functions to VW Navarra subsequent to the Landaben plant's full integration into the VW structures.

When we take a look at the tasks involved in a car model's production life cycle based on Section 4.2.1, we can distinguish the following stages.

At the outset of a car model's production life cycle a conceptual, design and product engineering part takes place. Second, together with the suppliers of production equipment and components a small set of pre-series is made. Third, final production engineering takes place. Finally, industrial mass manufacturing of the car model in question takes off.

With respect to the first stage, the VW headquarters and design studios are responsible. In general terms, the more strategic business functions, such as R&D, marketing, sales, strategic quality and logistics management, purchasing and selection of suppliers, are concentrated at corporate level. With respect to those strategic matters, the Landaben plant has always functioned as a branch location without autonomy (Sanchez Jauregui, 2001). This was the case during the AUTHI and SEAT period, and the situation under VW is therefore no more than a prolongation of the intra-firm distribution of competences of old. It is at the central level that the prototypes are designed and produced. It is also at the central level that suppliers are selected both for development tasks (the so-called 'development suppliers') and for final mass production (Busto, 1997).

Until the 1990s the second stage took place centrally in Germany. From the 1990s onwards, VW began to transfer responsibility to a so-called *'Leitwerk'* (*'fabrica lider'* or 'leading plant'), which could also be located outside Germany. This was the case with the Landaben factory with regard to the VW Polo A03, which first went into production in 1994. In short, the second stage of the above-mentioned process today no longer has to take place at company headquarters level or at home-based plants, but it can also be assigned to plants located outside of Germany.

The third stage of the production life cycle, regarding final production engineering of a new model, is assigned to the plant that is chosen as the leading plant for a particular model. The leading plant then takes the lead in production fine-tuning activities with component suppliers and production equipment providers (Sanchez Jauregui, 2001).

Once the production routines are put in place by the leading plant, they are also introduced at other factories where the same model will be assembled. This is done under the guidance and supervision of that same leading plant (Erro, 2001).

The fourth group of activities involved in the production life cycle of a car is, besides mass production, the purchasing of generic material – provided it stays under a limited cost (Busto, 1997; Longas, 1998; Sanchez Jauregui, 2001), plant-specific fine-tuning of mass production routines, final inbound logistics and operational quality inspection. These responsibilities are allocated at the level of all assembly plants involved in serial production of VW models.

Obviously, being elected leading plant for a specific model is something which accentuates the status and intra-firm network position of a plant as it involves the responsibility to prepare and manage the global production of that model. It also means the plant has to carry out a number of tasks with higher added value than pure assembly activities. Meanwhile, it receives considerable responsibility in the final engineering of production activities and the shaping of b2b relationships for the whole VW concern.[24] Implicitly, it also has an impact on the allocation and assignment of production shares of a specific model to plants, that is, which factory will obtain the largest share of the production of a specific model?

5.1.3   Corporate features of VW's management of inter-firm relationships

Data on the 1980s supplier practices at VW indicate that at that time the company worked on a rather geographically scattered basis with suppliers, emphasizing local-for-local production due to local content prescriptions (VW, 1981, p. 14): 'Generally speaking, the foreign branch plants are advancing very well in developing their own networks of suppliers for local procurement of parts. Thanks to that, we have been able to live up to local content standards imposed on us by various national governments. It also allowed us to reap additional technical know-how by interacting with new suppliers' (our translation).

Similarly, the outsourced production tasks were considerably fragmented and allocated to small and medium-sized enterprises (SMEs) in the beginning (VW, 1982, p. 15): 'In 1981 the Volkswagen concern worked worldwide with 30,000 supply companies of which approximately 90% can be categorized as SMEs' (our translation). Also in 1983, the annual report still mentions VW works worldwide with 30,000 suppliers, 15,400 of which were from Germany. The small and medium size of the bulk of its suppliers is also emphasized (VW, 1984, p. 37). All this accentuates the sustained local-for-local and fragmented character of VW's outsourcing practices in this period.

In the 1984 annual report (VW, 1985, p. 33) it is again acknowledged that global activities require international procurement. In that edition it is also indicated that foreign suppliers are responsible for increasing shares of the total expenses on parts procurement by VW plants (VW, 1985, p. 33): 'Building upon the highly competitive supplier conjoint from Western Germany, our international purchasing serves to complement our global procurement needs' and '... the production of certain models at different places around the globe has already led to a significant increase in international exchange of parts and integrated components' (our translation).

As regards the strategic involvement of suppliers, until the early 1980s this was limited to production tasks, largely based on design specifications of VW. Development and design activities were only to a very limited extent the domain of the contracted suppliers. Suppliers were largely selected on the basis of their production cost structures and their logistics possibilities. Instead, the disposal of or the potential for technological and innovation capabilities was of marginal importance at that time (VW slide show, 2002).

Later a more globally integrated supplier management, centrally led and with global sourcing practices, was pursued. This can be illustrated via the following statements (VW, 1989, p. 13): 'Also in 1988 foreign purchasing increased sharper than the overall value of external purchasing. Especially procurement from suppliers with establishments on many international locations contributed to this. They made our company's car manufacturing activities abroad considerably easier' (our translation). Internationalization of the activities of supplier firms is also forwarded as a reason for enhancing and implementing global sourcing: 'The high relevance foreign suppliers represent to Volkswagen as a whole is also fruit of the internationalizing supply and purchasing business' (VW, 1992, p. 10).

Nevertheless, the emphasis that is put on the purchasing from suppliers based in West and East Germany, continues to indicate a strong embeddedness of VW in home base supply relationships (e.g. VW, 1991, p. 13, 1993, p. 9, 1994, p. 14, 1995, p. 13). In fact, relationships with suppliers of German origin continued to play a significant part in the company's overall purchasing activities at least until the mid-1990s (VW, 1996, p. 37): 'As in past years, also in 1995 the largest share of the global procurement volume was delivered by German suppliers. In total, German suppliers were good for approximately 70% of the global sourcing value, which underlines their international competitiveness' (our translation). Grohn (2002) argues that before 1995 the German suppliers' share was even higher than 70%. This insinuates that local procurement of parts does not imperatively imply that local-owned manufacturers made the parts in question. In fact, it is also possible that it is parts produced by German firms with a local presence abroad.

Afterwards, a decline in the value German suppliers represented to VW's procurement volumes could be observed. In 1996, the share of German suppliers in the grand total of exterior purchasing was 59.1% and in 1997 this had dropped to 52.8% (VW, 1998, p. 16). In 1998 it was 55.6% (VW, 1999, p. 22), in 1999 it was 56.6% (VW, 2001, p. 25) and in 2000 and 2001 it was 57.5% and 53.8% respectively (VW, 2002, p. 38).

The increased share of foreign suppliers in VW's exterior purchasing expenses can be attributed to VW's policy to actively increase foreign suppliers' involvement in its procurement relations (VW, 1998, p. 35): 'Internationalization of our purchasing activities is supported in the following way: foreign branch plants as well as purchasing agencies in areas of the world where we want to improve our market positions will become increasingly involved in our procurement processes' (our translation).

With respect to the increase of foreign suppliers' value in annual purchasing totals from 1995 onwards, Grohn (2002) argues that they are the outcome of the initiation of VW's global and forward sourcing policies in 1993. It can thus be seen as an effect of the more global approach to purchasing, which VW implemented at that time. It appears that from 1993 onwards VW truly widened its scope and started comparing potential suppliers with those that were already supplying VW. As a consequence, solid and embedded supplier relationships were thoroughly benchmarked with alternative suppliers and these 'bonded' relationships were no longer prolonged automatically. The purchasing team also started to function more proactively, scanning the world for potential suppliers. This approach increased the chances for substitution of suppliers as contacts with new candidates were actively sought after and they were invited to bid. Rather than offering a 'last call' to incumbent suppliers,

suppliers were selected after offering equal chances for everyone to participate in competitive bidding. 'Loyalty' to incumbent suppliers was thus not practiced to extremes. In short, suppliers were selected on competitive grounds, but with freedom for VW purchasers to negotiate (Grohn, 2002).

In addition, VW evolved to procurement of more integrated components and a tiering of the supplier structure. Likewise, the selected suppliers became involved in more upstream development activities with regard to the components in question. This growing strategic importance of suppliers is already clearly acknowledged in the early 1980s (e.g. VW, 1984, p. 37, 1985, p. 17). Towards the second half of the 1980s, suppliers increasingly became involved as well in the early development stages through their inclusion in simultaneous engineering activities. Another illustration of suppliers' growing importance to VW is their inclusion in simultaneous engineering activities (e.g. VW, 1994, p. 14, 1995, p. 13, 1996, p. 36, 1997, p. 16). The conceiving and management of supplier relationships on the basis of limited stock and JIT at VW is also emphasized from the second half of the 1980s onwards (e.g. VW, 1987, p. 35, 1988, p. 37, 1990, p. 34). The implementation of JIT practices between suppliers and VW were, for instance, further emphasized in 1991 (VW, 1992, p. 21). The mentioning of practices of complete systems supply by first tier suppliers (e.g. VW, 1994, p. 14, 1997, p. 29), and forward sourcing (e.g. VW, 1996, p. 36, 1998, p. 34) are additional examples of the growing importance of the role of suppliers.

The former led to a reduction of the supplier base as more and more suppliers were selected to work for multiple VW plants, models and continents (see for example, Pries, 1999). Consequently, in 2001, VW worked with only 4,532 suppliers of automotive parts (Grohn, 2002) – as compared to 30,000 in 1983, as mentioned earlier.

From among this group of 4,532 suppliers, the bulk of VW's parts procurement comes from suppliers with an annual turnover below €125 million (VW slide show, 2002). This group of suppliers represents more than 50% of the total value of VW's external procurement. Companies from this turnover segment are considered SMEs by VW. Although their share in VW's total outsourcing expenses is lower than it was at the beginning of the 1980s (approximately 90%, as mentioned earlier), it still represents a considerable part of VW's external procurement. The majority of the indicated group of SMEs supplies VW with individual parts. The second most important group of suppliers are those with an annual turnover between €500–10,000 million. This group represents in particular suppliers of modules. Together, they account for around 20% of the total value of VW's external procurement. The fact that most suppliers have an annual turnover below €125 million, indicates that VW works mostly with parts suppliers. In fact, VW prefers to work largely on the basis of parts supplies and only to a limited extent with system and module supplies (Grohn, 2002). VW argues that this limits its (technological) dependence on suppliers.

To illustrate the value of independent suppliers to VW, it is stated that a supplier like Bosch (brakes, ignition, engine control systems, wiper systems, ...) possesses knowledge and capabilities VW does not possess. As such, VW can not do without this kind of suppliers and needs early consultation rounds with them (Grohn, 2002). This illustrates that not only asymmetric b2b relationships exist between VW and component suppliers, but also more symmetric relationships. In general terms, the ongoing specialization of suppliers in their respective fields means that asymmetry is contained in buyer–supplier relationships.

On behalf of VW, what is done to avoid too strong a reliance on suppliers is the following. VW prefers to keep the integration of automotive conjoints below the level of a system. Otherwise, it would lose grip on its conceptual and technological development and its product composition. Through less aggregated conjoints, the purchasing management is able to maintain a stronger hold on the overall design of a conjoint and the relationship with suppliers. This can be considered as practices of dependence and supplier autonomy containment in order to reduce the gap in know-how between supplier and assembler. Instead, when systems are more fragmented, VW is able to co-determine more easily the supply specificities of materials and the choice of lower tier suppliers that deliver these materials to a first tier supplier. It also allows VW to keep better sight on the processes and materials implied, thus ensuring that the gap between assembler's and suppliers' core competences and core knowledge is maintained below a certain critical level. Therefore, 'product fragmentation' is considered a key element for VW's purchasing strategies. Finally, it also favours cost transparency and therefore enhances cost containment possibilities. As a consequence, the total number of suppliers remains relatively high.

The *filialization*[25] or sell-off of in-house production activities is a method for externalization, which has been practiced rarely by VW. Grohn (2002) supposes that the marriage of VW cabling activities with *Bergmann Kabelwerke* and its transformation into '*Bordnetze*' around 1983 is probably the only case of filialization at VW. Rather than selling off activities that form no longer a core business for VW, such activities tend to be discontinued gradually and the VW workers involved are re-educated to fulfil other functions within the VW concern, whereas others leave the company via a social plan.

If we focus on the value that expenses for external development and purchasing of automotive parts and components represent compared to VW's turnover, Figure 5.1 demonstrates how this continually increases over time.

As can be derived from Figure 5.1, there was a steadily growing involvement of suppliers in VW's business activities. The intensified sourcing strategies from the middle of the 1990s onwards, in general, and the more strategic involvement of suppliers in the conceiving of VW car parts in particular, manifestly led to a continued growth in the value of suppliers' contributions to VW's turnover after 1995.[26]

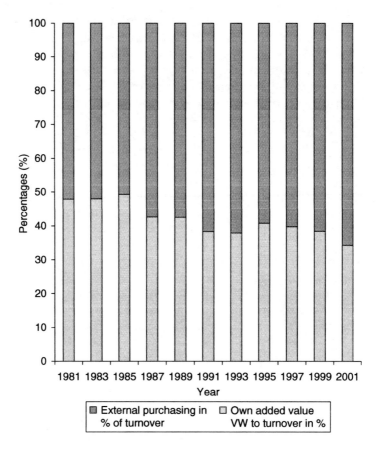

Figure 5.1 Implication of external suppliers in total VW turnover 1981–2001.

Source: Author's elaboration based on VW, Annual Reports 1981–2001, Wolfsburg, 1982–2002.

5.2   The VW Polo A02 production period

5.2.1   Analysis

In February 1984 the Landaben plant started producing the VW Polo. The first Polo model produced in Landaben, the Polo A02, stayed in production until 1994.

5.2.1.1   Volkswagen Navarra's share in total Polo production

The VW Polo A02 was also produced in Germany, at the Wolfsburg plant, where it had already been in production for several years. From 1990 onwards it was also produced at the VW site in Mosel near Zwickau, former East Germany (VW, 1991, p. 13). The following Table 5.1 illustrates how the

Table 5.1 Annual production volumes at VW Navarra and share in total production of Polo A02

Year	Polo A02 production in Landaben	Polo A02 production of VW Group in rest of Europe	Landaben share in total VW A02 Polo production in Europe (%)
1984	30,123	125,931	19.30
1985	75,778	109,315	40.94
1986	95,919	118,589	44.72
1987	116,02	116,138	49.97
1988	104,616	110,716	48.58
1989	124,115	104,752	54.23
1990	143,750	82,056	63.66
1991	191,700	133,582	58.93
1992	222,222	84,268	72.51
1993	176,327	0	100.00
1994	145,784	6,209	95.91

Source: Author's elaboration based on SEAT, Memoria y Balance ejercicio 1983–1986, Madrid, 1984–1987; VW, Annual Reports 1983–1994, Wolfsburg, 1984–1995.

VW Polo A02 production evolved in Landaben and at the conjoint of VW plants in Europe.

Although this term may not have been in use at the time, conceptually speaking Wolfsburg operated as the leading plant for the Polo A02 between 1984 and 1994. It was the main producer of VW Polos and it also provided managerial direction to other plants assembling the VW Polo.

In 1984, when the Landaben plant commenced with the production of the VW Polo, it started manufacturing a 'consolidated' product that was already firmly embedded in established intra-firm and inter-firm production and supply patterns set up around the assembly operations of Wolfsburg. These patterns were to a large extent also applied to the Landaben plant. This meant that many components the Landaben plant processed were provided by Volkswagen factories in Germany and by suppliers, mainly from Germany, that already delivered to the Wolfsburg plant.

As Marrodan (1999, p. 36) testifies: 'when Landaben started assembling the Polo A02, the totality of pieces was received from Germany. However, there was a firm intention to augment the degree of national inputs. This was achieved bit-by-bit' (our translation). The VW annual reports published between 1984–1994, those of SEAT between 1984–1986, as well as the various interviews held with representatives from VW Navarra (Marrodan, 1996; Busto, 1997, 2000; Sanchez Jauregui, 2001) confirm this picture. The factory evolved from a situation where the bulk of the assembled pieces came in from Germany, towards a situation where a considerable share was supplied by the SEAT factories in Catalonia, supplemented with parts produced at the Landaben factory itself and supplies from independent suppliers with (in certain cases newly set-up) production centres in Spain.

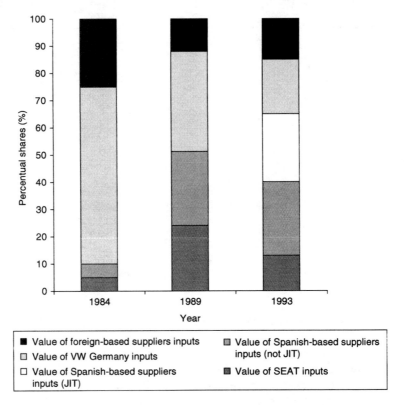

Figure 5.2 Breakdown of the origins of supplies to VW Navarra for the Polo A02.

Source: Author's elaboration based on VW Navarra S.A. Direccion Logistica, 1989, 1995; Marrodan, 1999; Sanchez Jauregui, 2001.

Especially as the annual amount of Polos that Landaben assembled kept growing and its position in the gross European production virtually reached a monopoly status in the early 1990s (see Table 5.1), continuing to import pieces from Germany on a massive scale became far too costly. Therefore, from the end of the 1980s onwards a supply structure emerged that reflected more strongly the increasing importance of the Landaben plant in the production of VW Polos. The importance of the Landaben plant not only grew from an intra-VW perspective, but also from the point of view of the growing number of independent suppliers. For the latter, Navarra gradually replaced Niedersachsen as 'the place to be' to set up production or assembly centres for Polo parts deliveries.

5.2.1.2   Evolution of supply origins

In order to analyse the supply origins with regard to the Landaben plant, the following Figure 5.2 presents a quantitative breakdown of the external supply flows. This figure allows observing the evolutions in supply origins that were characteristic for the Polo A02 production period.

Figure 5.2 illustrates that the role of the parts manufactured internally (VW produce) was still quite important at the start of this period, representing the majority of the external inputs to the car production activities at the Landaben plant. The role of independent suppliers was, at the same time, relatively limited at the beginning of the A02 period. Nevertheless, their role would gain rapidly in importance. Especially towards the end of the A02 production period it can be seen that the contribution in value of the independent suppliers surpasses that of inputs from sister VW and SEAT plants. This indicates the increasing (accumulated) strategic importance of the independent suppliers towards the end of this period.

Regarding the geographical constellation of the supply network in this period we see the following. At the outset of the A02 period, there is a complete embeddedness of the Landaben plant in the supply and production structures of the VW mother company and its Wolfsburg plant that also produces the A02. The level of Spanish inputs, either by SEAT or by Spanish suppliers, is negligible and the dependence on foreign supply is complete.

It is also evident that supplies from Spain became increasingly important towards the end of the A02 period. For this, two main reasons can be forwarded. First of all, the initial dependence on inputs from abroad was substituted as soon as possible by product flows from SEAT branch locations in Spain. Second, the shift from in-company production towards outsourcing to independent suppliers, either from Spain or with production and assembly bases in Spain is intensified. The following illustrations are indicative of these two trends.

As regards the substitution of supplies from German VW centres by products from SEAT, the following highlights should be mentioned. In 1991 SEAT took over the supply of gearboxes via its El Prat de Llobregat plant, discontinuing another import flow. The same had happened before with the production of a considerable number of small metal parts for the Polo A02, the supply of which was moved from Germany to SEAT plants in Catalonia.

In relation to the shift from imports towards national supplies one sees how, after the initial dependence on VW Germany for material, the following Navarra-based companies, among others, regained their supplier positions vis-à-vis the Landaben factory: FADASA (integrated into Arvin Exhaust in 1988) for exhaust pipes, *Industrias Esteban* (whose plant dedicated to the Landaben deliveries was later converted into *Tecnoconfort*) for seats, TRW for steering systems, and Unicables (later integrated into Delphi) for cabling.

From the national *ambito*, there were suppliers of metal sheet, large exterior body parts and small metal devices that replaced the German supply as of 1985 (SEAT, 1986, p. 31). From 1991 onwards, the Landaben plant itself carried out the stamping of large exterior body parts, due to quality problems with suppliers (Sanchez Jauregui, 2001).

Finally, at the beginning of the 1990s a first group of suppliers – that already supplied to VW Germany – set up new facilities near the Landaben factory to supply material from greenfield plants. This was the case with *Dynamit Nobel Ibérica* for interior trims, and rear-end bumpers in 1991, and *Lunke Navarra* for pedals and certain synthetic interior pieces in 1992.

The creation of new local production centres by suppliers was clearly induced by the growing production volumes of the Landaben plant and by the demand for JIT delivery. Especially German firms set up supply plants near the Landaben factory (e.g. Lunke, Ibérica) or took over local firms (e.g. *Archter und Ebels* entering in the capital of *Industrias Esteban*). As a consequence, an important part of the Germany-based b2b relationships was transformed into Landaben-specific supply structures, resulting in a modified, but ongoing, German hegemony of Landaben's b2b relationships during the A02 production period.

The fact that the Landaben plant started to demand JIT delivery standards regarding the supply of many components was certainly an important additional reason for independent suppliers to set up branch locations near the Landaben plant. However, it can not be seen as a sufficient explanatory factor behind the many co-location decisions. Especially because many of these newly created supply centres in Navarra were also used to service other customers (Navarra Empresarial, 1994, pp. 10–39; Sodena/Conway, 1997, p. 14; Longas, 1998, pp. 213, 274–275; Expert, 2000; Lunke Navarra, 2000). Moreover, it is argued that JIT supply can also be practiced from distant locations – upto several hundreds of kilometers (Logistica Navarra, 1996). Therefore, the large and growing production share Landaben had in the A02 assembly during this period (see Table 5.1), and the future strategic role the Landaben plant was to play in future Polo models (see for example, the previous comments regarding the preparatory investments in the Landaben plant during the early 1990s – VW Navarra, 1995, p. 3), are presumably more important in explaining the fact that multiple suppliers to the Landaben plant decided to operate from nearby located sites.

In reality, the fact that many of the supply centres in Navarra were not 100% Landaben-dedicated or site-specific (Navarra Empresarial, 1994, pp. 10–39; Expert, 2000; Longas, 2000; Lunke Navarra, 2000; Zabalo, 2000), emphasizes that – of the various clients serviced by these centres – the Landaben plant was certainly the most important one in terms of influencing their decision as to choose from where to operate.

As such, the supplier settlements taking place during the A02 period can be seen as preparatory moves in view of an expected improvement of the intra-firm network position of the Landaben plant within the VW concern with regard to the then and coming Polo models. That way, they aimed to maintain or conquer supply positions with respect to the Landaben plant.

5.2.2   Conclusions

As far as the period 1984–1994 is concerned, it is clear to see that a strong embeddedness of the b2b relationships in a German context prevailed.

The reason that German suppliers in particular managed to set up supply relationships with the Landaben plant in this period was because the Landaben plant started assembling an already consolidated product. The solid embeddedness of VW's procurement in German supply relationships at the outset of the Polo production in Landaben did the rest. In fact, around the middle of the 1980s it appears that VW's supply relationships had not yet quite globalized and instead it functioned more on a home-based supplier basis.

The strong reliance on home-based suppliers at a time when information technology possibilities and supply relationships that extended national borders had not yet grown to full maturity, is an understandable phenomenon. For especially in such circumstances nearby located partners are the ones with whom loyalty (bonding) and trust can most easily be established. Mainly because trust and getting on the same wave length with business partners is typically built up over time, through learning about the idiosyncrasies of actors, through experience, repeated interaction and consecutive (re-) contracting (Becattini, 1992; Harrison, 1992; Kamp, 1994). Evidently, in a pre-globalization era and at a time when information technology possibilities can only be exploited suboptimally, suppliers who are located in the vicinity offer the best basis for 'gearing' inter-firm co-operation and for developing trust. Moreover, partnership, loyalty and trust will also develop more easily if partners have shared backgrounds due to social, cultural and geographical proximities. As such, it made sense that Landaben initially relied on German suppliers, especially in the light of its dependence on the Wolfsburg plant.

Thus, in the case of the Landaben plant, the suppliers with strong inter-firm network positions vis-à-vis VW in its home base also gained easy access to VW's ventures abroad at the outset of Polo production at Landaben. Consequently, they delivered to the Landaben plant either through exports (in the first half of the A02 period) or through foreign branch plants (in the second half of the A02 period). This also illustrates that when the Landaben plant was incorporated into the VW hierarchy, it was especially the suppliers of the dominant actor in the transaction (VW) that obtained most business opportunities from the 'new' branch location. Simultaneously, it implied that the suppliers of the dominant actor were handed opportunities to internationalize together with the dominant actor in the transaction, that is, VW.

It also testifies that, at the time the Landaben plant started producing the Polo A02, the way VW planned future internationalization projects was clearly something which was done within a limited geographical perimeter and partner community. Also as VW at that time did not dispose of experiences in Spain. The reliance on already established relationships was perhaps also enhanced by the fact that the amount of strategically important suppliers could probably be limited to a few, as outsourcing did not reach its mature stage until the late 1980s.

As a result, it was mainly those suppliers with whom prior relationships existed that would be informed about and involved in projects abroad.

This situation fits with the assumption that b2b acquaintance with specific partners, mutual trust and perceptions of the other party's loyalty and morality play a crucial role when entering insecure or new business circumstances. In this case, VW's buyer–supplier relationships were extended across national borders when it started its Spanish venture. This indicates that the company made use of partners whose behaviour they could predict or monitor easily and with whom relationship management seemed easiest. VW's relying on familiar input providers to the Landaben plant can, therefore, be interpreted as a way to reduce the uncertainty of the well-functioning of its newly acquired plant. Similarly, it was a time-efficient way to get its operations on track.

5.3 The VW Polo A03, GP 99 and A04 production periods

5.3.1 Analysis

In 1994, production of the Polo version A02 stopped and only 15 days afterwards assembly of its successor, the Polo version A03, started. This way, the mono-product character of the factory was extended.

5.3.1.1 Volkswagen Navarra's share in total Polo production

In 1994, Landaben became the leading plant ('*Leitwerk*') with respect to the management of worldwide manufacturing and final production engineering of the VW Polo A03. The accompanying preparation tasks *ex ante* to serial production, which were previously carried out in Wolfsburg, were consequently transferred to Landaben. Both the substantial production share of the Landaben plant in the European Polo production in which this resulted (see Table 5.2),[27] and the final engineering competences assigned to the Landaben plant, testified the improved intra-firm network position of the plant. This resulted in important incentives for suppliers to locate near the Landaben factory. From then on, Landaben would be the plant around which all Polo activities following the development stage would be concentrated. This leading plant status was confirmed for the GP 99, which was produced from 1997 onwards. For the GP 99, Landaben was also the main producer.[28]

For the Polo A04, which first went into production in 2001, the Landaben factory was again elected leading plant, responsible for the final production engineering for this model and the co-ordination of the production activities at other VW centres which would also build the Polo A04 (Erro, 2001, p. 38). In practical terms this implied responsibility for final engineering of the series production, to be achieved in cooperation with the first tier suppliers. The knowledge and routines obtained from this were then spread to the other production centres of VW that also built the Polo A04 (i.e. in Slovakia, Brazil and China). Suggestions for improvement after

Table 5.2 Annual production volumes at VW Navarra and share in total production of Polo A03, GP 99 and A04

Year	Polo A03, GP 99, A04 production in Landaben	Polo A03, GP 99, A04 production of VW Group in rest of Europe	Landaben share in total European A03, GP 99, A04 Polo production (%)
1994	145,784	6,209	95.91
1995	239,428	104,957	69.52
1996	251,805	207,860	54.78
1997	274,000	180,112	60.34
1998	311,136	132,326	70.16
1999	291,900	23,600	92.52
2000	298,387	77,777	79.32
2001	239,809	88,733	72.99

Source: Author's elaborations based on VW, Annual Reports 1983–1994, Wolfsburg, 1984–1995, varia VW Navarra and Diario de Navarra.

implementation of the large series production may come from the other centres, but product and production changes can only be introduced after their implications have been studied and approved by VW Navarra.

Thus, since 1994 Landaben serves as the central plant with regards to all stages following the conceptualization, product engineering and supplier selection stages.

In production terms, VW Navarra remained the main production centre in Europe for the VW Polo during the A04 period. On average two-thirds of the A04 would be assembled in Landaben. The other third was assembled in Bratislava, Slovakia.

5.3.1.2 Evolution of supply origins

The fortified network position of the Landaben factory within the VW concern did indeed result in a situation whereby an increased delivery of inputs from external providers was conducted through nearby located suppliers (see Figure 5.3 and Table 5.3). The more widespread adoption of JIT and modular supply practices further strengthened the network position of the Landaben factory within the VW concern, although the adoption of these practices did not necessarily imply that suppliers had to be located in the plant's vicinity (*Logistica Navarra*, 1996). However, they did contribute to suppliers' decisions to locate activities particularly near high volume clients. In this respect, it is also noteworthy to mention that several of the suppliers eventually located near VW Navarra – and also the Landaben plant itself – supply to Bratislava: the other VW Polo production centre in the second half of the 1990s (Renfe, 2000; Sanchez Jauregui, 2001). This indicates that suppliers prefer to set up establishments near those buyer plants that offer the highest possible turnover or strategic opportunities rather than locating near

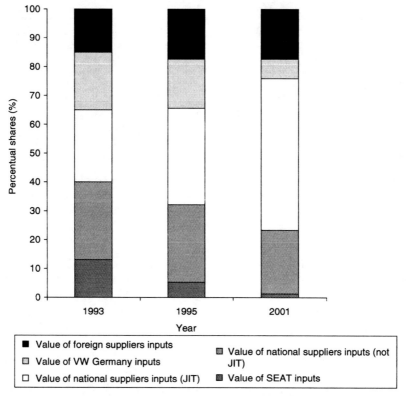

Figure 5.3 Breakdown of the origins of supplies to VW Navarra for the Polo A03, GP 99 and A04.

Source: Author's elaboration based on VW Navarra S.A. Direccion Logistica, 1995, 2001.

every individual customer. The latter is not something suppliers are willing to do unconditionally, as it is costly and it leads to a fragmentation of activities and assets, and it results in substantial dependence (see for example Grupo Antolín, 2000; Muruzabal, 2000; Valeo, 2000).

The former graph shows that the suppliers from whom the Landaben plant sourced its inputs underwent a process of spatial concentration in the direct vicinity of the Landaben plant. This went notably in favour of intra-Spain (JIT-based and non JIT-based) establishments and supplies. Whereas in 1993 JIT supplies only represented a quarter of all deliveries in value terms, by 2001 this had more than doubled. The importance of almost all other supplies retroceded. Value of SEAT inputs decreased from some 13% to slightly more than 1%, whereas also the value of inputs from Germany dropped sharply from some 20% to less than 7% of the value of all the incoming supplies processed by the Landaben plant. The value of the supplies delivered by national input providers went down less considerably: from some 27 to some

22%. The value of foreign inputs originating in other countries than Germany augmented slightly, going from 15 to some 17%. In all, the value of all supplies being brought in from within Spain grew from +/−65% to over 75% between 1993 and 2001. The massive shift from notably German supplies to supplies from within Spain is in line with the previous observations. It was a result of basically two trends. One, pioneer firms from abroad that had acquired or set up production centres near Landaben earlier (e.g. *Lunke, Dynamit Nobel* and *Archter und Ebels*) now started to work on cruising speed. Two, the establishment of additional foreign suppliers near the Landaben plant that took place from 1994 onwards (e.g. Expert, Borgers, KWD, ESSA). Together this resulted in a further shift from export to FDI and supply from local bases among suppliers.

5.3.1.3 Geographical and actor breakdown of the supplier network

To illustrate the geographical developments in the supplier network for the Polo production at the Landaben plant further, we refer to Table 5.3. This table reveals both the geographical and the actor composition changes of the supply network to the Landaben plant via a reconstruction of the suppliers involved in this network and their locations over time based on a sample of 20 automotive parts. This sample embodies a representative cross-cut of parts that nowadays are typically sourced out by car constructors. We have focused on interior and exterior trim components. Also propulsion and chassis components (gearbox, engine, brake devices, transmission, steering system and power train) are included as they are vital components of the final product assembled in a car factory.

To analyse the geographical evolutions and the major inter-firm network changes during the Polo production period until the present, we will now forward comments based on a comparison between the Polo A02 period (1984–1994) and the Polo A04 era (2001–2003). These two periods mark the first and the latest time segment in Polo production at the Landaben plant of the time frame we analysed.

5.3.1.4 Analysis of the geographical articulation of the supplier network

Table 5.3 shows a clear tendency of spatial concentration of suppliers in the direct vicinity of the Landaben plant itself towards the end of the period we analysed. We see how – among the 20 components under consideration[29] – for 11 components there is clear geographical approximation involving 15 cases of on-site investments. That is to say, in the direct vicinity of the Landaben factory. The number is somewhat inflated due to the counting of the recent location of four suppliers of metal parts, that is, KWD, ESSA, Metal Bages and DOGA. But even when these four are left of, the number of 11 on-site investments is still impressive. Furthermore, there are 3 cases of

Table 5.3 Composition of supplier network around VW Navarra 1984–2001

Component	1984–1994 (*Polo A02*)			1994–2001 (*Polo A03 and Polo GP 99*)			2001–2003 (*Polo A04*)		
	Supplier	*Origin of capital*	*Location*	*Supplier*	*Origin of capital*	*Location*	*Supplier*	*Origin of capital*	*Location*
Exhaust pipe	VW	D	Kassel (D)	Arvin Cheswick	USA	Orcoyen (Navarra)	50%–50% Arvin Exhaust Faurecia	USA + F	Orcoyen (Navarra)+ Landaben (Navarra)
Rear end bumper	German supplier or VW + Dynamit Nobel Ibérica from 1991 onwards	D + D	(via) Wolfsburg (D) + Tudela (Navarra)	Dynamit Nobel Ibérica	D	Tudela (Navarra)	Mecaplast	F (Monaco)	Madrid
Front-end bumper	German and Spanish part supplier(s) + VW	D + E	(via) Wolfsburg (D)/Navarra + Catalonia	Expert components from 1994 onwards	D	Beriain (Navarra)	Peguform Ibérica & Expert components (both firms entered in 'VEAS' in 2001)	D – USA	Palencia + Beriain (Navarra)
Fuel tank	VW	D	Wolfsburg (D)	Dynoplast from 1993 onwards/ Walbro from 1995 onwards (through take-over of Dynoplast in 1995)	NO – USA	Berrioplano (Navarra)	Kautex	D	Pamplona (Navarra)

Seats	Industrias Esteban (E) from 1984 onwards, later converted into Tecnoconfort when Archter und Ebels and RHW (Bertrand Faure) entered	E → D – F	Pamplona (Navarra)	Tecnoconfort	D – F	Pamplona (Navarra)	Tecnoconfort	D – F	Pamplona (Navarra)
Steering system	TRW + VW	USA + D	Landaben (Navarra)+ Braunschweig (D)	TRW + VW	USA + D	Landaben (Navarra)+ Braunschweig (D)	TRW	USA	Landaben (Navarra)
Cabling	VW + Bordnetze from 1986 onwards + Unicables	D + D + E	Germany + Landaben (Navarra)	Unicables (Unicables became property of Delphi in 1995)	E – USA	Landaben (Navarra)	Bordnetze from 2001 onwards	D	Pamplona (Navarra)
Cockpit	VW/Factoria de Landaben	D	Germany/ Landaben (Navarra)	Unicables (Unicables became property of Delphi in 1995)/SAS-Lignotock from 1997 onwards (in 1999 Sommer	E – USA + E → D – F (Siemens & Sommer Allibert)	Landaben (Navarra) Almussafes (1997–1999) – Pamplona (Navarra) from 1999 onwards	Sommer Allibert Siemens (SAS)	D – F (Siemens & Sommer Allibert)	Landaben (Navarra)

(Table 5.3 continued)

Table 5.3 Continued

Component	1984–1994 (Polo A02)			1994–2001 (Polo A03 and Polo GP 99)			2001–2003 (Polo A04)		
	Supplier	Origin of capital	Location	Supplier	Origin of capital	Location	Supplier	Origin of capital	Location
Isolating floor coverings	Factoria de Landaben	D	Landaben (Navarra)	Allibert took over Lignotock); Borgers from 1994 onwards	D	Mutilva Baja (Navarra)	Borgers	D	Mutilva Baja (Navarra)
Interior trims and consoles	Factoria de Landaben + Dynamit Nobel Ibérica from 1991 onwards	D + D	Landaben (Navarra) + Tudela (Navarra)	Dynamit Nobel Ibérica	D	Tudela (Navarra)	Mecaplast	F (Monaco)	Madrid
Door and roof panels	Küster GmbH (major supplier) + Irausa from 1990s onwards	D + E	Wustrow (D) + Burgos	Küster GmbH + Irausa	D + E	Wustrow (D) + Burgos/ Landaben (Navarra) from 1999 onwards + Wustrow (D)	Irausa (80% of supplies) + Küster GmbH (20% of supplies)	E + D	Landaben (Navarra) + Wustrow (D)
Lights	Hella	D	Germany	MAESA-Hella	D	Madrid/Venta de Baños Palencia from 1999 onwards	Yorka (majority of shares owned by Magneti Marelli)	E – I	Llinars del Vallès
Stamping of small metal devices	VW/SEAT + Landaben factory workshops +	D + E	Germany/ Zona Franca de Barcelona + Landaben	Metal Bages from 1994 onwards + Alcala +	E + E + E – D	Zona Franca de Barcelona/ Landaben (Navarra) +	Alcala + Metal Bages + KWD +	E + E + D + E – D + D + E	Madrid + Landaben (Navarra) + Landaben

Component	Spanish suppliers (a.o. BINASA, Alcala, …)	(Navarra) + Pamplona, Madrid, …	Novel Lahnwerk	Madrid + Noain (Navarra)	Novel Lahnwerk Navarra + ESSA + DOGA	(Navarra) + Noain (Navarra) + Landaben (Navarra)
Gearbox	VW/ Gearbox del Prat from 1991 onwards (D / D)	Kassel (D)/ El Prat de Llobregat	Gearbox del Prat (D)	El Prat de Llobregat	Gearbox del Prat (D)	El Prat del Llobregat
Engine	VW (D)	Salzgitter (D)	VW (D)	Salzgitter (D)	VW (D)	Salzgitter (D)
Brake devices	VW (D)	Braunschweig (D)	VW (D)	Braunschweig (D)	VW (D)	Braunschweig (D)
Transmission Motor propulsion group (power train)	VW (D) / VW (D)	Salzgitter (D) / Braunschweig (D)	VW Navarra VW/VW Navarra + Expert Components from 1998 onwards (Expert: front trains) (D+D)	Landaben (Navarra) Braunschweig (D) + Landaben (Navarra) Braunschweig (D) + Beriain (Navarra)	VW Navarra VW + Expert Components (Expert: front trains) (Expert entered in 'VEAS' in 2001) (D + D – USA)	Landaben (Navarra) Braunschweig (D) + Beriain (Navarra)
Gearstick	VW (D)	Kassel (D)	Heidemann Novel Ibérica from 1994 onwards (taken over in 1997 by Adwest PLC) (D – E → UK)	Noain (Navarra)	Dura (through takeover of Adwest in 1999) (USA)	Noain (Navarra)
Pedals	SEAT + Lunke Navarra from 1992 onwards (D + D)	Zona Franca de Barcelona + Beriain (Navarra)	Lunke Navarra from 1992 onwards (D)	Beriain (Navarra)	ATESO (CZ)	Jablonec (CZ) (Navarra)

Source: Author's elaboration.

Note
If under the columns with location details no country code is added to a city name, the city in question is located in Spain. For a further assessment of the location evolutions per component see also Table A.10 under Appendix A.

intermediate geographical approximation, where the components in question currently come from within Spain but from outside Navarra, after they were first imported from Germany and later – for a while – from within Navarra. The on-site investments involved in these cases of intermediate geographical proximity are included in the 15 cases mentioned above. In addition, in four cases there was no change. This occurred especially among the propulsion parts. Finally, in two cases the successive suppliers involved result in longer supply distances to the plant: pedals (which now are imported from the Czech Republic) and interior trims and consoles (whose current main supplier is located in the Madrid area).

The same trends can be observed when we look at the number of suppliers located in Navarra and the Pamplona area itself respectively. From those countings, it can be deduced that, whereas during the A02 period in all a mere 5.75 of the 20 components were mainly delivered from within Navarra, during the A04 period it was 11.75.[30] If we focus on the Pamplona area itself, we see the following. Of the sample of 20 components in the first period 4.75 and 11.75 in the last period respectively were delivered from within the Pamplona area itself.[31] These figures also reveal clear co-location patterns.

Typically, the arrival of companies to Navarra in the 1990s was of a greenfield investment type. In contrast, the more ancient foreign-owned companies in Navarra (mostly American and English investments) had mostly been in the form of takeovers. This illustrates that the more recent investments were related to VW's ownership of the Landaben plant and the competence assignments allocated at this plant and to the way a large part of its supplier base chose to locate near Landaben and the Pamplona area. The older investments, on the other hand, were rather made to tap into strategic technological or production competences and to gain a commercial foothold in Spain in general. In fact, many of the companies acquired by overseas companies were already established in Navarra before the Landaben plant was set up and before VW or even SEAT became its owner. Moreover, several of these long-standing firms in Navarra have never been suppliers of the Landaben plant. This indicates that certainly the recent settlements can be explained through a buyer–supplier network perspective, whereas the older investments are associated with more generic foreign entry mode choices (choice between, for instance, FDI via takeover of or capital participation in existing plants, or the setting up of new wholly owned or joint venture plants) and with more classical location choices.

5.3.1.5　Analysis of the actor composition evolutions in the supplier network

Similar to the number of changes in locations of suppliers, we see a fairly significant frequence of substitutions among the suppliers involved in subsequent versions of the VW Polo for specific components, even in cases where a supplier already owned nearby supply establishments (e.g. *Dynamit Nobel Ibérica*, Dynoplast, Unicables, *Lunke Navarra*).

For the period 1984–1994 it is clear that a strong embeddedness of the b2b relationships within a German context prevailed.

For a further assessment of the changes related to the suppliers involved in the delivery of our sample of components, we will elaborate on the periods 1994–2001 and 2001–2003. We focus on these time segments as the information obtained with respect to the period 1994–2001 is more complete and accurate than the information relating to the period 1984–1994, and thus provides a better basis for comparison with the situation in the period between 2001 and 2003.

When taking the Polo A03 – launched in 1994 – as the point of departure we see that, in the subsequent periods, 1994–2001 and 2001–2003, two new product versions were launched, that is, the Polo GP 99 and the Polo A04. Based on the Landaben-specific component sample, this offers – *ceteris paribus* – two times 20 components makes 40 possibilities to change the actor composition of the network.

To characterize the changes between 1994–2001 and 2001–2003 in the actor composition of VW Navarra's supplier base, we distinguish between the kinds of changes forwarded in Section 4.2.3. Based on that categorization of changes, the following overview emerges.

Table 5.4 shows that out of a total of 20 components – whose supply would be reconsidered twice from 1994 onwards $16\frac{1}{4}$ changes with regard to the suppliers responsible for their delivery were observed.[32] Seven changes were a consequence of take-overs of or joint ventures with incumbent suppliers resulting in virtual supplier substitutions (oligopoly-related substitutions). Eight and a half as a consequence of the involvement of entirely new suppliers (competitiveness-oriented substitutions) and $\frac{3}{4}$ as a consequence of the first-time externalization of the production of an automotive part. Of the 7 oligopoly-related substitutions, it appears that $5\frac{1}{2}$ of them were changes in which the leading entities in the takeovers or joint ventures were companies that were completely new to VW Navarra, and which, consequently, can be judged as genuine substitutions. In terms of 'genuine' substitutions, we then observe $5\frac{1}{2}$ oligopoly-related substitutions plus $8\frac{1}{2}$ competitiveness-related substitutions makes 14 in total.

Table 5.4 Changes in the actor composition of VW Navarra's supplier network

(A) oligopoly-related substitutions	(B) competitiveness-oriented substitutions	(C) first-time externalizations	(D) re-internalizations
7	$8\frac{1}{2}$	$\frac{3}{4}$	0

Source: Author's elaboration.

When applying the previous data to the formula presented in Chapter 4 for measuring longevity of b2b relations, we get the following result.

Degree of longevity of b2b relationships around VW Navarra from 1994 to 2003

$$L_{1994-2003} = 100\% * \left(1 - \frac{140}{40.0}\right) = 65.0\%$$

Source: Author's elaboration.

This proxy indicates that a substantial number of changes in the actor composition have occurred during the period under consideration. It reveals that more than one-third of all initial supplier relationships were completely exchanged. The outcome appears to contradict the longevity expectations one would have with regard to the constellation of suppliers surrounding a buyer firm, based on claims of the N&I approach to b2b relationships, the network view on the IPM and the F/5P model. If we take into account that the Landaben plant worked almost exclusively on the basis of single sourcing, these outcomes contradict such expectations even more. In that context, substitutions have a much stronger impact. Finally, the time period under consideration was rather short, as it only spanned nine years. The picture would be even starker, if we were to leave out the propulsion and chassis components (gearbox, engine, brake devices, transmission and power trains), which were subject to few changes, as they were principally manufactured in-house for the entire period under analysis.

By all means, it is clear that the dominant form under which changes took place during the observed time period were rather radical through substitutions of incumbent suppliers by entirely new supplier relationships. As such,

Table 5.5 Origin of capital of supplier sample for VW Navarra

Nationality	1984–1994	1994–2001	2001–2003
D	16.75	13.125	10
F	0.25	0.625	3.5
USA	0.5	3.00	3.25
E	2.5	2.5	1.75
NO	0	0.5	0
I	0	0	0.5
UK	0	0.25	0
CZ	0	0	1
Total	20	20	20

Source: Author's elaboration.

it questions the longevity thesis. Regarding the nationality mix involved in the supplier network for the analysed sample, we see the following evolution.

Table 5.5 clearly illustrates how the changes in the supplier network are accompanied by a shift away from a strong embeddedness in German supply relations.[33] Whereas at the outset German suppliers accounted for more than 80% of the supply relationships of the components we analysed, in the period 2001–2003 its share fell to 50%. At the same time, the French and US suppliers improved their inter-firm network position vis-à-vis the Landaben plant most strongly, augmenting their presence from 1.3% and 2.5% to 17.5% and 16.3% respectively. Presence of suppliers of Spanish capital went down from 12.5% to 8.75% in the observed period.

These results also indicate an increased multinational diversification of the Landaben plant's supplier base and thus a detachment of long-lasting relationships embedded in a mutual home base for buyer and supplier.

5.3.2 Conclusions

Regarding the geographical constellation of the supplier network around the Landaben plant between 1994 and 2003, we see a clear tendency of spatial concentration of suppliers in the direct vicinity of the Landaben plant.

There is also a clear correlation between, on the one hand, assignment of leading plant competences to the Landaben plant and, on the other hand, the settlement *in situ* of a large share of its suppliers as an expression of their desire to improve or maintain their inter-firm network position. As a matter of fact, in many cases we are talking about suppliers that service multiple clients (Expert, 2000; Longas, 2000; Lunke (Navarra), 2000; Zabalo, 2000). These suppliers chose to set up an establishment near the Landaben factory, indicating the comparative importance of this plant compared to their other clients.

It should also be stressed that among these co-located suppliers there are many which do not deliver unit-specific components and thus do not need to adapt their final product to, for instance, the colour of the respective Polos for which the components are supplied. Valid examples are: fuel tanks, steering columns, shock absorbers, gearsticks, pedals, isolating floor covers and small metal devices.

Furthermore, a significant substitution can be observed among the suppliers involved in subsequent versions of the VW Polo. This even happened in cases where suppliers were already located in the vicinity (e.g. *Dynamit Nobel Ibérica*, Dynoplast, Unicables, *Lunke Navarra*).

In this context, from 1994 onwards as regards the supply relationships for 20 components, we witnessed that the degree of longevity with regards to the actor composition around the Landaben plant was rather limited. Both the number of and especially the kind of changes perceived do not support the claim that the buyer-supplier relationships will display a high level of stability. In this case, it is clear that competitive pressure from rival firms and oligopolization tendencies in the industry were an important source for genuine substitutions.

In all, the situation outlined above clearly shows that (rival) suppliers strived to occupy improved inter-firm network positions in view of the improving intra-firm network positions of VW Navarra. Improvement or maintenance of such inter-firm network positions either took place via takeovers or through competition, which fueled substitution of b2b relations. As can be derived from this case, this substitution process was intensified over time. This may indeed have been connected to ongoing organizational learning and internationalization processes on behalf of both VW as the car constructor and of supplier companies.

As regards the origin of suppliers delivering to VW Navarra, during the period 1984–1994 a strong embeddedness of the b2b relationships in a German context prevailed. Later on, a more diversified national background of suppliers is observed.

The analysis of the origin of capital behind the suppliers that deliver to the Landaben plant serves as a further indicator for changes of b2b relationships around the Landaben plant. They reveal that there is an increased presence of US and French capital in the supplier network around the Landaben plant at the expense of German capital. This also confirms the previously established signs of b2b relationship substitutions and a stronger inclusion of non-German relationships into the Landaben plant's supplier network over time.

As a final observation, we can conclude that b2b relationships that at the outset of foreign ventures tend to be conceived around previously established relationships at home, over time undergo significant changes through competitive behaviour of firms, and the internationalization of buyers and suppliers. Ultimately, this leads to an increased inclusion of alternative and foreign b2b relationships.

6 Empirical results with respect to FASA-Renault Valladolid

This chapter presents the results of the empirical case study with respect to the FASA-Renault Valladolid plant and its supplier network during the period the Valladolid factory produced the latest version of the Renault 5 (the Supercinq) and its successor: the Renault Clio.

6.1 Empirical study on the Renault Clio era

6.1.1 Introduction: FASA's consolidation into the Renault hierarchy

The establishment of '*Fabricacion de Automoviles Sociedad Anonima de Valladolid*' (FASA) took place in 1951 in Valladolid. It was local entrepreneurs obtaining a Renault production licence who set up the FASA project. In its early years it operated on a relatively autonomous basis and Renault did not play a large financial or managerial role. Indeed, FASA – in product terms – depended entirely on the French company. In 1965 Renault increased its share in FASA from 15% to 49.9% (Pedrosa Sanz, 1983, p. 72; Carreras and Estapé-Triay, 1998). As a result, the venture changed its name to FASA-Renault (Ortiz-Villajos, 2001, p. 22). After this, activities expanded from merely assembling Renault models to include genuine engine production and the manufacturing of other mechanical and propulsion components. Likewise, FASA-Renault acquired the company '*Industrias Subsidiarias de Aviacion*' to produce gearboxes on an in-house basis. In 1974 FASA-Renault started to build a second assembly factory in Palencia, which became operational in 1978. In 1976 Renault was allowed to become the major shareholder in FASA-Renault.

Around the mid-eighties, several circumstances led to a full integration of the Spanish FASA-Renault apparatus into the Renault hierarchy and its competence structures. Until then, the FASA-Renault apparatus – in spite of its strong ties with the Renault Régie – had continued to function on a highly independent basis (Manero Miguel, 1997; Pedrosa Sanz, 1997; Peran Gonzalez, 1997).

The first circumstance that led to FASA-Renault's integration was the approaching entry of Spain into the European Union and the increased possibilities for cross-border trade flows and management of multinational firms that followed from this. In 1979, in view of Spain's European Union entry, a smoother automobile regulation was adopted by the Spanish state. This led to a lowering of the obligatory minimum of 90% Spanish components incorporation per car to 60% of local content from 1984 onwards (Bueno Lastra and Ramos Barrado, 1981, p. 54). Also import contingents were eliminated and custom tariffs were reduced from 70–80% to 40% (FASA-Renault, 1986, p. 9; Manero Miguel, 1997; Gilodi, 2001). Thus, companies gradually obtained greater freedom in their purchasing and sourcing choices and they could now choose more freely between Spain-based and foreign-based providers.

Consequently, when constraints on cross-border co-ordination and foreign trade flows started to disappear, Renault was able to optimize and integrate its Spanish activities and product flows within its European business apparatus. As a result, it gradually replaced local autonomy in favour of central co-ordination (Parnière, 2001).

The second circumstance that contributed to a full integration of the Spanish FASA-Renault apparatus into the Renault business structures was the fact that Renault went through a series of financially weak years in the mid-eighties (Renault, 1985, p. 4, 1986, p. 4, 1987, p. 4, 1989, p. 4; Layan, 1997, p. 141; Gilodi, 2001). To overcome this situation an internal rationalization of competence assignments and, simultaneously, a centralization of competences took place. As Layan (1997, p. 141) states: 'Renault terminated the simultaneous existence of functions and responsibilities at group level and at the level of FASA-Renault' (our translation).

The third relevant circumstance was the fact that a nation-by-nation approach to car products became less and less necessary. Not only was there an increased harmonization of consumer taste between Spanish and other western European consumers, but there was also a slow but sure assimilation of purchasing power between the first and the second group of buyers. Additionally, technical norms became increasingly uniform. As a result, Renault could phase out a large part of the design and research activities FASA-Renault had carried out until then and the company was able to streamline its product range for the whole of western Europe (Rombo 83, p. 30; Layan, 1997, p. 146; Parnière, 2001).

As a consequence, FASA-Renault was fully integrated into Renault in the second half of the 1980s (Fernandez Arrufe and Pedrosa Sanz, 1997, p. 216). From 1988 onwards, formal integration into the Renault ranks and complete subjection of FASA-Renault to the decisions of the Renault Régie was a reality. From that point on, the necessity of investing or divesting in the FASA-Renault apparatus was decided on the basis of the needs of the whole Renault apparatus of which FASA-Renault from now on formed a mere part (see for example, Renault, 1988, p. v, 1990, p. 9; Manero Miguel and Pascual Ruiz de Valdepeñas, 1998, p. 137). This integration of FASA-Renault into Renault went hand in hand with a reinforcement of the headquarters' financial control over the peripherally located '*sociétés nationaux*' through their conversion into branch locations (Layan, 1997, p. 150).

This also resulted in practices of company-wide supplier relationships and intra-firm exchanges of mechanical components, as is testified by many sources, for example, Renault (1991, p. 19), Muruzabal (2000), Gilodi (2001), Parnière (2001), Rivas (2001) and Torrico (2002): 'In our search to manage costs, considerable savings have been obtained from purchasing and supply cooperation with FASA-Renault in Spain (the largest industrial establishment of Renault outside of France). This cooperation allowed putting in place a provisioning system that bundles the supply needs of the various assembly centres and links these centres to suppliers from France or the Iberian peninsula. As a consequence, they share suppliers for the same inputs' (our translation). As a consequence, annual reports reveal an increase in incoming component flows from sister Renault sites to FASA-Renault, and a stronger intra-firm integration of FASA-Renault's production activities into the overall production schemes of Renault as a whole (FASA-Renault, 1988, p. iii, 1989, p. iii, 1990, p. 10). Eventually, this went at the expense of production of mechanical parts and organs by FASA-Renault itself.

An intra-firm division and rationalization of the production of the complete Renault product range, that is, the assignment of the production of a limited amount of car models to individual plants, did not take place until the late 1990s. Therefore, the FASA-Renault plants continued to produce a large variety of Renault models until the end of the 1990s, albeit more for international markets (*FASA-Renault Memoria y Balance/Informe Anual*, various editions of the 1990s).

The transfer of FASA-Renault competences to the Renault headquarters took place via a gradual, but progressive process in different stages. With respect to several of the management functions, like production, purchasing, supplier selection, design, responsibilities were centralized little by little (Gilodi, 2001; Parnière, 2001; Torrico, 2002). During a certain period several director positions existed parallelly in Spain and France and for instance purchases from Iberian peninsula-based suppliers were arranged by the Spanish purchasing directors (see for example, Mandos 26, p. 7). Afterwards, the Spanish directors were subjected to their French counterparts and the former were still able to take autonomous decisions, although they were obliged to consult and report to their French superiors in advance. In this second period, a direction level for the Iberian peninsula existed as an intermediate layer (Pedrosa Sanz, 1993, p. 103): 'The Renault unit in Valladolid forms an integrated part of the FASA-Renault division within the divisional and financial organization of the Renault Group. It is the general direction of Renault for the Iberian peninsula that controls and co-ordinates the activities of FASA-Renault, those of its Spanish subsidiaries and those of the Portuguese subsidiary' (our translation). Finally, the Spanish director positions were 'erased' and they were transformed into members of the European team of, for instance, production directors. As a consequence, they were subjected to

Renault's headquarters who now had full discretionary powers over the FASA-Renault apparatus.

In 1999 and 2000 Renault obtained all remaining FASA-Renault shares in a complete buy-out (Renault, 2000, p. 6). By the end of December 2000 FASA-Renault was fully owned by the Renault Group (Renault, 2001, p. 6).

6.1.2   Corporate features of Renault's headquarters–subsidiary relationships

In order to interpret the Valladolid plant's intra-firm network position within the Renault concern over time, we will now discuss the hierarchical and intra-firm distribution of competences at Renault and, related to this, the assignment of business functions to the Valladolid plant subsequent to FASA-Renault's full integration into the Renault structures.

When we take a look at the tasks involved in a car model's production life cycle based on Section 4.2.1, we get the following breakdown.

At the first stage of a car model's production life cycle a conceptual, design and product engineering part takes place. Afterwards a small set of pre-series is built together with the suppliers of production equipment and components. Then final production engineering takes place. In a fourth and final stage, industrial mass manufacturing of the car model in question takes off.

With respect to the first stage, the Renault headquarters and design centre are responsible for the conceptualization of the car models. In general terms, the more strategic business functions, such as R&D, marketing, sales, strategic quality and logistics management, purchasing and selection of suppliers, are managed centrally by Renault since the early 1990s (Renault, 1992, p. 6, 1995F, p. 27, 1996, p. 6).

Consequently, the FASA-Renault apparatus lost virtually all autonomy in terms of strategic or conceptual tasks that are related to production, R&D, supplier selection, design, marketing, sales and purchasing. For R&D this had always been the case to a large extent, although a certain degree of autonomy regarding product development did exist before (Gilodi, 2001). The latter led, for example, to the 'Renault Siete': a sedan version of the Renault 5, which was exclusively developed and produced by FASA-Renault Valladolid (Renault, 1997, p. 42). For other strategic business functions such as production, purchasing and sales, either the Valladolid plant or the FASA-Renault headquarters in Madrid enjoyed full autonomy until the integration of FASA-Renault into Renault.

The full integration of FASA-Renault's purchasing activities into and its subjection to the Group structure was to all intents and purposes completed at the start of 1994 (Rombo 112, pp. 3, 23–26). Today, purchasing decisions are completely centralized at the Renault headquarters in France and it is Renault France who relates to the headquarters of potential suppliers. This is also reflected in the number of persons employed in purchasing tasks by FASA-Renault. FASA-Renault used to have a central purchasing department in Madrid with some 400 people working there (Torrico, 2002). Today staff is reduced to only 50–60 employees (Gilodi, 2001; Torrico, 2002).

From the second half of the 1980s onwards, external suppliers have become increasingly involved in the early development stages through their inclusion in simultaneous engineering activities (see for example, Renault, 1988, p. 30, 1994, p. 13, 1995F, pp. 4, 23–24, 1996F, p. 28, 1997F, p. 75, 1998, p. 72; FASA-Renault, 1991, p. 11; Layan, 1997, p. 144). In line with the overall centralization strategy pursued at Renault from the mid-1980s until the early 1990s, supplier selection now also takes place at the general headquarters of Renault in Boulogne-Billancourt, including the selection of suppliers to foreign car assembly subsidiaries of the group, that is, outside France. This is both the case for suppliers involved in the exploratory product phase, the so-called 'expert suppliers' (Florence, 1996; Bonzemba and Okano, 1998), for the product development phase where Renault involves 'pilot suppliers' (ibid.), and for the final mass production where Renault involves 'leader suppliers' and possibly 'additional subcontractors' (ibid.).

As part of supplier involvement in early development stages, expert and pilot suppliers are also involved in the second stage of the production life cycle of a car model, that is, the design and construction of prototypes of new Renault car models. Since 1995, these development activities take place at Renault's Technocentre in Guyancourt (Renault, 1995, pp. 5, 46–48, 1996F, pp. 28–29, 1998, p. 69). It is here that engineers of suppliers are gathered (the so-called: *'ingénieurs résidents'*) to carry out simultaneous engineering and virtual tests for prototyping components, platforms and entire end product (Layan, 1997, p. 144; Parnière, 2001). Furthermore, tests with new car models and components are carried out at the trial complex in Lardy, near Paris (Yeboles, 1997).

The third part around a car model's production life cycle includes the more tactical tasks surrounding its production, that is, the final preparation and engineering for serial production. These tasks are carried out before mass production of the model commences. Renault usually assigns these tasks to a plant in its traditional production home base (north-west of Paris). This has at least been the case over the last decades with respect to 'fast moving' models like the Clio and Renault 5 (coordinated at the Flins plant), Renault 9, 11, 19 and Mégane (co-ordinated at the Douai plant), and the Renault 21, 25, Laguna, Safrane, Espace and Vel Satis (co-ordinated at the Sandouville plant). For niche products several peripheral factories have recently been appointed as leading plants as well: Palencia for the Mégane Coupé and the Mégane Classic (FASA-Renault, 1996, p. 26, 1997, p. 30, 1999, p. 16, 2001, p. 22) and Bursa, Türkiye, for the Mégane Break (Renault, 1998, p. 30). Once the production routines are put in place by the 'leading plant' they are introduced in the other factories where the same model will be assembled. Typically, workers from the other plants come and learn about new production aspects of a new model in the leading factory. For instance, workers of FASA-Renault Valladolid come to the Flins plant to be trained with respect to the

Clio. This clearly indicates that there is a certain car model-specific hierarchy among Renault plants.

The fourth group of activities involved in the production life cycle of a car includes production, purchasing of generic material below a specific cost threshold (Yeboles, 1997; Gilodi, 2001; Torrico, 2002), final production engineering in the plant, final inbound logistics and operational quality inspection. These responsibilities are allocated at the level of individual car manufacturing plants. FASA-Renault Valladolid also carries out these activities.

With respect to the car model-specific assignment of serial production shares, it is noteworthy that Renault has a long tradition (until the late 1990s) of spreading production per model over several plants. Only those models that need to be produced in a limited quantity (like the Renault Safrane, the Renault Vel Satis, the Renault Espace, Renault sport cars and previously the Renault 25, 20 and 30) are produced in a single plant. Consequently, many of the plants (certainly the Spanish ones) have a long tradition of manufacturing a large variety of models at the same time. This was the case until long after the integration of FASA-Renault into the Renault structures. As a consequence, many factories (except for the ones in Sandouville and Douai) produce a relatively small part of the overall production of a certain model, independently of the question whether or not a factory has a leading factory status. Today, for example, the Mégane is produced in Douai, Palencia and Bursa (Türkiye), and it also used to be produced by *Renault Industrie Belgique* (Vilvoorde, Belgium). Likewise, the Clio is produced in Flins, Valladolid and Novo Mesto (Slovenija). Previously, this model was also assembled in Vilvoorde (Belgium) and Setubal (Portugal).

In addition, Renault's car model offer was for a long time characterized by a product range that was heavily diversified, based on a set of platforms that was very diverse, which did not allow for a rigorous simplification of plant-specific production programmes until the mid-1990s (Layan, 1997, p. 142). In certain years its production programme counted no fewer than 8 models, that is, the Renault 4, 5, 9, 11, 18, 19, 21 and 25 (Renault Annual Report, various editions from the 1980s and 1990s). Such fragmentation of production shares led to low quantities of model-specific production at most plants until the late 1990s. It is only since 1998, when Renault moved towards 'mono-product oriented factories', that the model-specific quantities of production at individual plants became substantial.

6.1.3   *Corporate features of Renault's management of inter-firm relationships*

Until the mid-1980s, outsourcing and supplier selection practices was organized on a nation-by-nation basis at Renault. Thus, FASA-Renault had a considerable degree of autonomy with regard to purchasing policies (FASA-Renault, 1988, 1989; Renault, 1991; Manero Miguel, 1997; Pedrosa Sanz, 1997; Gilodi, 2001; Rivas, 2001; Torrico, 2002). Consequently, there was only limited overlap between FASA-Renault's supplier base and that of the

Table 6.1 Change in the number of direct suppliers to Renault

	1984	1985	1986	1987	1988	1989	1990	1991	1992
Q	1800	1415	1246	1100	968	810	720	680	630
Year	1993	1994	1995	1996	1997	1998	1999	2000	2001
Q	585	543	527	512	497	506	500	616	507

Source: Author's elaboration based on Gorgeu and Mathieu, 1995; Renault, Annual Reports, Paris, various editions; Renault, Atlas économique, Paris, various editions.

French Renault factories. In the second half of the eighties this autonomy ceased to exist (Renault, 1988, p. v, 1990, p. 9; Fernandez Arrufe and Pedrosa Sanz, 1997, p. 216; Manero Miguel and Pascual Ruiz de Valdepeñas, 1998, p. 137; Gilodi, 2001; Parnière, 2001; Torrico, 2002).

The centralization pursued by Renault led to a company-wide reduction of the number of direct supply relationships (see for example Renault, 1991, p. 19). Centralization of purchasing competences allowed for a higher level of uniformity of supplier networks around all of the company's plants (Parnière, 2001). Therefore, nowadays the composition of plant-specific supplier bases shows a high degree of communality as regards the participating suppliers. This is reflected in the decreasing number of direct suppliers to Renault (see Table 6.1).[34] The introduction of strict quality requirements (the PSA-Renault quality evaluation programme *'Evaluation Aptitude Qualité Fournisseur'*, short: EAQF) and tiering practices among suppliers as well as single sourcing practices contributed further to this reduction, see for example, Renault (1987, p. 21, 1987F, p. 34, 1988, p. 30, 1989, p. 27, 1991, p. 19, 30), Gorgeu and Mathieu (1995), Florence (1996), Gilodi (2001). One of the parameters for the EAQF is a supplier's capacity to '... *accompany Renault abroad* ...' (Renault, 1991, p. 19, 1999, p. 28). This criterion also contributed to a reduction of the overall supplier base as it stimulates the selection of suppliers that can attend multiple Renault sites.

Similarly, from the second half of the 1980s onwards a stronger perform-ance was demanded on behalf of the suppliers in logistics (see for example, Renault, 1987, p. 21, 1989, p. 27, 1994, p. 13, 1995F, pp. 4, 23–24, 1996F, p. 28, 1997F, p. 75, 1998, p. 72; FASA-Renault, 1989, p. 11, 1990, p. 21, 1991, p. 11, 1992, pp. 17, 26).

In addition to the afore-mentioned developments with regard to the uniformity and centralization policies adopted by Renault, as well as the developments surrounding quality management, there are two other important factors explaining the diminishing number of supply relationships Renault maintained.

1   Renault's intention to stimulate the creation of large '... *groupes franco-françaises ou à défaut franco-européens*'. (FASA-Renault, 1989, p. 17; Gorgeu and Mathieu, 1995, p. 44)

2   The filialization of in-house departments, which were acquired a posteriori by large international supply groups that offered a wide array of automotive inputs, and which ended the previous supply situation in which Renault worked with multiple smaller firms (Renault, 1988, p. 18; Gorgeu and Mathieu, 1995, pp. 51, 53, 58; La Lettre du GERPISA, No. 121, mars 1998; Parnière, 2001).

Ad 1: 'The reduction in direct supplier relationships may also be due to mergers in the supplier segment, because both Renault and PSA have been encouraging supplier firms with complementary capabilities to join forces or forge alliances over the past years. Most efforts have been deployed towards creating French groupings or, if that were not possible, pan-European groupings' (own translation based on: Gorgeu and Mathieu, 1995, p. 44). By extension, it seems fair, however, to state that the accent was not so much on maintaining a French touch among the suppliers base. Non-French and even non-European partners were also seriously considered as supply partners. It is, thus, more fair to state that patriotic sentiments did not play a dominant role in fostering the creation of large supply groups (FASA Calidad, 1989, p. 5; Parnière, 2001). Examples of *regroupements* with relevance to Renault, are the creation of Sommer Allibert and Siemens' *société commune* 'SAS' in 1996 (Siemens, 1996, 1999), the incorporation of Reydel into Plastic Omnium (Plastic Omnium, Shareholders Letter No. 7, June 2001), Sylea's absorption by Labinal, followed by Sylea's sale to Valeo (Hoover, 2002), Roth Frères' take-over by Johnson Controls (Rombo 72, p. 12; Renault, 1988, pp. 18, 30, 1989, p. 27; IFA, 1999; Johnson Controls, 2001), Tubauto's incorporation into Bertrand Faure (Parnière, 2001), and the joint ventures between Solvay and Plastic Omnium (Solvay, 2002) and between Inoplast and Plastic Omnium (Entreprises Rhône-Alpes, septembre 2000, No. 1439).

With respect to the Spain-based FASA-Renault suppliers, Renault pursued a similar strategy. There, too, an approach between local suppliers and large international groups was fostered or looked upon benevolently (FASA-Renault, 1989, p. 17, 1990, p. 21, 1991, p. 10–11; ITEC, 1998). Illustrative examples of this are: Mecanismos Auxiliares Industriales' (MAISA) takeover by UTA, and later by Lear (Generalitat de Catalunya, 2001, p. 115), the takeover of S.G. Hules by Solvay (Solvay, 2002), of ATEPSA by Reydel and later by Plastic Omnium (Plastic Omnium, Shareholders Letter No. 7, June 2001), of Gunasa by Sommer Allibert (Automotive Information Centre – MIRA, May 1998), the joint venture between FASA-Renault's supplier *Trety from Maçanet de la Selva* (Girona, Spain) and Alsace (France)-based seat component supplier Trèves which led to the creation of *Ibérica de Asientos* (Mandos 16, p. 8; Rombo 79, p. 6) and the subsequent takeover by Johnson Controls of the *Ibérica de Asientos* factory (*El Norte de Castilla*, 14 *de abril de 2002*, p. 11). Take note that Johnson Controls, via its acquisition of Roth Frères and the 1998 purchasing of Trèves' production centres devoted to Renault Clio seat supplies, is not just a supplier to FASA-Renault, but also a partner of Renault

France in seat production all around Europe (see for example, TPV Johnson Controls d.o.o., 2001).

Ad 2: Throughout the last two decades of the twentieth century, Renault has been very active in reshaping the *perimeter* of its activities (Parnière, 2001). This led to the filialization of several activities or to the sell-off of these activities to third parties. Here we witness the same as regards the nationalities of the suppliers implied. Marriages have been sealed between previous in-house activities and both French and non-French suppliers. The main criterion to choose the partners in question has been to secure the highest component quality (FASA Calidad, 1989, p. 5; Parnière, 2001).

The following is an anthology of cases of filialization–externalization at Renault.

First of all, the sell-off of Renault's entire seat production and development activities (previously filialized under the Sotexo umbrella) to Bertrand Faure, to Roth Frères and to Johnson Controls should be mentioned (Renault, 1988, pp. 18, 30, 1989, p. 27; Rombo 72, p. 12; Johnson Controls, 2001).

Renault's navigation electronics department was externalized through the set-up of 'Renix'. At the outset, this company was a joint venture between Renault and Bendix. Later, Renault withdrew completely from this joint venture and when Allied Signal took over Bendix, the electronics activities were completely externalized as far as Renault was concerned. Eventually, Siemens acquired Renix (Siemens, 1999; Parnière, 2001).

Cabling activity is another component from which Renault actively withdrew through a filialization strategy. Simultaneously, it involved Rheinshagen/Delphi, Labinal and UTA in its initial projects to externalize the cabling activity (see for example, Renault, 1990, p. 9, 1997, p. 15; Gilodi, 2001; Parnière, 2001). Its branch Tecnoffra ended up in the hands of UTA. All in all, several Renault plants that were dedicated to cabling activity ended up in the hands of companies specialized in cabling: '... the factory that was already engaged in a partial reconversion towards cabling activities was incorporated into the ranks of an international specialist in this field' (own translation based on: Renault, 1990, p. 9).

The production and development of several chassis and power train elements have also been sold off. For instance, the valve production at Renault Orléans was transferred to TRW (Renault, 1997, p. 15; *La Lettre du GERPISA*, No. 121, mars 1998).

Another example was the combined externalization–filialization of transmission axles. Until the beginning of the 1980s these were 100% manufactured by Renault. Then GKN took over part of the production, while the other part was filialized. The intention was that this filial would also service other clients, but this was not achieved. Moreover, it appeared to be increasingly difficult to keep up with and master the necessary technologies to stay in the vanguard of this business. As a consequence, Renault decided to stop producing transmission axles itself (Gilodi, 2001).

Also in relation to other transmission parts, in 1997 (*La Lettre du GERPISA*, No. 121, mars 1998; Renault, 1998, p. 69) Renault opened discussions with NTN, a Japanese automotive components supplier in the field of universal transmission joints, which led to a joint venture in the Le Mans region. In 1999 the materialization of this joint venture was confirmed (Renault, 2000, p. 37).

In 1989 a start was made with transferring SMI (*Société Mécanique Irigny*: steering directions) to Koyo. Little by little, Koyo's participation in SMI's steering direction activities grew: 'Since the Japanese firm Koyo took control [of SMI] its participation in the entity's capital increased from 35% to 75%' (own translation based on: Renault, 1994, p. 44).

In 1989, SMM (*Société Mosellane de Mécanique*), involved in pieces for gearboxes, was sold to Kolbenschmidt (Gorgeu and Mathieu, 1995, p. 58).

Various metal and stamping activities have also been filialized or externalized. Chausson Outillage was sold to Italian Magnetto, specialized in the engineering and production of stamping tools (Renault, 1998, p. 69). In the first half of 1999, Renault pooled foundry activities with FIAT's '*Teksid Spa foundries*' (Renault, 1999, p. 34, 2000, p. 37). This involved, among others, *Fonderies du Poîtou* and Funfrap (Portugal). Also the Le Mans' '*fonderie est filialisé*' (*La Lettre du GERPISA*, No. 121, mars 1998). Other parts ended up in the hands of Hayes (Gorgeu and Mathieu, 1995, p. 58). Likewise, several steel operations ended up in the hands of third parties through a filialization-externalization sequence, that is, transfers to Usinor Salicor (now Arcelor) and Ascometal in the 1980s (Gorgeu and Mathieu, 1995; Parnière, 2001).

In the mid-1980s Renault's paint activities at Le Mans were filialized through the setting up of the '*Société des Peintures Le Mans*' subsidiary. Afterwards, Renault agreed to subcontract entire functions such as paint lines to outside partners (Renault, 1988, p. 30). In the end, it was sold to Hoechst (Gorgeu and Mathieu, 1995, p. 58).

The production of rubber items by Renault was sold to Laird and Sommer Allibert (Gorgeu and Mathieu, 1995; Parnière, 2001) in the second half of the 1980s. Since then, it has changed ownership a number of times (Parnière, 2001) ending up principally in the hands of Sommer Allibert and Plastic Omnium.

Also by transferring the activities mentioned earlier to large internationally active groups, Renault was able to achieve a sharp reduction of direct supply relationships, as reported in Table 6.1. Likewise, it enabled the various Renault plants, whether located inside or outside of France, to work with similar supplier bases.

From the previous analyses of Renault's filialization-externalization activities and its policy of encouraging inter-supplier cooperation, it becomes clear that a growing variety of nationalities and origins of capital became involved in the supply base with which Renault maintains direct relationships. This is further enhanced by the many examples that can be forwarded regarding alliances and takeovers as such in the automotive supply world

(Parnière, 2001). The official statement is that Renault explicitly follows a policy of widening its geographical scope in its supplier search activities (Renault, 1991, p. 19). The individual examples that were mentioned earlier illustrate this. More significantly, company-wide statistics also confirm the gradual increase in sourcing from foreign suppliers as is testified by the following figures.

Table 6.2 shows a relatively stable situation. France and Spain are the main *Standörter* from where suppliers physically ship their components to the various Renault plants. Table 6.3 instead shows a gradual erosion of the positions of suppliers of French and Spanish capital in favour of notably Japanese, German and US suppliers. As Table 6.3, like Table 6.2 is based on purchasing value, it is likely that the percentages involved are also influenced by the fact that the suppliers from the latter countries are especially active in high-value propulsion, steering, electronics and power train components (e.g. TRW, LucasVarity, Siemens, Bosch, NTN, Koyo...), whereas Spain and France have above all prominent suppliers in the interior trim segments (e.g. Plastic Omnium, Sommer Allibert, Faurecia, Irausa...). The latter represent a remarkably smaller share in the overall value of (Renault's) car models (see for example, Renault Atlas économique, Edition 1995, p. 27). According to Parnière (2001), the value of French capital within Renault's supplier base was even higher before 1990, that is, before the waves of acquisitions and alliances in the automotive supply business rolled in. The same seems to be the case with respect to suppliers of Spanish capital.

The increasing shares of US, German and Japanese suppliers in Renault's total purchasing combined with a relatively stable location picture (see Table 6.2), implies that the former capital changes had no great impact on the places from which the physical supply is carried out.

Table 6.2 Location of Renault's supplier base in function of supply value

Country	1990(%)	1992(%)	1994(%)	1995(%)	1996(%)	2000(%)
F	75.0	76.0	74.6	75.0	74.2	72.0
E	0.0	11.1	11.4	11.5	11.2	12.4
D	0.0	4.8	5.9	4.9	6.0	6.8
I	0.0	2.8	2.5	2.7	2.2	1.7
P	0.0	0.0	0.9	1.0	0.9	1.7
Rest of Europe	0.0	0.0	3.1	3.8	4.3	0.0
Rest of the World	0.0	0.0	1.6	1.1	1.2	0.0
USA	0.0	3.0	0.0	0.0	0.0	0.0
J	0.0	1.4	0.0	0.0	0.0	0.0
UK	0.0	0.9	0.0	0.0	0.0	1.6
B	0.0	0.0	0.0	0.0	0.0	1.0
Rest	25.0	0.0	0.0	0.0	0.0	2.3

Source: Author's elaboration based on Renault, Atlas économique, Paris, various editions.

Table 6.3 Origin of capital of Renault's supplier base in function of supply value

Country	1990(%)	1993(%)	1999(%)	2000(%)	2001(%)
F	50.0	47.0	44.4	40.4	39.0
E	0.0	4.5	3.4	3.2	3.0
D	0.0	15.0	17.8	18.9	22.0
I	0.0	13.0	2.7	5.5	6.0
P	0.0	0.0	0.0	0.6	0.0
S	0.0	0.0	1.8	2.3	3.0
USA	0.0	9.0	137	17.0	17.0
J	0.0	1.0	4.2	3.6	3.0
UK	0.0	6.0	6.9	3.8	3.0
B	0.0	0.0	1.6	0.7	0.0
Rest	50.0	4.5	3.5	4.0	4.0

Source: Author's elaboration based on Renault, Atlas économique, Paris, various editions.

The rise of Japan as the country of origin of Renault suppliers has to do, above all, with the Renault-Nissan alliance at the end of the 1990s and the intention to come to a joint purchasing approach between the two allies (Renault, 2000, pp. 2, 27, 31–34, 2001, pp. 30–32, 36, 2002, pp. 37–42; Parnière, 2001).

The marginal presence of Swedish suppliers among Renault's supplier base, notably for the year 1993, reveals that the Renault-Volvo alliance plans and the expressed desire to purchase jointly up to 80% of Renault and Volvo's accumulated procurement (Renault, 1990, p. 47, 1993, p. 40; Yeboles, 1997), never passed the stage of good intentions.

The various filialization–externalization steps taken by Renault that were documented earlier, also underline the increasing importance of third party contributions to Renault's final products (Renault, 1991, p. 19, 1994, p. 13, 1995F, pp. 4, 23–24, 1996F, p. 28, 1997, p. 75, 1998, p. 72). This is also confirmed by statistics with respect to outsourcing vis-à-vis turnover figures at Renault (see for example, Renault, 1995F, p. 24, 1996F, p. 28, 1997F, p. 75, 1998, p. 16, 2000, p. 37).

When using data from the various editions of Renault's Atlas économique and from the company's annual reports regarding purchasing and turnover totals, in order to reconstruct the changes in outsourcing intensity at Renault, one obtains the following picture.

We emphasize that these percentages are considerably lower than the outsourcing indications Renault provides in its annual and financial reports (see for example, Renault, 1995F, p. 24, 1996F, p. 28, 1997F, p. 75, 1998, p. 16, 2000, p. 37). For instance, with regard to 1999 Renault (2000, p. 37) argued that '...outsourced procurement accounts for about 80% of the assembly cost of its vehicles'. The reason for the substantial difference between our own-reconstructed and Renault's reported percentages is that the indications mentioned in the annual report only represent external purchases vis-à-vis

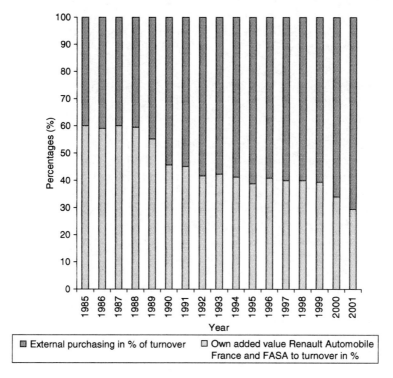

Figure 6.1 Implication of external suppliers in total Renault turnover 1985–2001.

Source: Author's elaboration based on Renault, Annual Reports 1985–2001, Paris, 1986–2002; Renault, Atlas économique, Paris, various editions.

production (and probably product R&D) costs. They do not take into account distribution and general overhead expenses (Florence, 1996, p. 34), where the balance inclines much more towards in-company costs. Neither are marketing costs included in the outsourcing percentages Renault forwards in its annual reports, for which the balance also inclines much more towards in-company costs. The percentages presented in Figure 6.1 are indeed based on the integrated cost structure of the Renault business apparatus, and not solely on the costs related to 'production' and 'R&D'.[35]

When combining the contents of Tables 6.2, 6.3 and Figure 6.1, and the reflections that were presented subsequent to Table 6.3, it appears that the centralization of purchasing activities coincided in time with the rise of the outsourcing phenomena. In fact, a slow but sure absolute and relative increase in outsourcing can be observed from the 1990s onwards, which is also the decade in which Renault intensified its filialization and externalization policies. Furthermore, to keep the supplier base within manageable proportions, a policy towards working with a limited amount of suppliers for a larger or richer package of products was followed, as is evidenced by Table 6.1. It is also against this 'multiple background' that an encouragement of approaches between local, in this case Spanish, suppliers and large MNEs and vice versa should be understood.

6.2   The Renault 5 and Clio production periods

6.2.1   *Analysis*

In 1990, the Renault 5 had been in production at FASA-Renault Valladolid for almost 18 years. The latest generation of the Renault 5, *le Supercinq*, was launched in 1984. Serial production of this model started in Valladolid in December 1984 (Rombo 49, p. 4).

From 1990 onwards Renault started producing the Renault Clio as the follow-up to the Renault Supercinq (Renault, 1991, pp. 7, 16, 23–24). The first units were assembled in the Flins factory in France from February 1990 onwards (Rombo 83, p. 4). Soon afterwards, in April 1990, serial production also commenced in Valladolid (Rombo 83, p. 4; FASA-Renault, 1991, p. 8).

The first Clio generation stayed in production until March 1994 (FASA-Renault, 1995, p. 19) when it was replaced by the second generation Clio (Renault, 1995, p. 22).

6.2.1.1   *FASA-Renault Valladolid's share in total Supercinq and Clio production*

The Renault Supercinq production process had been piloted at the Flins factory (Rombo 49, p. 5). As Flins had started serial production of the Supercinq several months before Valladolid, it provided assistance in production engineering to the Valladolid plant and the Flins experiences were transferred to the Valladolid plant (Rombo 49, p. 5). Apart from Valladolid and Flins, the Supercinq was also produced in Vilvoorde, Belgium (Renault, 1986, p. 25) and at Renault's manufacturing subsidiary 'Renault Portuguesa' in Setubal, Portugal.

Production piloting for the first Clio generation was again carried out at the Flins factory (Rombo 83, pp. 4, 23). The initial division of Clio production was as follows (Renault, 1991, p. 24): Flins (1,430 cars per day), Valladolid (550 cars per day), Vilvoorde (500 cars per day) and Setubal (150 cars per day).

Data on the annual production shares of the Valladolid plant related to the Supercinq and the first Clio generation result in the following overview.

The figures in Table 6.4 indicate that, from an intra-firm network perspective, the Valladolid production site was of marginal importance with regard to the models indicated in the period in question. Nevertheless, the Valladolid plant played a much more important role – from a model-specific and cross-border perspective on production – during the Clio era (from 1990

Table 6.4 Annual production volumes at FASA-Renault Valladolid and share in total production of Supercinq and Clio first-generation

Year	Supercinq and Clio first-generation production by FASA-Renault Valladolid	Total production of Supercinq and Clio first-generation by Renault	FASA-Renault Valladolid share in total Renault Supercinq and Clio first-generation production (%)
1985	36,635	498,394	7.4
1986	25,496	484,537	5.3
1987	36,435	515,673	7.1
1988	23,915	559,400	4.3
1989	19,688	513,991	3.8
1990	43,404	446,329	9.7
1991	121,433	668,125	18.2
1992	140,541	730,072	19.3
1993	107,046	482,071	22.2
1994	128,940	524,146	24.6

Source: Author's elaboration based on FASA-Renault, Memoria y Balance 1985–1994, Madrid, 1986–1995; Renault, Annual Reports 1985–1994, Paris, 1986–1995.

onwards) than during the Renault Supercinq era (until 1990). The factory also produced other models, but throughout the whole period under consideration the Supercinq and the Clio respectively were its most important products.

Among the initial factories to produce the Renault Clio, production-wise the Flins plant and – followed on a distance – the Valladolid plant were the most important ones. Not only in terms of yearly production shares, which grew significantly for the Valladolid plant (see Table 6.4), but also in terms of the production and supply to the other 'Clio plants' of large body parts and propulsion elements. Both factories provided large coachwork parts, such as doors, hoods and roof elements, and engine and exhaust parts to Vilvoorde and Setubal, the other Clio factories (Rombo 83, pp. 23, 25). As such, Flins and Valladolid functioned as real production centres, whereas the others were mere assembly plants.

6.2.1.2 *Evolution of supply origins*

During the Renault Supercinq production period, production at the Valladolid plant was still largely fed by and embedded in national (Spanish) supply structures, with limited interchange of pieces with other Renault plants or import of pieces from suppliers abroad. Overviews of supplier relationships of FASA-Renault with respect to the years 1988–1989 reveal a Spain-based constellation of suppliers with concentrations throughout

Castilla y Leon, the Madrid area, Catalonia, the Basque Country and Andalusia (FASA Calidad, 1989; Pedrosa Sanz, 1993). Moreover, it reveals a fairly fragmented supply structure in terms of multiple suppliers per component and direct supply relationships for several small individual pieces of what would later be supplied as integrated components or modules. This was notably the case for seating parts, dashboard and bumper pieces.

From the Clio era onwards, a tiering system among suppliers was introduced. As a consequence, only certain upstream supply actors maintained their direct relationships with FASA-Renault, whereas many suppliers of less integrated pieces and parts ended up supplying to these first tier suppliers.

Also a more uniform purchasing policy for all Renault plants was applied from the Renault Clio era onwards. This led to a linking of FASA-Renault with companies that were also working for other Renault plants. It also gradually led to a stronger embeddedness of production at the Valladolid plant '*au sein du groupe Renault*' with more intra-group transactions and product flows.

This intensified outsourcing and a stronger anchoring of the Valladolid plant in the Renault Group structure can be illustrated via the following graphic, in Figure 6.2, which is expressed in million pesetas (MPTAS).

As the main point of comparison to comprehend the evolutions pictured in the previous figure, we mention the fact that in the period in question FASA-Renault's turnover grew by a factor of 1.47. In the same period, inputs from third parties located within Spain increased considerably stronger due to intensified outsourcing practices (growth multiplier: 2.28).

However, geographically speaking the origins remained more or less unchanged compared to the years 1988–1989 (see FASA Calidad, 1989; Pedrosa Sanz, 1993). A breakdown in October 1991 of the suppliers for the first Clio generation (Mando 26, p. 6), confirmed the picture of a supplier base scattered across Spain with selective inputs from suppliers based in France and Portugal. The attempts to introduce JIT practices for delivery to FASA-Renault (see for example, FASA-Renault, 1989, p. 11, 1990, p. 21, Renault, 1989, p. 27) from the Clio production period onwards, apparently did not present a problem for FASA-Renault's scattered supplier base. For when the Clio came into production, many of these suppliers were able to comply with JIT or other tight logistics delivery schemes (Rombo 15, p. 8).

The integration of FASA-Renault into Renault-wide intra-firm component transactions did not yet lead to a marked increase in inputs from other Renault plants (growth multiplier: 1.08) for the period 1987–1994. The main reason for this is that until the mid-1990s, FASA-Renault kept producing most chassis and propulsion parts in-house: power trains, steering directions, engines and gearboxes (Renault Atlas économique, Editions de 1990, 1993 and 1995; Rombo 83, p. 30). The incoming chassis components were supplementary to the company's own production and were thus of a relatively small quantity. The following overview of the 1992 situation illustrates this point. In 1992 FASA-Renault (both for Valladolid and

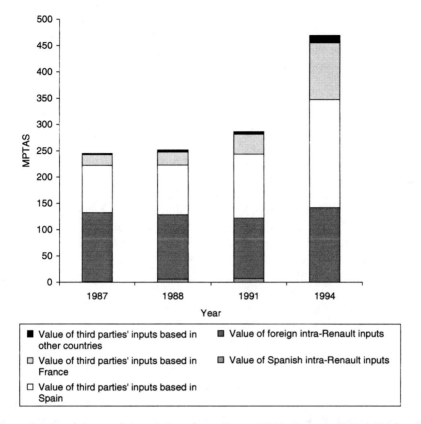

Figure 6.2 Breakdown of the origins of supplies to FASA-Renault Valladolid for the Supercinq and the Clio first-generation.

Source: Author's elaboration based on FASA-Renault, Memoria y Balance, Madrid, various editions; Mandos, various editions; Pedrosa Sanz, 1993.

Palencia) received 200,000 gearboxes from Sevilla (considered as FASA-Renault production), 74,000 steering directions from SMI (Renault France), 56,000 gearboxes and 45,000 engines from Cacia (Renault Portugal), 115,000 motors and 108,000 gearboxes from Cléon (Renault France). The Valladolid plant produced 191,000 engines, 290,000 steering directions and 716,000 front and rear power trains for its own purposes (Renault Atlas économique, Edition 1993, p. 29). In addition to the chassis flows, incoming Renault flows to FASA-Renault were mostly concentrated around comparatively lower added value foundry pieces from, for example, *Fonderies du Poîtou* and *Funfrap* (Renault Annual Report, various editions).

Furthermore, the previous figure clearly indicates that there was an ongoing shift from intra-group provision of parts towards procurement from third parties. Imports of parts from third party suppliers grew very strongly between 1987 and 1994 (growth multipliers for third party inputs from France and elsewhere were 5.33 and 6.25 respectively). Although in absolute terms these imports were still of relatively marginal importance, the fact that they grew a lot stronger than FASA-Renault's overall turnover in this period (growth multiplier 1.47), made that their shares in total turnover increased significantly. In fact, the geographical origins of inputs shown in Figure 6.2 reveal a connection with France-based supply locations that grows stronger over time. Notably as regards the increased involvement of third party suppliers from France, a trigger moment was the preparation of the Clio production and the integration of FASA-Renault into the Renault Group structure, that is, around the year 1990.

The trend towards increased outsourcing combined with a concerted reliance of FASA-Renault on inputs from Renault sister plants can also be deduced from the following figures, as detailed in Table 6.5.

The steep increase in outsourcing from 1985 onwards is basically due to the two factors mentioned above (see also Figure 6.2). First of all, a steady level of incoming components, notably chassis and foundry parts, from other Renault plants (Renault, 1986; FASA-Renault, 1988, pp. ii–iii; Pedrosa Sanz, 1993, p. 103; Muruzabal, 2000, Renault Atlas économique, various editions). In second place a stronger reliance on independent suppliers.

Given the content of FASA-Renault's president's discourse at the start of the 1987 annual report, we have reasons to argue that the increase in outsourcing by FASA-Renault between 1985 and 1987 is completely due to an increase in intra-firm component flows (FASA-Renault, 1988, pp. ii–iii): 'Our companies are rigid, both when business flourishes and when there is lack of demand after our products. Labour questions are to a large extent

Table 6.5 Implication of external suppliers in total FASA-Renault turnover 1985–1994

Year	Turnover FASA-Renault in MPTAS	Value of external purchasing in MPTAS	External purchasing as share of turnover (%)
1985	289,510	143,638	49.6
1986	342,490	175,598	51.3
1987	424,985	245,023	57.7
1988	451,212	251,459	55.7
1989	515,919	299,448	58.0
1990	429,937	292,710	68.1
1991	453,739	286,252	63.1
1992	537,514	368,466	68.6
1993	483,796	344,317	71.2
1994	622,771	469,423	75.4

Source: Author's elaboration based on FASA-Renault, Memoria y Balance 1985–1994, Madrid, 1986–1995.

responsible for our possibilities to adapt to fluctuating situations. For that reason we have been obliged to diminish our export activities and to increase our import activities. This policy has been adopted by all [Spanish] car constructors but perhaps – for being more integrated [in the production structure of our mother company, that is, Renault] – we have applied it more intensively. As a consequence of growing market demand, we have had to import components and cars to come up with a sufficient product offer' (our translation).

We stress that FASA-Renault booked incoming intra-firm product flows as purchasing activities.[36] Consequently, they form a relevant explanatory factor for the evolutions presented in Table 6.5. For Renault as a whole evidently these intra-firm transactions were not booked as external procurement. This explains the rather big difference as regards the percentages indicated per year on FASA-Renault level in Table 6.5, and on group level in Figure 6.1. Moreover, as all kinds of corporate matters such as R&D, design and sales expenses are not booked on subsidiaries' accounts the purchasing-turnover quotient at the level of subsidiaries tends to be higher also. By all means, Table 6.5 provides clear indications regarding FASA-Renault's reliance on external input providers, whether these were legally independent entities or not.[37] Thus, we can argue that the steep increase in FASA-Renault's reliance on external inputs is both due to an increased reliance of the Renault Group as a whole, and thus also FASA-Renault, on external suppliers (see for example, Figure 6.1, Figure 6.2, and the mentioned growth multipliers for FASA-Renault's purchasing from third parties compared to growth of its overall turnover) and on the enhancement of FASA-Renault's anchoring '*au sein du groupe Renault*' (see for example, FASA-Renault, 1988, pp. ii–iii; 1989, p. iii; 1990, p. 10; Renault, 1991, p. 19, Layan, 1997).

From the increased reliance on third party suppliers and on intra-firm supply of components – notably from French Renault subsidiaries as pictured in Table 6.5, it follows that FASA-Renault's own added value vis-à-vis its turnover figures shrank from approximately 50% in 1985 to around 25% in 1994. When breaking down geographically the external purchasing figures behind Table 6.5 we see the following. The value share of external suppliers located in Spain vis-à-vis FASA-Renault's turnover grew from around 20% in 1985 to 33% in 1994. Consequently, the overall Spanish value of FASA-Renault's turnover (FASA-Renault own added value, inputs from other Spain-based Renault sites and from independent Spain-based external suppliers) dropped from around (50% + 20% =) 70% in 1985 to (25% + 33% =) 58% in 1994. Thus, foreign inputs as complementary factor grew from around 30% to approximately 42% in the same period.

With respect to the external suppliers located in Spain, the following investment and location details should be highlighted.

As indicated before, Renault and FASA-Renault's intended to harmonize the supplier bases of their various plants (Renault, 1988; FASA-Renault, 1989; 1990; 1991; Gorgeu and Mathieu, 1995; *La Lettre du GERPISA*, No. 121, mars 1998; Parnière, 2001). Also, they intended to encourage the creation of a supplier base for FASA-Renault that consisted of '. . . a texture of Spanish and foreign suppliers that must be competitive from an international point of view. With that goal in mind, we have facilitated approaches between Spanish suppliers and internationally active manufacturers of components, in order to cosolidate companies that used to operate only locally' (own translation based on: Pedrosa Sanz, 1993, p. 107). The former implied that an important part of FASA-Renault's Spain-based suppliers was taken over by foreign groups or that their supplies were replaced by component flows coming from greenfield investments by foreign groups in Spain. Alternatively, incumbent suppliers were encouraged to pursue internal growth strategies, sustained by Renault. This was, for example, the case with the Burgos-based (*Grupo Antolin*) *Irausa*.

As noteworthy cases of foreign capital intervention with respect to FASA-Renault suppliers located in Castilla y Leon, we can mention the following examples for the period in question: Trèves in car seating (F), Plastic Omnium and Reydel in synthetic components (F), Sommer Allibert in carpeting (F), Solvay in deposits (B), Inerga/Eurotec in front and rear end pieces (D), and Johnson Controls in car seating (USA). Apart from Trèves' and Plastic Omnium's ventures, all these investments were made in already existing establishments. This indicates that most investments were takeovers instead of greenfield investments.

It turns out that most of the investments, and also many suppliers to FASA-Renault in general were located on the axis Jaén-Madrid-Vigo through which the Renault sites (Sevilla, Valladolid and to a lesser extent Palencia) and the also French-owned PSA sites (Peugeot Madrid and Citroën Vigo) are linked. In fact, many of the suppliers operate sites on this axis from which they simultaneously attend several of these Renault and PSA sites (see for example, Plastic Omnium Annual Report, various editions; ECIA Annual Report, various editions; Bertrand Faure Annual Report, various editions; Faurecia Annual Report, various editions; Solvay Annual Report, various editions; ITEC, 1998). Since FASA-Renault Valladolid was not the leading factory in terms of production engineering or production share of the Renault Clio or of any other Renault model, it is questionable whether the Valladolid plant was the primary or decisive client of these suppliers and thus, whether it would pay-off to set up buyer-specific sites for such a client. Therefore, the location of the Valladolid plant alone appears not to have been determinant for suppliers in deciding where to settle. Instead, they took the location of all their clients into account. The fact that – apparently with the approval of FASA-Renault and Renault – the accent was placed on takeovers rather than greenfield investment as entry mode stimulated this further. As a consequence, the creation of (semi-)dedicated supply sites vis-à-vis FASA-Renault Valladolid was the exception rather than the rule and the overall outcome was a rather fragmented supplier base from a geographical point of view.

6.2.2 Conclusions

During the transition period from the Renault Supercinq to the Renault Clio, the strategy Renault followed with regard to FASA-Renault's supplier base was to upgrade the incumbent suppliers to partners that could satisfy the quality demands of Renault according to its 'EAQF' standards. That way, several former in-house operations were to be externalized. One way to achieve this, and at the same time harmonize the supplier bases of the different Renault plants, was encouraging incumbent FASA-Renault suppliers to approach or merge with large international groups that were already working for Renault plants elsewhere (notably in France). The start of the Clio era – coinciding with an intensification of outsourcing practices and FASA-Renault's integration into the Renault Group – was seized by Renault as the starting signal to implement this supplier 'partnering' strategy and assure a certain form of 'continuity' in the traditional supply relationships of FASA-Renault Valladolid. Both in terms of the final actors involved in FASA-Renault's supply relationships, and in terms of their location. Through this approach, in very few cases suppliers moved closer to the Valladolid plant. The exception was the creation of Ibérica de Asientos (car seats) in Mojados, near FASA-Renault Valladolid, created by Catalonia-based Trety and France-based Trèves, later taken over by Johnson Controls.

It appears that the rather fragmented and distant relationships – spatially speaking – that characterized FASA-Renault's supplier base were not an impediment for complying with lean and sequenced logistics requirements. FASA-Renault succeeded in operating JIT delivery schemes with suppliers from as far away as Andalusia, Portugal and the Basque Country.

In terms of inter-firm network positioning, it appears that those suppliers that already had a strong connection to Renault as the mother company of FASA-Renault or those that were willing to invest in such a relationship (for instance through internal growth or the acquisition of or linking up with incumbent suppliers to Renault), achieved pole positions with respect to FASA-Renault Valladolid in the early 1990s.

Furthermore, it appears that relationship-specific assets or geographical proximity were not necessary in this positioning process. The fact that the Valladolid plant was not the leading factory in terms of production engineering or production share of the Renault Clio or of any other Renault model, is arguably an important factor in explaining the absence of on-site investments. It hampered possibilities for economies of scale or learning effects in the engineering field. Consequently, investors or acquirers preferred to maintain or place their establishments in areas from where they could attend multiple clients. The non-assignment of leading factory 'features' to the Valladolid plant was in line with Renault's choices at the time in favour of maintaining strategic and piloting activities in centrally located sites and fragmenting model-specific production over a large number of factories. The Renault tradition of producing multiple car models based on different platforms under one roof also continued at FASA-Renault. This was another barrier for the factory to reach high production volumes of any single car model and, therefore, reduced the Valladolid plant's possibilities of offering large site-specific economies of scale to suppliers.

6.3   The Renault Clio second-generation and subsequent versions production periods

6.3.1   *Analysis*

The second-generation Clio went into production in March 1994 (FASA-Renault, 1995, p. 19; Renault, 1995, p. 22). It was initially produced in Flins, Vilvoorde, Setubal, Valladolid and Novo Mesto (Slovenija) (Renault Atlas économique Edition 1995, 1996, p. 23). Again, the Flins plant was the most important production hub and the plant to carry out fine-tuning of production engineering before serial production would commence at the other production sites. In April 1996, the second-generation Clio was restyled (Mandos 75, p. 1). Apart from the esthetic and equipment *retouches* to the model itself, this caused no changes to the intra-firm production organization described above.

In 1997 Renault presents a completely new Clio, the Clio II (Renault, 1998, pp. 12, 70; Renault, 1999, pp. 26, 32; Mandos 94, pp. 1, 3). The start of its production from 1998 onwards is accompanied by a radical reorganization of plant-specific production assignments. Stimulated by a loss in 1996 (Renault, 1997, pp. 6, 14–15; Rombo 143, pp. 12–13) and by losses at the level of FASA-Renault in the years 1996 and 1997 (FASA-Renault, 1997, pp. 6–7, 1998, p. 7; Rombo 143, pp. 10–11), Renault decided to rationalize its business apparatus seriously and to hive off its least profitable branch locations.

This led to the sale of the Setubal plant (Portugal) in 1996 (FASA-Renault, 1997, p. 10; Renault, 1997, p. 15). It also led to the closure of the plant in Vilvoorde (Belgium) in the second half of 1997 (Rombo 151, p. 21; Renault, 1997, p. 15; Renault, 1998, pp. 18, 26; FET, *1 maart 1997, L'Echo, 1er au 3 mars 1997*, p. 2; *Le Monde, 1er mars 1997*, p. 20; Renault, 1998, p. 16). Furthermore, it led Renault to reconsider its FASA-Renault assets and opt for a single product factory concept at the FASA-Renault plants (FASA-Renault, 1997, p. 7, 1999, p. 16; Renault, 1999, p. 27).

Consequently, production of the Clio II took place in Flins, which at the same time acted as the piloting plant for Clio II production engineering (see for example, Renault, 1997, p. 14, 1998, p. 17; Rombo 153, p. IV), Valladolid and Novo Mesto (Slovenija): 'To increase efficiency, we cut the number of sites to three – Flins in France, Valladolid in Spain and Revoz [Novo Mesto] in Slovenija – setting high standards for each' (Renault, 1997, p. 14). The plant-specific production quantities were then foreseen at 980 units daily at FASA-Renault Valladolid, 840 at Flins and 480 at Novo Mesto (Rombo 153, p. V).

A further implication was that the Valladolid plant manufactured its last Renault Twingo in 1997, after having produced its last Renault Express in 1996 (FASA-Renault, 1997, 1998). Consequently, from 1998 onwards the Valladolid plant was solely dedicated to Clio production. The same happened with the FASA-Renault Palencia plant, which shifted from Mégane and Laguna production to 100% Mégane production in 1998 (FASA-Renault, 1997, 1998, 1999).

Another completely new Clio was launched in the first half of 2001 (Mandos 129, p. 1; Renault, 2002F, pp. 3, 43, 51). Production of this model was again divided among Flins, Valladolid and Novo Mesto (Slovenija). FASA-Renault Valladolid started producing this Clio model on April 2001; the same day as the Flins plant did (Mandos 129, p. 1; Renault, 2002F, p. 51). Again, the Flins plant served as the piloting plant for preparing the prototypes, testing the first preseries production and fine-tuning production engineering for serial assembly (Renault, Global Magazine 4, Mayo 2001, p. 13).

6.3.1.1   FASA-Renault Valladolid's share in total Clio production

Obviously, both the closure of Vilvoorde and the sale of Setubal (Renault, 1997, pp. 6, 14–15), the partial shift of Clio production towards Valladolid and the switch to a mono-product factory concept favoured the Valladolid plant's Clio assembly activities both in absolute and in relative sense. The figures in the following Table 6.6 illustrate this.[38]

It is clear to see that the overall production figures at FASA-Renault Valladolid grew substantially after 1997, the year in which Vilvoorde was

Table 6.6 Annual production volumes at FASA-Renault Valladolid and share in total production of second-generation and subsequent versions of Clio

Year	Production of Clio second-generation and subsequent versions by FASA-Renault Valladolid	Total production of Clio second-generation and subsequent versions by Renault	FASA-Renault Valladolid share in total production of Clio second-generation and subsequent versions (%)
1994	128,940	477,529	27.0
1995	91,992	428,799	21.5
1996	125,483	409,354	30.7
1997	136,607	412,383	33.1
1998	205,669	507,485	40.5
1999	275,058	571,878	48.1
2000	280,667	640,252	43.8
2001	277,188	648,346	42.8

Source: Author's elaboration based on FASA-Renault, Memoria y Balance 1994–2001, Madrid, 1995–2002; Renault, Rapport Annuel 1994–2001, Paris, 1995–2002.

closed and the mono-product factory philosophy was adopted at FASA-Renault Valladolid. It turns out that the Valladolid plant is the site that has assembled most Clios since 1998, surpassing even the Flins plant (Perfiles 3, p. 3). Additionally, as a consequence of the Clio production concentration in Flins and Valladolid, at both sites a paint shop and plastic injection work shop was installed in order to paint all the bumpers in the same colour of the main coachwork and to assemble the various front-end pieces into one module (Renault, Global Magazine 2, Marzo 2001, pp. 40–42; Renault, Global Magazine 6, Julio 2001, pp. 40–42; Perfiles 3, pp. 3, 11). Thus, from a Clio-specific intra-firm network position it is clear to see this contributed to the importance of the Valladolid plant. Consequently, the Valladolid plant also became more important from a viewpoint of Clio-specific physical supply. However, in managerial and conceptual terms and from a viewpoint of proximity to the Renault Clio development and piloting centre, the Valladolid plant did not become more attractive. As such, in terms of the more tactical and strategic activities as regards the Renault Clio, Valladolid still holds second place to Flins.

A salient detail is the fact that the other FASA-Renault plant, the one in Palencia, also saw its production share in the Mégane assembly grow after the monoproduct philosophy was applied to the FASA-Renault factories and part of the Mégane production from Vilvoorde was assigned to Palencia in 1998. Moreover, Palencia was appointed pilot factory for the Mégane Coupé and the Mégane Classic (FASA-Renault, 1996, p. 26, 1997, p. 30, 1999, p. 16, 2001, p. 22; Renault, 1997, p. 12), thus also creating further incentives for suppliers to settle closer to the plant.

6.3.1.2   *Evolution of supply origins*

In line with Figure 6.2, charting the changes in supply origin between 1987 and 1994, the following Figure 6.3 shows the evolution, in value terms, of the external input for the assembly activities at the Valladolid plant in the years to follow.

As the point of reference to comment upon the evolutions presented in the previous figure, we mention the fact that in the period in question FASA-Renault's turnover grew by a factor of 1.92. In the same period, 1994–1999, the input provided by France-based third parties grew by a factor of 2.55. As such, this was the fastest growing supply origin. This trend can be explained by pointing at the filialization and sell-off of several Renault activities to independent suppliers. Noteworthy cases during these years are the creation of Auto Chassis International and the sale of Renault sites in Le Mans and Villeurbanne to Koyo, NTN and TRW (Muruzabal, 2000; Renault Atlas économique, various editions; FASA-Renault Memoria y Balance, various editions). Also the trend towards cross-model part communality to achieve better economies of scale from selected supply centres and the subsequent termination at FASA-Renault of several chassis and propulsion

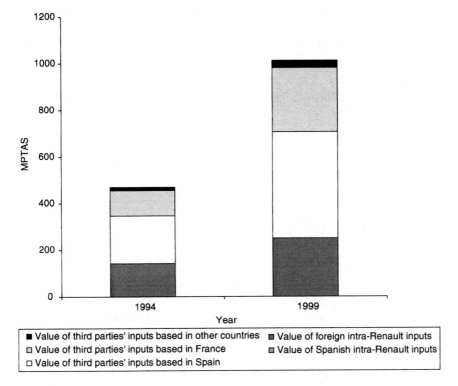

Figure 6.3 Breakdown of the origins of supplies to FASA-Renault Valladolid between 1994–1999.

Source: Author's elaboration based on FASA-Renault, Memoria y Balance, Madrid, various editions.

related manufacturing activities is an important explanatory factor here (Renault, 1994, p. 44, 1997, pp. 12, 14–15, 1998, pp. 16, 68–69, 1999, pp. 14, 16, 26–27, 36, 2000, p. 36; FASA-Renault, 1996, p. 27, 1997, p. 31, 1999, pp. 16, 28, 56, 2000, pp. 19, 28, 56; Rombo 153, p. VI; Renault Atlas économique, various editions; Muruzabal, 2000). This led to a situation whereby several chassis and propulsion components, which until then had been produced by FASA-Renault itself, were now being imported from France-based production centres. Concrete examples are steering directions and rear trains (FASA-Renault, 1996, p. 27, 1997, p. 31, 1999, pp. 16, 28, 56, 2000, pp. 19, 28, 56). The sale of former France-based Renault centres to third parties also led to the fact that imports from Renault France itself (legally speaking) grew with a smaller factor (1.77) than FASA-Renault's turnover (1.92). The factor by which third parties' inputs based in Spain (2.21) or in other countries other than France (2.15) grew, was slightly higher than the one with respect to FASA-Renault's turnover (1.92), but smaller than the one with respect to France-based third parties' inputs (2.55). In all, we see a further intensification of foreign-based supplies to FASA-Renault Valladolid.

In percentage terms, in 1994 external suppliers located in Spain provided some 33% of FASA-Renault's turnover. In 1999, this had grown to around 38%. Nevertheless, the overall Spanish value of the FASA-Renault production vis-à-vis FASA-Renault's turnover in 1999 (FASA-Renault own added value, inputs from other Spain-based Renault sites and from independent Spain-based external suppliers) dropped from 58% in 1994 to 53%. Within this Spanish component, the share of FASA-Renault's in-house added value vis-à-vis its own turnover fell, dropping from around 25% in 1994 to approximately 15% in 1999. The foreign input component grew consequently from about 42% to around 47% over the same period.

The growing emphasis on imports from abroad are furthermore explained by the fact that – with the exception of a part of the engine production and the gearbox production which are still under control of FASA-Renault – the most expensive mechanical and electronic propulsion parts come from abroad, notably from France and Germany. On the other hand, it is especially the interior trim and exterior trim components, which represent less value, that are provided by Spain-based supply sites.

The spectacular growth in purchasing value between 1994 and 1999 that is portrayed in Figure 6.3 (from approximately 450 million pesetas to some 1000 million pesetas) is also due to the fact, that outsourcing and processing of inputs manufactured outside the walls of FASA-Renault also grew quicker in this period than turnover at FASA-Renault. This increasing reliance of FASA-Renault on external input procurement is illustrated in the next Table 6.7.[39]

As a closing word on procurement from third parties, it appears that the absence of a strong local link with Castilla y Leon or Valladolid-based

Table 6.7 Implication of external suppliers in total FASA-Renault turnover 1994–2001.

Year	Turnover FASA-Renault in MPTAS	Value of external purchasing in MPTAS	External purchasing as share of turnover (%)
1994	622,771	469,423	75.4
1995	671,051	518,761	77.3
1996	716,507	562,704	78.5
1997	778,550	626,477	80.5
1998	1,024,328	852,142	83.2
1999	1,195,478	1,011,274	84.6
2000	1,208,859	1,027,530	85.0
2001	1,181,191	1,004,012	85.0

Source: Author's elaboration based on FASA-Renault, Memoria y Balance 1994–2001, Madrid, 1995–2002.

suppliers – in particular with regard to the higher-value components, as is illustrated Figure 6.3, is also found in analyses by Pedrosa Sanz (1993) and Fernandez Arrufe and Pedrosa Sanz (1997). They report on the limited effects FASA-Renault produced in labour terms among suppliers in the province of Valladolid and Castilla y Leon. Likewise, it is supported by the statements of various automotive enterprises on the limited regional connections between FASA-Renault and automotive supply companies of Castilla y Leon: '.. the major manufacturers do not have many suppliers in this region [Castilla y Leon] ... contrary to what might be expected, the Renault, Nissan and Iveco plants in the autonomous community do not demand a great deal of work and services' (Autorevista, 2001, pp. 53, 60–61). Further support for these findings can also be found in the many local press releases that report on production interruptions due to insufficient supply of foreign, notably engine, parts (see for example *El Norte de Castilla*, 04/10/2000, 21/11/2000, 03/12/2000, 09/12/2000, 11/12/2000, 03/01/2001). Finally, the picture of FASA-Renault's 'non-locally anchored supplier base' is also supported and strengthened by statements made by Carlos Ghosn (one of Renault's main leaders). His comments reveal that, in spite of the lower labour costs at Renault's Spanish plants, their unit-specific production cost is on a par with their French *homologues'* production cost due to the fact that on average the French plants have their suppliers a lot closer and thus have lower logistics-related costs (*El País*, 31 de mayo 1998, p. 9). Also many of the consulted experts indicate that it is especially the centralization of purchasing powers from FASA-Renault to Renault Paris at the end of the 1980s that caused a rift between FASA-Renault and many local suppliers (see for example, Manero Miguel, 1997; Pedrosa Sanz, 1997, 2000; Peran Gonzalez, 1997; Muruzabal, 2000; Gilodi, 2001; Rivas, 2001). This image is further illustrated in the coming paragraph and Table 6.8, which show how the importance of several local supply actors retroceded over time.

6.3.1.3   *Geographical and actor breakdown of the supplier network*

In order to further illustrate the geographical and actor composition developments in the supplier network for the Clio production at FASA-Renault Valladolid and to reveal the changes at the level of the individually suppliers involved, the Table 6.8 presents a longitudinal reconstruction of the supplier network surrounding FASA-Renault Valladolid and the locations of the involved companies for a sample of 16 automotive parts. This sample embodies a representative cross section of parts that are currently typically sourced out by car constructors. Also propulsion and chassis components (gearbox, engine, brake devices, transmission, steering system and power train) are included as they are vital components of the final product assembled in a car factory.

In order to analyse the geographical developments and major changes among the actors involved in the delivery of the components presented

Table 6.8 Composition of supplier network around FASA-Renault Valladolid 1984–2001

Component	1984–1990 (Superving)			1990–1996 (Clio first generation)			1996–2001 (Clio II)			2001–2003 (New Clio)		
	Supplier	Origin Of capital	Location	Supplier	Origin of capital	Location	Supplier	Origin of capital	Location	Supplier	Origin of capital	Location
Exhaust pipe	FASA	E – F	Factoria de Carroceria (Valladolid)	Norma + Ekin SCI (ECIA)	E + F	The Basque Country + France	Silenciadores PCG SA (ECIA) until 1998/ Faurecia from 1999 onwards (finalization of merger between ECIA and Bertrand Faure in 1999)	E – F	Madrid	Faurecia	F	Madrid
Front-end and rear-end bumper	FASA	E – F	Factoria de Carrocerias (Valladolid)	Plastic Omnium + Inerga (Eurotec Group) + Matriplast (Fagor-MCC)	F + D + E	Arevalo (Avila) + Villamuriel (Palencia) + Zamudio (Bizkaia)	Peguform (via take over of Inerga in 1996) + Plastic Omnium + Sommer Allibert	D + F + F	Villamuriel (Palencia) + Arevalo (Avila) + Fuenlabrada (Madrid)	Faurecia-Sommer Allibert + FASA + IPO (Inoplast-Plastic Omnium) + Peguform	F + E–F + F + D–USA (as Peguform forms part of US' Venture' since 2001)	Fuenlabrada (Madrid) + Valladolid + Arevalo (Avila) + Villamuriel (Palencia)
Fuel tank	S.G. Hules + Draft. Airex + Carbureibar	E–B + F + E	Valladolid + France + Abadiano (Bizkaia)	S.G. Hules (taken over by Solvay) + Draft. Airex + Carbureibar	E–B + F + E	Valladolid + France + Abadiano (Bizkaia)	S.G. Hules (Solvay) until 2000/ Inergy (= J.V. between Solvay and Plastic Omnium) from 2000 onwards +	E–B + USA	Valladolid + Palencia	Inergy + Bundy/ TI Group	B–F + USA	Valladolid + Palencia

Seats	FASA + Trey S.A. Promotriz + Irausa	E–F + E + E + E	Factoria de Carrocerias (Valladolid) + Maçanet de la Selva (Girona) + Valladolid + Burgos	Ibérica de asientos (J.V. by Trety S.A and Trèves)	E – F	Mojados (Valladolid)	Bundy/ TI Group Ibérica de asientos (taken over by Johnson Controls)	USA	Ibérica de asientos	USA	Mojados (Valladolid)
Steering system	FASA	E–F	Factoria de Motores (Valladolid)	FASA + SMI	E–F + F	Valladolid + Irigny (France)	Koyo + TRW	J + USA	Koyo + TRW	J + USA	Irigny (F) + Landaben (Navarra)
Cabling	FASA + MAISA	E–F	Factoria de Montaje-2 (Valladolid) + Valls (Tarragona)	CETASA + REICAB + MAISA	E + E + E	Tarazona (Zaragoza) + Portugal + Lleida/ Valls (Tarragona)	CETASA (incorporated by Delphi + MAISA (incorporated by UTA and later by Lear)	E-USA + E – USA	Delphi	USA	Tarazona + Valls (Tarragona)
Cockpit	FASA	E–F	Factoria de Carrocerias (Valladolid)	Atepsa– Reydel + Sommer Allibert + Jaeger + Zanini	E–F + F + F + E	Medina de Rioseco (Valladolid) + Olmedo (Valladolid) + Barcelona + Barcelona	Atepsa-Plastic Omnium (Reydel was acquired by Plastic Omnium in 1995)	F	(Plastic Omnium-)Visteon (in 1999 Plastic Omnium automotive interiors was acquired by Visteon)	USA	Medina de Rioseco (Valladolid)
Isolating floor coverings	FASA	E–F	Taller de Montaje (Palencia)	CEFSA + Ekin SCI+ (ECIA)+ Trety + Gunasa (incorporated by Sommer Allibert)	E + F + E+ E–F	Madrid + France + Girona + Olmedo (Valladolid)	Sommer Allibert	F	Faurecia-Sommer Allibert (due to merger between the two companies in 2000)	F	Olmedo (Valladolid)

(Table 6.8 continued)

Table 6.8 Continued

Component	1984–1990 (Supercinq)			1990–1996 (Clio first generation)			1996–2001 (Clio II)			2001–2003 (New Clio)		
	Supplier	Origin Of capital	Location	Supplier	Origin of capital	Location	Supplier	Origin of capital	Location	Supplier	Origin of capitall	Location
Interior trims, consoles, door and roof panels	FASA	E–F	Confeccion-Pozuelo (Valladolid)	Irausa + Simoldes + Sommer Allibert	E + P + F	Burgos until 1993/ Valladolid from 1993 onwards + Portugal + France until 1993/ Fuenlabrada (Madrid) from 1993 onwards	Plastic Omnium + Sommer Allibert + Irausa Valladolid	F + F E	Arevalo (Avila) + Olmedo (Valladolid)/ Fuenlabrada (Madrid) + Valladolid	Plastic Omnium + Faurecia-Sommer Allibert + Irausa	F + F + E	Arevalo (Avila) + Olmedo (Valladolid)/ Fuenlabrada (Madrid) + Valladolid
Lights	Faespa-Valeo Iluminacion + Yorka	E–F + E	Martos (Jaén) + Barcelona	Faespa-Valeo Iluminacion + Yorka	E–F + E	Martos (Jaén) + Barcelona	Hella-Maesa + Faespa-Valeo	D + E–F	Madrid + Martos (Jaén)	Hella-Maesa + Valeo	D + F	Venta de Baños (Palencia) + Martos (Jaén)
Stamping of small metal devices	FASA + Fonderies du Poitou + Samber + Funfrap + Alcala Industrial + Alumalsa	E–F + F + E + P– F + E + E	Factoria de Carrocerias (Valladolid) + France + Madrid + Portugal + Madrid + Zaragoza	Alcala Industrial + Funfrap + Mikalor + Alumalsa + Inyectametal + Acenor	E + P– F + E + E + E + UK	Madrid + Portugal + Sabadell + Zaragoza + the Basque Country + Vitoria	Sofedit Ibérica + Alcala industrial + Estampaciones Bizkaia	F + E + E	Valladolid + Madrid + Dueñas (Palencia)	Sofedit Ibérica + Alcala industrial + Estampaciones Bizkaia	F + E + E	Valladolid + Madrid + Dueñas (Palencia)
Gearbox	FASA	E–F	Sevilla	FASA + Renault (Portuguesa)	E–F + P–F + F	Sevilla + Cacia (P) + Cléon (F)	FASA + Renault (Portuguesa)	E–F + P–F + F	Sevilla + Cacia (P) + Cléon (F)	FASA + Renault (Portuguesa)	E–F + P–F + F	Sevilla + Cacia (P) + Cléon (F)
Engine	FASA + Renault	E–F + F	Factoria de Motores (Valladolid) + Cacia (P) + Cléon (F)	FASA + Renault (Portuguesa)	E–F + P–F + F	Factoria de Motores (Valladolid) + Cacia (P) + Cléon (F)	FASA + Renault (Portuguesa)	E–F + P–F + F	Factoria de Motores (Valladolid) + Cacia (P) + Cléon (F)	FASA + Renault (Portuguesa)	E–F + P–F + F	Factoria de Motores (Valladolid) + Cacia (P) + Cléon (F)

Brake devices	FASA + Bendix España/ Bendiberica + Lingotes Especiales	E− F + E− USA + E	Factoria de Motores (Valladolid) + Santander + Valladolid	FASA + Bendix España/ Bendiberica + Lingotes Especiales	E− F + E− USA + E	Factoria de Motores (Valladolid) + Santander + Valladolid	FASA (until 1999) + Lingotes Especiales/ Bradling Conjuntos (until 1999) + ACI from 1999 onwards + Fagor Ederlan + TI Group/ Bundy	E− F + E + F + E + USA USA	Factoria de (Valladolid) + Valladolid + Le Mans (F)/ Villeurbanne (F)+ Gipuzkoa + Palencia	ACI + Fagor Ederlan + TI Group/Bundy	F + E + USA	Le Mans (F)/ Villeurbanne (F)/ Palencia from 2002 onwards + Gipuzkoa + Palencia
Transmission	Ayra Durex + FASA + Ascometal (Renault Safe was bought up by Ascometal – Usinor Salicor- in 1982)	E − UK + E−F + F	Gipuzkoa + Factoria de Motores (Valladolid) + France	Ayra Durex + FASA + Ascometal	E-UK + + E−F + F	Gipuzkoa + Factoria de Motores (Valladolid) + France	FASA (until 1999) + ACI from 1999 onwards + Renault	F + F	Factoria de Motores (Valladolid) + Le Mans (F) + Villeurbanne (F) + Le Mans (F)	ACI + NTN	F + J	Le Mans (F)/ Villeurbanne (F)/ Palencia from 2002 onwards + Le Mans (F)
Motor propulsion group (power train)	FASA + Fagor + Valeo + Femsa (owned by Bosch)	E−F + E+ F + E−D	Factoria de Motores (Valladolid) + Usurbil (Gipuzkoa)/ Tafalla (Navarra) + Madrid + Barcelona	FASA + Fagor + Valeo/ Siemens (in 1995 Siemens took over Valeo's motor and electricity activities) + Femsa (owned by Bosch)	E−F + E+ F− D + E− D	Factoria de Motores (Valladolid) + Usurbil (Gipuzkoa)/ Tafalla (Navarra)+ Madrid/ Toulouse (F)+ Barcelona	FASA (until 1999) + ACI from 1999 onwards + Renault + Siemens + Bosch	E−F + F+ F + D + D	Factoria de Motores (Valladolid) + Le Mans (F)/ Villeurbanne (F) + Le Mans (F)+ Madrid/ Toulouse (F)+ Barcelona	ACI + NTN + Bosch + Delphi-Lucas Varity + Siemens	F + J + D + USA + D	Le Mans (F)/ Villeurbanne (F)/ Palencia from 2002 onwards + Le Mans (F)+ Barcelona + Barcelona + Madrid/ Toulouse (F)

Source: Author's elaboration.

Note

If under the columns with location details no country code is added to a city name, the city in question is located in Spain. For a further assessment of the location evolutions per component see also Table A.11 under Appendix A.

in Table 6.8, we will elaborate on a comparison between the Renault Clio first-generation period (1990–1996) and the Renault new Clio era (2001–2003). Within our time frame of analysis these two periods mark the first and the most recent time segment in which the Clio is produced. Moreover, we find that the information obtained with respect to the period 1990–1996 is more complete and accurate than the information relating to the period 1984–1990, and thus provides a better basis for comparison with the situation during the period 2001–2003. Finally, the period 1984–1990 mainly concerns the production period of the Clio's predecessor: the Renault Supercinq. In order to be able to make statements regarding model-specific evolutions it is therefore also best to take the 1990–1996 period as the point of reference. Finally, as the selection of suppliers for the Clio that went into production in 1990 took place between 1985–1988 (Rombo 83, p. 4), it can be argued that the selection of suppliers for component delivery to the Valladolid plant in relation to the first Clio should reflect the historical supply relationships between FASA-Renault and its suppliers fairly well.

6.3.1.4   Analysis of the geographical articulation of the supplier network

Based on a comparison between the Renault Clio first-generation period (1990–1996) and the Renault new Clio era (2001–2003), the contents of Table 6.8 indicate the following. We see that – for the supply of the 16 components under consideration –[40] there are 6 that undergo a geographical approximation without any on-site investments. They result from a shake-out and tiering process among FASA-Renault's multiple suppliers until 1990. The only true approximations are the creation of a new seat production centre in Mojados, (Grupo Antolín) Irausa's approximation from Burgos to Valladolid through the creation of its '*Revestimientos y Asientos*' branch location in Valladolid and the creation of the Bundy plant in Palencia. The first one is a 'dedicated' production centre. The second one is a production centre that serves multiple clients. Bundy's fuel alimentation plant concerns the establishment of a client-specific storage sink. Bundy's major production centre in Spain is located in Barcelona and it opened satellite units, among others, in Palencia for FASA-Renault, in Madrid and in Vigo for PSA plants (ITEC, 1998). Furthermore, there are four cases where the successive suppliers involved are located further away, resulting in longer supply distances to FASA-Renault Valladolid. These are all due to the change to France-based supply of certain propulsion and chassis components as a consequence of Renault's centralization policies. Subsequently, we find six cases of geographical status quo. In all, Table 6.8 shows a supplier network that is rather scattered over western Spain, some isolated supply establishments from the Ebro Delta (the Basque Country, Zaragoza and Tarragona-Barcelona) and

France. The supplier base of the Valladolid plant by no means has become concentrated in or around Valladolid itself over time. Whereas for the Clio first-generation 4.74 of the components we analysed were mainly delivered from within the province of Valladolid, for the new Clio era (2001–2003) this is the case for 5.41 of the 16 components. If we focus on Castilla y Leon as the host region for FASA-Renault Valladolid's suppliers base, we see a growth from 5.58 to 7.67. This means that more than half of the analysed components are provided from outside the autonomous community of Castilla y Leon. At the same time, around two-thirds of the analysed sample comes from outside FASA-Renault Valladolid's host province. This clearly underlines the previous indications of an absence of tendencies of geographical concentration and co-location around FASA-Renault Valladolid.

As reported above, to the extent that geographical approximation did occur, it appears to be especially related to a tiering process of FASA-Renault's supplier base in which those suppliers that are most nearby located emerge as first tier suppliers and in which the suppliers that are located further away lose their direct relationships with FASA-Renault Valladolid.

6.3.1.5 Analysis of the actor composition evolutions in the supplier network

For many components a tendency to go from fragmented to integrated (modularized) outsourcing can be observed in Table 6.8. See, for example, fuel alimentation, seats, cockpits, isolating floor covers and small metal devices. Nonetheless, with regard to certain other components 1+n module-specific supplier relationships stay intact. This is for instance the case with steering systems, interior trims and bumpers. According to Torrico (2002) this may occur – in order to spread risks – with those components where Renault has or expects good relationships with several suppliers.

In many cases the tiering processes coincided with the acquisition of traditional suppliers to FASA-Renault by MNEs that already delivered to Renault France and or which were involved in one of the filialization operations of Renault France. Consequently, many of the suppliers that emerge as tier one supplier to FASA-Renault were familiar ones, both to FASA-Renault Valladolid and to Renault France. Thus, a status quo as regards many main suppliers to FASA-Renault was the outcome. Most companies that acted as suppliers of a certain component during the initial production period of the Renault Clio still do so today. Consequently, rather than genuine supplier substitutions, what has taken place are virtual substitutions via takeovers and incorporations of early FASA-Renault suppliers into the ranks of MNEs that functioned as suppliers to Renault France.

This was the case with exhaust pipes, rear and front-end bumpers, fuel tanks, seats, cabling, cockpits, floor covers, transmissions and to a lesser extent for brakes, engine propulsion group, steering systems and interior trims, consoles and door and roof panels. As such, in terms of ownership structures of the suppliers, when we consider FASA-Renault as an integrated part of Renault, there were also very few genuine substitutions.

As regards exhaust pipes, rear and front end bumpers, fuel tanks and transmissions, we see that FASA-Renault's 'French connection' in the long run proves to be stronger than FASA-Renault's long time relationships with, notably Basque, supply companies. Take note that a US specialist company in fuel tubes complemented the Franco-Belgian supplier for fuel tanks.

Likewise, in cabling, interior trims and consoles and door and roof panels we see that FASA-Renault's traditional Portuguese suppliers lost their direct supply relations. Here, first tier supply relationships end up at traditional France-based Renault partners and at local multinational (Grupo Antolín) Irausa: another classic FASA-Renault supplier.

Cockpits and floor covers are textbook examples of how a shake-out among several partial suppliers leads to the emergence of one first tier supplier who co-ordinates and integrates the efforts of several other lower tier suppliers. Here also, a French company came to the front as the exclusive direct supply relation.

Seats ended up in the hands of Johnson Controls, a well-known company to the Renault Group. It took over Roth Frères, one of Renault's long-lasting supply partners, as well as several seat activities of another classic Renault supplier: Trèves.

Steering systems, transmissions, motor propulsion groups and brakes show clear signs of Renault's company-wide rationalization policy which resulted in a depending of FASA-Renault on supply relationships with production centres in France, notably around Le Mans. Additionally, with regard to steering systems a Spanish branch plant of American TRW was involved. For the non-mechanical parts of the motor propulsion group, Spanish branch locations of foreign companies dedicated to, for example, electronic ignition systems maintained their first tier supplier position.

Gearbox and motor supply also show how the full integration of FASA-Renault into the Renault business apparatus led to intra-group supply origins for these *organs*.

Lights and the stamping of small metal devices were two exceptions to the rule. Neither of them went through any specific changes that can be related to FASA-Renault's integration into Renault's hierarchy and the accompanying centralization of purchasing competences, or to a linking up with specific Renault France suppliers.

As such, most cases of supplier involvement around component delivery reveal a survival of the fittest process whereby the ultimate supplier was already a FASA-Renault supplier at the end of the 1980s. Only in the case of fuel tanks, steering systems, interior trims and consoles, door and roof panels, motor propulsion group and lights, we see that one or two suppliers obtained a first tier supplier relationship while not being a first tier supplier at the start of the

Renault Clio production period. However, all these cases were governed by multiple sourcing. Meaning that the 'new' suppliers that obtained first tier supplier status shared this status with another (standing) supplier. Moreover, in all cases the standing supplier had been in business with FASA-Renault at least since the end of the 1980s. This strengthens the picture of continuity.

For a further assessment of the changes in the actor composition of the supplier network for the Clio production at FASA-Renault Valladolid between 1990–1996 and 2001–2003, we will now attempt to characterize the changes that took place during the last decade of the twentieth century based on the typology of changes presented in section 4.2.3.

When taking the first Clio generation Clio, launched in 1990 as the point of departure, in the subsequent periods, 1996–2001 and 2001–2003, two product versions were launched, the Clio II (1996) and the New Clio (2001). Based on the Valladolid-specific component sample, this offers – *ceteris paribus* – two times 16 components; makes 32 possibilities to change the actor composition of the network

Based on the categorization of changes forwarded in Section 4.2.3, the following overview emerges.

From Table 6.9 it follows that in particular a large number of oligopoly-related changes took place.[41] These are due to the many joint ventures and mergers among a select group of suppliers to the Valladolid plant who were involved in the supply of multiple components (like Plastic Omnium, Sommer Allibert and Faurecia).

Of the 15 oligopoly-related substitutions, it appears that 7 of them were changes in which the leading entities were companies that were completely new to FASA-Renault Valladolid, and which, consequently, can be considered as genuine substitutions. The others were changes in which the new leading partner was already a supplier of other components to FASA-Renault Valladolid (and who now converted into 'multiple components supplier') or had been in the past.

In terms of 'genuine' substitutions, we then observe 7 oligopoly-related substitutions plus 3.57 competitiveness-related substitutions.

When applying the previous data to the formula presented in Chapter 4 for measuring 'longevity' of b2b relationships, we get the following result.

Table 6.9 Changes in the actor composition of FASA-Renault Valladolid's supplier network

(A) oligopoly-related substitutions	(B) competitiveness-oriented substitutions	(C) first-time externalizations	(D) re-internalizations
15	3.57	2.08	1

Source: Author's elaboration.

Degree of longevity of b2b relationships around FASA-Renault Valladolid from 1990 to 2003

$$L_{1990-2003} = 100\% * \left(1 - \frac{10.57}{32.0}\right) = 67.0\%$$

Source: Author's elaboration.

This proxy indicates that a substantial number of changes in the actor composition took place. It reveals that almost one-third of all initial supplier relationships were completely exchanged. Therefore, it seems to be at odds with what one might expect with regard to the longevity of the relationships between a buyer firm and its suppliers, according to N&I approach to b2b relationships, the network view on the IPM and the F/5P model. However, in view of the much larger number of stability-oriented changes that were detected, that is, the domination of oligopoly-related substitutions in which many long-standing suppliers to (FASA-)Renault were involved and which were explicitly directed at maintaining relationships with traditional suppliers to the Valladolid plant as well as the various cases of re-internalization, it should be acknowledged that this research case is in fact very much in line with the propositions of the mentioned frameworks, that it is especially changes and adaptations with regard to existing relationships that take place. Certainly, when taking into account that the Valladolid plant worked for various components with multiple suppliers. In that context, the substitution of one out of several suppliers for a specific component embodies a less drastic change. Finally, the time period that was analysed spanned more than a decade.

Still, the large number of oligopolization-inspired substitutions also supports the claim that (rival) suppliers tried to improve their relationship with (FASA-)Renault in an attempt to upgrade their network position and to generate business.

Regarding the nationality mix involved in the supplier network of the sample we analysed, we see the following developments.

Table 6.10 shows a significant loss of first tier supply relationships by Spanish suppliers and the appearance of several American and Japanese suppliers. The latter penetrated especially into FASA-Renault's supplier network through takeovers of activities that were previously conducted either by Renault or by suppliers of Renault, as was also documented in Table 6.8 and the subsequent analysis. Moreover, there is a relatively stable situation as regards French capital involved behind the suppliers to the Valladolid plant. The same can be said about the involvement of German capital. It appears that both the French consolidation and the Japanese and US advance went at the expense of the foothold of Spanish suppliers.

These results also indicate – in spite of the French consolidation – an increased multi-national diversification of the supplier base of the Valladolid

Table 6.10 Origin of capital of supplier sample for FASA-Renault Valladolid

Nationality	1990–1996	1996–2001	2001–2003
D	0.58	1.23	1.02
F	6.23	7.25	6.25
USA	0.17	2.67	5.16
E	7.63	3.68	1.79
J	—	0.5	1.2
P	0.74	0.33	0.33
B	0.33	0.33	0.25
UK	0.32	—	—
Total	16	16	16

Source: Author's elaboration.

plant and thus a detachment of long-lasting relationships embedded in a mutual home base for buyer and supplier, both seen from a branch location and from a mother company perspective.

6.3.2 Conclusions

Data analysis with respect to FASA-Renault's 1990–2003 supplier base points at a strategy towards unified supplier bases for all (European) Renault plants. As part of this strategy, many newly related suppliers to FASA-Renault Valladolid bought existing establishments owned by companies that were traditional suppliers to FASA-Renault. This was due to Renault's and FASA-Renault's explicit desire to continue incumbent supply relationships. Acquisition moves by 'new' suppliers were especially targeted at establishments on the Jaén-Vigo axis, from where it was possible to attend both FASA-Renault and other car manufacturing plants in Spain.

Renault and FASA-Renault's attempts to pair supplier relationships can be interpreted as a concerted form of 'bonding': allying or aligning incumbent suppliers of FASA-Renault with Renault France suppliers instead of replacing the former by the latter. It appears that such actions were orchestrated simultaneously with a further integration of FASA-Renault into the Renault hierarchy, and when replacing production of one car model or model version by a subsequent one.

As a consequence, we witnessed a rather reduced number of radical changes from the first-generation Clio production period (1990–1996) to the New Clio production period (2001–2003). Instead, what dominated were the more incremental changes. We observed a very large number of virtual substitutions through the creation of joint ventures with and takeovers of incumbent suppliers, or the filialization of activities. From a corporate perspective there was, therefore, a striking continuity in b2b relationships.

Obviously, the type of 'bonding' as described above prevented suppliers from moving closer to FASA-Renault Valladolid. This was also true when the intra-firm network position of this Renault branch location improved from 1998 onwards.

When analysing the developments of the nationality of capital involved behind the supply relations, we see a steady presence of French capital, and an important rise of Japanese and especially American capital. This indicates a gradual multinationalization of the supplier network over time. This must first of all be attributed to a general internationalization of business by supplier companies from around the globe and to the fact that Renault externalized and sold a lot of its activities, many of them ending up in the hands of foreign companies.

Geographical inertia on behalf of the Spain-based suppliers of the Valladolid plant also appears to have been fostered by their non-client specific character. Moreover, many of these establishments had already been able to implement JIT and sequenced delivery schemes to the Valladolid plant – in spite of being located at a distance – and, thus, felt no need to move closer for logistics reasons either. In addition, the fact that very few supplier substitutions were forced, contributed further to the geographical status quo and to the near absence of on-site greenfield investments close to FASA-Renault Valladolid.

In most cases where it seems that the supply chain did move closer, this is mostly due to the implementation of a tiering system, from which the suppliers located closest emerged as first tier suppliers, and not due to a relocation of one supplier or another.

In fact, the strongest geographical dynamism could be observed with respect to several chassis components whose supply origins underwent serious changes in a two-step way. The first step was the termination of certain in-house activities at the Valladolid plant and their substitution for supplies from Renault production sites in France. The second step was the filialization and externalization of these production sites to independent suppliers that were specialized in the components in question. *Per saldo*, at the end of our period of analysis such components came from further away than at the start.

In all, therefore, there was not a trend of suppliers moving closer to the Valladolid plant. Its integration into the Renault ranks and its submission to Renault's strategic competences led to a rationalization of the activities of the Valladolid plant from a group viewpoint. As a consequence, FASA-Renault Valladolid became firmly connected to the Renault Group's independent supply partners and to Renault's other production centres. This led to many virtual substitutions of the Valladolid plant's third party supply relationships, which in practice still meant continuity with previous supplier relationships and locations. In addition, it led to the outsourcing of previous in-house activities of the Valladolid plant that were now supplied in their majority from France.

In summary, it appears that FASA-Renault and Renault's early insisting on a continuity of the Valladolid plant's supplier relationships and the limited importance of the Valladolid plant with respect to the Renault Clio led to an initial geographical deconcentration of the supplier network surrounding the Valladolid plant. Additionally, the fact that most of suppliers' production centres had a multiclient vocation fostered geographical inertia further. Consequently, even when the Valladolid plant's intra-firm network position improved, that is, in terms of its share in the overall production of the Clio, this did not lead to co-location processes.

The actor composition reconstruction (see Table 6.8) clearly reveals that Renault stayed loyal to long-lasting b2b relationships and did not implement substantial supplier substitutions. This can also be considered a major factor explaining the absence of co-location processes. What is more, with respect to those components where supplier changes occurred, that is, where FASA-Renault in-house production was substituted for alternative sourcing, without exception the ultimate suppliers would be located further away. The newly appointed suppliers (Renault production centres) were all located in France, where they were best placed to attend the Renault assembly sites. After the majority of these production centres came into the hands of independent suppliers, these suppliers did not think it worth their while either to locate closer to FASA-Renault Valladolid.

7 Discussion of research results and conclusions

The central objective of this study has been to analyse and conceptualize the formation and evolution of international business networks and in particular of satellite business networks in peripheral regions. In brief, how these networks are shaped and evolve over time, especially with respect to:

- Their geographical articulation: the (non-)practicing of co-location by suppliers and the degree to which a conjoint of suppliers is geographically concentrated around the focal buyer of an international business network.
- Their actor composition: continuity and discontinuity, for example, through substitutions or exit, of suppliers in international business networks.

To analyse these network characteristics, a conceptual framework was designed and presented in Chapter 3.

This conceptual framework builds upon the assumption that international business networks are characterized by a deep structure that can undergo changes in terms of the geographical articulation and actor composition of buyer–supplier networks. The term 'deep structure' refers to the fundamental choices which sets of business actors have made regarding who they are connected to (Gersick, 1991; Halinen et al., 1999). In this respect our conceptual framework distinguishes between two types of change. The first type of change is incremental change: adjustments within ongoing business relationships and overall stability of the deep structure of the network. The second type of change is radical change: changes of entire relationships including their termination and a substitution of partners, which cause modifications of the network's deep structure. As a trigger for changes, our conceptual framework makes use of the concept of 'critical event', which refers to those events that have a decisive effect on the development of relationships.

Subsequently, the following four hypotheses were formulated.

Hypothesis 1: The degree of co-location on the part of suppliers pertaining to a satellite network in a peripheral region is the result of intra-firm assignment decisions taken by the focal buyer firm of the network, followed by inter-firm network dynamics with the relevant b2b relationships.

Hypothesis 2: The co-location thesis combined with the theoretical and empirical observations that most inter-firm relationships have long-standing traditions, suggests that satellite business networks in peripheral regions should show a strong participation of companies originating from the same country as the focal buyer firm, certainly at the outset.

Hypothesis 3: The actor composition of business networks evolves significantly over time. Homogenization of economic space, competitive behaviour of rival firms, sector oligopolization and learning experiences as regards b2b relationships and internationalization are facilitating factors in this respect.

Hypothesis 4: Other b2b relationships and component-intrinsic logistics and production requirements determine to a larger extent whether or not a supplier will make site-specific investments than a (mutual) aim for exclusive relationships and or supplier status.

In the following paragraphs we will discuss the findings that our empirical research cases rendered in the light of the presented conceptual framework and the formulated hypotheses.

7.1 Comparative findings of the empirical research cases

7.1.1 Synthesis

When synthesizing the observed location patterns as well as the actor composition trajectories of the supplier bases surrounding the two car manufacturing plants we analysed, we can forward the following characterizations.

With respect to FASA-Renault Valladolid, there were two different periods revealing change processes to the deep structure of its supplier network. The first one, around 1987, witnessed changes in the deep structure regarding the b2b relationships around components that by then were already procured from third parties. The second period of change was related to changes in the deep structure with respect to the supply of components that were purchased externally at the end of our period of analysis, but which were an in-house activity at FASA-Renault Valladolid at the start. This second period was situated in the second half of the 1990s. The first period was predominantly evolutionary characterized by incremental changes. The changes taking place in the second period were of a more radical nature.

The incremental changes from the first period were highly orchestrated and guided by Renault's top management in the form of concerted bonding actions. These incremental changes took place after FASA-Renault was fully integrated into Renault's business structure around 1987. They took place during the course of the Renault Supercinq production period and they intended to anticipate the creation of a uniform supplier base for all Renault Clio assembly centres in Europe from 1990 onwards. This uniform third party supplier base – once it was set up – only underwent gradual adaptations through tiering processes among the supplier base of that time and via acquisitions, mergers and joint ventures between suppliers of Renault, on the one hand, and suppliers of FASA-Renault, on the other. Thus, it was the full submission of the Valladolid plant to the orders of Renault's headquarters that functioned as a critical event. The 1987–1990 events surrounding FASA-Renault Valladolid and its integration into the Renault Group hierarchy formed an evolutionary period during which the foundations were put in place for the deep structure of its third party supplier base (both geographically speaking and actor-wise). This supplier base was rather stable and would only be gradually adapted in the years that followed.

Also with regard to the FASA-Renault Valladolid case, it is indicated to highlight separately the components that were purchased externally at the end of our period of analysis, but which were an in-house activity at FASA-Renault Valladolid at the start. This part of the supplier base was submitted to radical changes and critical events in the second half of the 1990s. These were inspired by a series of losses at Renault (1993 and 1996) and FASA-Renault (1996 and 1997) and led Renault to appoint other Renault production centres than FASA-Renault Valladolid itself as the provider of all kinds of chassis and propulsion parts. Subsequently, Renault decided to externalize or filialize the production of these parts. As a consequence, the supply of these components and the b2b relationships behind it went through a revolutionary period. During the second half of the 1990s, the production of several chassis and propulsion parts moved from the Valladolid plant to Renault production centres in France. A posteriori these production bases were filialized or taken over by third parties, while maintaining their first tier supplier status vis-à-vis FASA-Renault Valladolid. This meant radical changes to the deep structure of this part of the supplier base, both in terms of the geographical origin of supplies, the actor composition and the origin of capital behind suppliers.

As regards VW Navarra, it experienced several turbulent – revolutionary – periods with regard to the geographical evolution and actor composition of its supplier base. From an actor composition perspective these changes occurred more or less continuously. From a geographical viewpoint, especially the period 1984–1994 was a highly revolutionary period with radical changes, whereas the changes that took place from 1994 onwards had a more evolutionary and incremental nature.

As regards the overall location of the suppliers to VW Navarra, the plant witnessed a complete U-turn between 1984 and 1994. At first, it changed from a largely Spain-based supplier conjoint to a Germany-based one. Subsequently, it shifted back to a Spain-based supplier network. Generally speaking, the process of intensified co-location of suppliers near the Landaben plant towards the year 1994 continued afterwards, notably through the subsequent model changes in 1994, 1997 and 2001. Thus, from 1994 onwards the supplier network to the Landaben plant witnessed incremental changes in spatial terms, with more and more suppliers setting up factories near the VW Navarra plant due to the ever-improving intra-firm network position of the plant.

At the same time, each model change resulted in a considerable number of supplier substitutions, leading to relatively radical changes to the deep structure of the actor composition of its supplier conjoint with each launchment of a new Polo model. This was notably the case with the model changes of 1984, 1994 and 2001.

As such, not only the integration of the Landaben plant into VW's industrial apparatus proved to be a critical event spurring radical changes, but also most of the model changes. As regards the first-time externalizations at VW Navarra, these were rare during our period of analysis. In broad terms, what was an in-house activity until 1984 either was externalized in (the beginning of) the Polo A02 period – thus coinciding with the first period of radical change – or was still an in-house activity at the end of our period of analysis.

7.1.2   Geographical articulation of buyer–supplier networks

As regards the determinants for location behaviour of suppliers vis-à-vis focal buyer plants of international business networks, our research findings reveal the following.

Both of our research cases showed similar tendencies towards the implementation of modular conception and JIT supply of components. These logistics and product conception practices have become relatively universally applied concepts by all car manufacturing companies. Many scholars hold them responsible for co-location processes (e.g. Mair, 1991a,b; Wells and Rawlinson, 1992; Aláez *et al.*, 1999; Adam-Ledunois and Renault, 2001). Nonetheless, we saw great differences in the location behaviour of suppliers surrounding the two car manufacturing plants that functioned as focal buyers of the respective business networks. On the one hand, there was a supplier conjoint densely localized around the VW Navarra plant, and a more geographically dispersed supplier conjoint in the case of FASA-Renault Valladolid, on the other. The former tendencies could therefore not be held responsible for the differences in the location logics we observed.

Instead, our headquarters–subsidiary and b2b relationship-oriented research focus leads us to establish that the comparative value of a network's focal buyer is a trigger for suppliers to move closer to this buyer and thus forms an important basis for the location behaviour of suppliers.

From our research cases it can be established that the primary determinant for co-location is the intra-firm network position of a buyer plant with respect to the product(s) it manufactures. We defined intra-firm network position in terms of model-specific production share and model-specific strategic and tactical responsibilities at plant level. It appears that the car manufacturing plant that developed a strong intra-firm network position (VW Navarra) had a considerably larger number of dedicated supply plants in its vicinity. Instead, the car manufacturing plant with a less important intra-firm network position until the late 1990s (FASA-Renault Valladolid) did not see its suppliers locate nearby in large numbers. The rise of dedicated supply plants is a first exponent of the way in which the intra-firm network position of a buyer plant exercises an influence on the location decisions of suppliers. For it determines the relative value it represents to its suppliers. The higher this value, through possibilities for learning or economies of scale, the stronger the attraction a buyer plant will exert on suppliers.

As such, we found convincing proof for our first hypothesis, which argues that the degree of co-location on the part of suppliers is the result of intra-firm assignment decisions taken by the focal buyer firm, followed by inter-firm network dynamics with the relevant b2b relationships.

A second exponent, through which it became manifest that the intra-firm network position of a focal buyer plant acts as a spatial magnet on suppliers, was the correlated venue of supply sites near the respective focal buyer plants that suppliers use for multiple client attendance. As such, it could be demonstrated that this approximation is not fully dependent on the degree of exclusivity that characterizes the relationship between one supplier and a specific buyer plant. The supplier samples around our two focal buyer plants included many cases of supplier plants that manufacture or assemble for multiple clients. But there were more of these near VW Navarra than near FASA-Renault Valladolid. Thus, intra-firm network position also determines a buyer plant's value to suppliers, in comparison to the value that other clients represent to these suppliers. As a consequence of the differences in intra-firm network positions of the respective car manufacturing plants we analysed, we also witnessed a significantly stronger co-location trend of supply sites attending multiple clients around VW Navarra than around the FASA-Renault Valladolid plant.

Moreover, we established that in both cases those suppliers that delivered highly unit-specific components, that is, which are dependent on the exterior colour of the car and or on the specific design of a car, like seats and door panels, tended to locate near the focal buyer plant of the network. This indicates that component-intrinsic logistics and production requirements definitely influence decisions on location choice on the part of suppliers.

As such, we found convincing proof for our fourth hypothesis. This hypothesis states that other b2b relationships and component-intrinsic logistics and production requirements determine whether or not suppliers are willing to make site-specific investments to a larger extent than a (mutual) aim for exclusive relationships and or supplier status.

All together, it could be established that the geographical articulation of a follow-the-client phenomenon (Forsgren, 1989; McKiernan, 1992; Lagendijk, 1995; Balcet and Enrietti, 2001) clearly depends on the intra-firm network position of a buyer plant and its relative value vis-à-vis that of suppliers' other clients.

It also appears that the more continuity there is in terms of manufactured products at the level of a buyer plant, the more likely it is that suppliers will set up establishments in the vicinity of a buyer plant.

From our findings we also conclude that dense and localized supplier networks are most likely to emerge around strategically important buyer plants. Furthermore, that such concentrated networks tend to have an importance, that is, network-transcending. As they tend to serve − more strongly than networks around strategically inferior plants − as an operating base for supplies to other clients that are of relatively lesser value (see also Rutherford, 2000).

7.1.2.1 *Theoretical progress on topic in question*

For our conceptual framework of analysis we elaborated on the assumption that organizations can be viewed as networks themselves (Forsgren, 1989; Ghoshal and Nohria, 1989; Ghoshal and Bartlett, 1990, 1993; Forsgren and Johanson, 1992; Holm *et al.*, 1995; Jüttner and Schlange, 1996; Andersson, 1997; Andersson and Forsgren, 2000). Likewise, our analytical framework followed from a combination of headquarters–subsidiary and b2b relationships concepts.

By means of this conceptual framework for analysis we were able to demonstrate that intra-firm assignment processes determine the value that subsidiaries represent to their suppliers (see also, Nooteboom, 1996; Nooteboom *et al.*, 1997; De Jong and Nooteboom, 2000; Rutherford, 2000). Such value appeared to serve as a predictor for supplier location behaviour and their willingness to invest in a relationship from a geographical angle (see also, Helper, 1987; De Jong and Nooteboom, 2000; Frigant and Lung, 2002). This insight was achieved by designing an 'intra-firm network position' and an 'inter-firm network positioning' parameter, which were subsequently operationalized. For the first parameter, we applied indicators of intra-firm assignment of competences to car manufacturing subsidiaries. For the second, we looked at suppliers' physical location choices for supply sites. These two parameters proved to be applicable and valid in foreseeing supplier location behaviour. Causal relationships between them could be clearly observed.

Moreover, the observed location behaviour on the part of suppliers vis-à-vis the focal buyer plants we investigated and their other clients, provided insights with regard to the assumption that the design of a specific b2b relationship should be understood both in view of dyadic or relational complementarities of resources and rent perspectives (Håkansson, 1987, 1989, 1993; Forsgren *et al.*, 1995; Laage-Hellman, 1997; Dyer, 1998). Similarly, that they should be seen against the background of the other b2b relationships that the parties in question are involved in (Johanson and Mattsson, 1987; Forsgren, 1989; Laage-Hellman, 1997).

As a consequence, our findings provide ways to include a geographical and physical location dimension to network theory's understanding of the design of b2b relationships. That is, the comparative rating of b2b relationships to suppliers, that is, by operationalizing and analysing the 'intra-firm network positions' of buyer plants, proved to be a useful tool to explain the geographical articulation of 'inter-firm network positioning' of suppliers. As such, our findings extend the scope and ability of network theory to explain and foresee geographical and physical location processes over time.

Similarly, they enable the incorporation and explanation of phenomena and processes that tend to be treated separately by network or internationalization theories, on the one hand, and by geography or location theories, on the other hand, in an integrated way. In this regard, the interpretation and breakdown of MNEs into networks, plus the introduction of the concept 'intra-firm network position' and the assessment of MNE subsidiaries in terms of value to their inter-firm relationships, also proved to be both a workable extension to and a refinement of the standard network and internationalization theories' analytical toolkits for the explanation of location phenomena and processes in international business networks.

Thus, the coherent conceptual and terminological toolkit, which the constructed framework for analysis provided, allows explaining a wider array of location phenomena and processes. Moreover, it allows coming up with more profound explications on these issues than the current state of network and internationalization theories is able to do.

7.1.3   Longevity of buyer–supplier relationships

As regards the assumptions forwarded by network theorists (Håkansson, 1987, 1993; Rugman and D'Cruz, 2000) that longevity is the 'norm' for b2b relationships, our research established the following insights.

We witnessed a substantial difference in the degree to which the phenomenon of longevity existed in the two business networks that were analysed.

The FASA-Renault Valladolid supplier network displayed a fairly stable composition and as such corroborated the validity of the 'textbook' argument concerning longevity and continuity of buyer–supplier relationships and networks. The VW Navarra supplier network, however, saw a large number of changes in terms of its b2b relationships and a lot of suppliers that were substituted over time. Some of these substitutions even had to do with companies that had previously made co-location investments. It appears that Renault from the outset worked a lot at 'bonding' and conservation of b2b relationships around the Clio production, whereas VW seemed to leave the actor composition for the VW Polo supplier base more to free market forces.

In addition, from our case studies it appears that the factor 'continuity of b2b relationships' correlates negatively with spatial approximation in b2b relationships. We found that prolonging long-lasting relationships (mostly the case with FASA-Renault Valladolid) frustrated greater spatial proximity. Instead, the VW Navarra case witnessed a substantial amount of supplier substitutions from which spatial proximity benefited highly. With respect to VW Navarra, several cases of supplier substitutions were observed where subsequent suppliers opened co-located sites.[42]

As such, it appears that geographical co-location as a form of inter-firm network positioning on the part of suppliers does not only correlate with the intra-firm network position held by the buyer plant in question. In addition, the frequency with which subsequent (incumbent and rival) suppliers demonstrate co-location behaviour as a weapon to compete for a direct supply relationship with a certain buyer also correlates with the intra-firm network position of the latter. The former implies that there is especially a willingness on behalf of suppliers to invest in their network positions through co-location when the targeted buyer plant occupies a strong intra-firm network position. For example, with respect to the VW Navarra case (the buyer plant with a markedly strong intra-firm network position), almost all of the many supplier substitutions were accompanied by the creation of more nearby or equally close supply sites. With respect to the FASA-Renault Valladolid case (the buyer plant with a weaker intra-firm network position, comparatively speaking), few examples of co-location were observed. Nevertheless, in the few supplier substitutions that did occur, also in the FASA-Renault research case co-location was employed by rival suppliers as a means to assure a good position vis-à-vis FAS-Renault Valladolid.

Another difference between the two research cases was the fact that co-located supplier sites in relation to VW Navarra were created at a very short distance (many are so to say 'on-site'), whereas co-locations in relation to FASA-Renault Valladolid were situated at a much larger distance. This can also be interpreted as an outcome of the different intra-firm network positions the respective two plants held within their own hierarchies, combined with the relative value they represent to their suppliers in comparison to the other clients these suppliers service.

Furthermore, the emphasis on either b2b continuity or discontinuity on the part of the focal buyer firm also appears to determine the most frequently used modes of foreign market and network entry. The FASA-Renault Valladolid supplier base saw a lot of takeovers of incumbent suppliers by multinational supply relationships of the Renault Group. These were notably French business partners, certainly at the outset of FASA-Renault's full integration into the Renault hierarchy. The VW Navarra supplier base, instead, saw a lot of greenfield investments. In the beginning, the majority of these investments were made by long-standing relationships of VW with the same (= German) nationality. As such, we also found convincing proof for our second hypothesis, which claims that the co-location thesis combined with the observation that most inter-firm relationships have long standing traditions suggests that satellite business networks in peripheral regions should show a strong participation of companies from the same country as the focal buyer firm, at least at the outset. Proof for this hypothesis was complemented by the fact that both car manufacturing plants kept receiving the most strategic propulsion parts from their respective home bases.

The fact that suppliers to the VW Navarra plant opted especially for greenfield investments, meant they had greater freedom in selecting the ideal location. Combined with the value that VW Navarra represented as a client among the total of (potential) supplier-specific clients, the choice for greenfield investments as 'network entry mode' led to many co-located establishments.

As regards the evolution of the nationality mix of the supplier networks, the higher degree of genuine substitutions among suppliers of VW Navarra also led to a stronger erosion of the share of German companies in its supplier base. Instead, the share of French companies in the FASA-Renault Valladolid supplier base remained relatively stable due to the fact that rather few genuine substitutions took place. In fact, the large number of virtual substitutions among the supplier base of FASA-Renault Valladolid seems to have contributed to a consolidation of the share of French companies in FASA-Renault's supplier base. As regards the interference of non-French and non-Spanish suppliers in the FASA-Renault Valladolid supplier base, there was a striking presence of companies that were previously involved in the filialization of former in-house activities of Renault France or in takeovers of suppliers from France that supplied to Renault France. Here also, early stage concerted actions towards a greater uniformity of supplier bases of Clio production plants became visible. The bulk of the component supply flows to FASA-Renault Valladolid that were submitted to these concerted relationships and filializations did not undergo any major changes once they were set up. Therefore, this contributed to the overall picture of continuity of b2b relationships surrounding the FASA-Renault Valladolid plant.

From the radical changes with respect to the supplier base of VW Navarra, on the one hand, as well as from the more incremental changes with respect to the supplier base of FASA-Renault Valladolid, on the other, the following can be derived, that is, that homogenization of economic space, cross-border competitive behaviour of suppliers and oligopolization trends in the supply industry evidently play a major role in shaping international buyer–supplier networks. However, the way in which VW and Renault acted upon or regulated these processes appears to have been highly diverse. This refers to the idiosyncrasy of firms and the room for organizational choices with respect to this kind of forces or events (see also Håkansson and Johanson, 1993, p. 44). For VW Navarra this resulted in a large number of supplier substitutions and for FASA-Renault Valladolid in a fairly stable composition of its supplier base.

As a consequence, we found mixed support for our third hypothesis, which suggests that the composition of business networks evolves significantly over time. The VW Navarra case provided firm support for this hypothesis. With respect to FASA-Renault Valladolid these evolutions were a great deal less intense and the changes had a more incremental and 'virtual' character.

Both cases clearly show how at the outset of our period of analysis, the supply relationships of the focal firm of the network were conceived around previously established relationships, that is, based on the car manufacturing subsidiary's own supplier base and that of the mother company, respectively Renault and VW. In the case of FASA-Renault Valladolid suppliers from the mother company's home base were paired up with incumbent suppliers to

FASA-Renault Valladolid. In the case of VW Navarra many suppliers with whom the Landaben plant itself maintained long-standing relationships were abruptly replaced by traditional suppliers to its mother company. This was triggered by the fact that respectively the FASA-Renault and the Landaben subsidiary were to be managed in an integrated way from abroad together with the other plants of the respective mother companies. The dominant party in this integration process, that is, the headquarters of Renault and Volkswagen was thus able to impose its supplier selection and supplier base composition preferences. The empirical cases were therefore also able to demonstrate how in subsequent cases of hierarchical integration or takeovers, the suppliers that are related to the parts of the business apparatus which eventually dominate in the new organizational setting, are the ones to come out best of a reshuffling of supplier bases.

7.1.3.1 *Theoretical progress on topic in question*

All in all, our research findings with respect to the (dis)continuity of b2b relationships indicate that supplier substitution is a phenomenon that has to be taken into account in (international) business network research. Alongside others (see for example, Gadde and Mattsson, 1987; Halinen *et al.*, 1999), we argue that it deserves much more attention than it is currently receiving. In order to conceptualize actor composition changes in business network formations, we forward arguments from the following schools of thoughts:

1 Concepts of competitive behaviour of firms (Montgomery, 1995), which advocate that firms try to improve their network positions at the cost of rivals. That way, one is able to reason why rival firms will compete to conquer network positions currently not under their control whereas incumbent suppliers will attempt to maintain acquired network positions (see for example, Laigle, 1997).
2 Embeddedness theory's claim that firms will ultimately try to avoid lock-ins (Grabher, 1993; Uzzi, 1997) in order not to end up being path-dependent on long-standing relationships. This implies that not only rival firms exert pressures on b2b relationships trying to replace incumbent partners. It also implies that business instincts induce firms to consider sub-stitutions of partners and to foster multi-client attendance on the part of suppliers (see for example, Florence, 1996; Pries, 1999).[43] That way, one is able to explain why firms are willing to engage in new relationships and substitute current partners for new ones, or do business in places where they have no previous experiences (see for example, Laigle, 1997; Sadler, 1999).
3 Concepts of organizational learning (Cyert and March, 1963; Carlson, 1966; Levitt and March, 1988; Lane and Lubatkin, 1998), which emphas-ize how buyers and suppliers lose fear over time to internationalize inde-pendently. Similarly, how they learn to engage in b2b relationships with unknown partners after accumulating b2b relationship management

experience. That way, one is able to explain why firms are willing to engage in new relationships and substitute current partners for new ones, or do business in places where they have no previous experiences (see for example, Laigle, 1997; Sadler, 1999).

4   Lessons from generic change theories (Gersick, 1991; Van de Ven, 1992; Van de Ven and Poole, 1995). These lessons help to understand and conceive the impact of b2b-relationship intrinsic and extrinsic critical events and gradual processes on business network formation and evolution. That way, one is able to explain when adequate circumstances present themselves – enhanced by organizational learning, regulation of embeddedness and competitive behaviour of firms – for such substitutions to materialize.

By incorporating these elements into a network and internationalization theory-based conceptual framework, we are also able to explain how and why such supplier substitutions come about. As such, it paves the way for a substantial extension of the explanatory power of our reference frameworks: the N&I approach, the network view on the IPM and the F/5P model.

Our argument that the actor composition of business networks can change substantially over time is linked to one of the principles of internationalization theory. The theory of internationalization posits that internationalizing firms undergo gradual organizational learning processes. The accumulation of these learning processes makes firms dare to undertake continuously new, and more complicated, internationalization ventures (see for example, Carlson, 1966; Johanson and Vahlne, 1977, 1990; Sullivan and Bauerschmidt, 1990). It postulates that cognitive, linguistic, cultural, geographical policy disparities and barriers and fear of the unknown, form initial obstacles for firms to embark on foreign markets and to compete with local players. As a consequence, the internationalization of companies often goes through stages, both in terms of the markets to conquer, the entry mode to foreign markets and of activity assignments to MNE establishments at home and abroad.

Similar to these gradual and sequential processes involved in company-specific internationalization choices, our research indicates that inter-firm network formation in an international business context can follow a parallel trajectory:

- Once firms have, first, become acquainted to buyer–supplier relationships and networks as *modus operandi* for design, production and development operations, and so on.;
- Second, once they have learned that trustworthy relationships can be constructed with business partners;
- Third, once they obtain a clear view on the management and the (technical) content and activities of inter-firm relationships;

Then firms have more confidence in their own ability to manage b2b relationships and they feel freer to choose business partners from a wider (geographic) domain of candidates and possibly substitute current suppliers.

Subsequently, we argue that bonding and trust, which are supposed to make inter-firm relationships into a lasting experience are unable to explain sufficiently the outcome of business network formation processes over time. Although important in b2b relations, trust can not prevent rational actors from terminating incumbent b2b relationships. This is not because b2b partners suddenly become opportunistic. But due to the fact that they may also learn to trust (to get superior benefits from) new partners and have confidence in their own capacities to manage relationships with new partners. Thus, confidence in their own capacities and in those of new partners may help companies to revaluate current b2b relationships or networks. In this sense, ruptures between buyers and suppliers may also serve to avoid over-embeddedness and inter-firm inertia. As a consequence, firms then also look beyond their own region or nation for business partners that offer the most optimal complementarities.

The fact that, through a buyer firm's own international operations and through internationalization moves of other firms, all internationally active firms become exposed to and get into contact with other potential business relationships than merely the ones they traditionally do business with, means that an inclusion of new partners in business networks becomes more plausible as well. Consequently, buyer–supplier networks can become detached from a buyer firm's home base, from the specific country in which the focal buyer plant of the network is located and from the actor composition as it exists at the outset of a specific period of analysis, both in terms of the nationalities involved and of the specific partners.

As such, business relationships and networks – be they networks in one nation or region, or in some cross-border form – can evolve from relatively closed systems (with adaptations of the relationships between unchanged partners) into more open systems (with increased possibilities of including new partners, besides adaptations of relationships). Consequently, networks obtain more dynamism in terms of actor composition. It is this distinction that makes the traditional N&I approach to b2b relationships and networks (e.g. Håkansson, 1987, 1989, 1993; Johanson and Mattsson, 1988; Laage-Hellman, 1997), the network view on the IPM (Forsgren, 1989) or the F/5P model (Rugman and D'Cruz, 2000) different from the insights obtained in our research. We argue that the three reference frameworks fall short with respect to actor dynamism and could benefit from the conceptual progress booked via our research.

We elaborated our conceptual framework on the assumption that organizations are networks in themselves (Forsgren, 1989; Ghoshal and Nohria, 1989; Ghoshal and Bartlett, 1990, 1993; Forsgren and Johanson, 1992; Holm *et al.*, 1995; Jüttner and Schlange, 1996; Andersson, 1997; Andersson and Forsgren, 2000). The former design feature, and the fact that our conceptual framework was based on a combined headquarters–subsidiary and b2b relationship focus, allows us to explain that changing intra-firm power balances, notably as a result of macro-economic and firm-specific integration or takeover processes (Håkansson and Johanson, 1993; Hertz, 1993; Mattsson and Hultén, 1994; Halinen *et al.*, 1999), can lead to changes in the influence structures underlying the composition of supplier networks surrounding car constructor entities. Therefore, with respect to supplier selection responsibilities, the design of the parameter 'intra-firm network position' proves to be highly useful.

As a result, our conceptual framework is able to foresee how a power shift regarding 'who is to make supplier selection choices within a hierarchy?,' can lead to a considerable amount of virtual (takeovers of incumbent suppliers) or genuine (replacement by rival suppliers) substitutions of b2b partners in such supplier networks. Additionally, it is able to foresee which supplier relationships will get priority after such power shifts. For causal relationships between changes in the intra-firm *locus* of supplier selection responsibilities and changes in supplier network compositions could clearly be observed in our research cases. That is, both in terms of timing or sequence and in terms of the characteristics that would make up the subsequent supplier networks. In this respect, our conceptual framework also provides a valuable enrichment of current network and internationalization theories. Meanwhile, through the design of the intra-firm network position parameter, we were not only able to make conceptual progress in this respect, but we also managed to provide a sound analytical tool to test and verify these matters.

Thus, the coherent conceptual and terminological toolkit, which our conceptual framework offers, allows explaining a wider array of actor composition phenomena and processes than the current state of network and international business theories are able to do.

7.2   Predictive validity of obtained knowledge

To what extent can the obtained knowledge serve to foresee (a) the geographical articulation of suppliers' inter-firm network positioning around focal buyer plants in networks and (b) the evolution in the actor composition of international business networks in general? The present paragraph serves to further check the validity of our outcomes in these two respects. First, we will check the validity of our conclusions on geographical articulation of international business networks via a sample test, and then we will turn to the issue of actor composition.

7.2.1   *Geographical articulation of buyer–supplier networks*

With respect to the geographical articulation of suppliers' inter-firm network positioning around focal buyer plants in networks, we conclude that the likeliness of co-location processes depends, *ceteris paribus*, on the intra-firm network position of a focal buyer plant and, as a consequence, on the value it represents as a client to suppliers.

As a preliminary test of the validity of this conclusion, we looked at a sample of car assembly plants from FIAT, Audi, Renault and Ford that house a supplier park in their vicinity *anno* 2003, as an expression of co-location processes. The results are as follows.

The FIAT Melfi plant produces FIAT Puntos only. Production of the Punto is shared with the FIAT plants in Mirafiori and Termini Imerese. They have a joint production target of 600,000 to 700,000 units a year. Of this total 450,000 are to be produced at Melfi. Adjacent to the factory, 22 component suppliers produce everything from seats and dashboards to bumpers. Housed in a cluster of buildings – dubbed Melfi City, they make 1,000 deliveries a day directly to the plant.

The Audi Ingolstadt complex produces the Audi A4 and the Audi A3. These are conceived on the same platform. Audi Ingolstadt has an annual production of around 400,000 cars. The models in question are not assembled elsewhere. In the supplier park, adjacent to the Audi factories, over 10 independent suppliers are housed.

Renault has supplier parks near its production plants in Sandouville (the leading plant for the Laguna, the Espace and the Vel Satis), Douai (the leading plant for the hatchback Mégane) and Flins (the leading plant for the Clio and the Twingo). Meanwhile, Renault has also been setting up a supplier park near Palencia (the leading plant for the Mégane Classic and Coupé).

Ford has supplier parks near Ford Almussafes (the exclusive manufacturing site of the Ka and the main production centre of the Fiesta), Saarlouis (the leading plant for the Focus) and Genk (the leading plant for the Mondeo).

These examples support the claim that the model-specific intra-firm network position of a car manufacturing plant is an indicator and a predictor for co-location processes.

In a similar vein, it appears that the degree 'product exclusivity' of a network's focal buyer is important as this enhances economies of scale, both for the final assembler and for the suppliers. Consequently, if a focal buyer plant is characterized by a strong model-specific intra-firm network position or has an exclusive production mandate with regard to one or more specific models, suppliers have a much stronger incentive to break down their production apparatus and set up a dedicated or semi-dedicated plant adjacent to such a client.

Thus, this scan provides additional proof for the proposition that supplier parks typically tend to emerge around those plants that enjoy model exclusivity or are responsible for a major share in the production of a certain model.

Evidently, the present scan represents a relatively static test of insights that were obtained through a longitudinal analysis. Moreover, we realize that this scan refers to the same sector as the one where our empirical research cases came from. Finally, in the sample scan we did not control for the learning possibilities the respective buyer plants provide to their suppliers. However, we argue that also for this sample it would be logical to expect a correlation between being the major producer of a certain car model and being responsible for more upstream tasks related to the final engineering of production, and so on. Thereby providing further incentives to (and co-explaining why) suppliers (decide) to settle near such leading plants.

When we compare these findings to our own empirical research findings, we see the following connections.

The VW Navarra plant developed into a major production centre with regard to the Polo after its incorporation into the VW hierarchy. Therefore, ongoing co-location processes – fuelled additionally by the acquisition of more strategic tasks related to the production of the Polo model – can be understood according to the same logics as exposed in the above paragraphs. Moreover, also the loss of value to suppliers from which the plant 'suffered' recently, that is, both due to a transfer of Polo production to VW Bratislava (Slovakia) and VW Vorst (Brussels, Belgium) and to stagnating sales of the Polo (especially from 2002 onwards), indeed brought about a certain erosion with regard to the continued presence of some of its suppliers. Therefore, also these recent dynamics are in line with our propositions.

With respect to FASA-Renault Valladolid we can make the following interpretations. Since 1999 the FASA-Renault Valladolid plant is a single product factory and since 1998 it produces the largest share of Clio production in Europe (although this represents only 40% of the overall figure). According to the propositions we forward an intensification of co-location processes surrounding this plant ought to be expected. For it now provides additional incentives to attract new investments in its proximity through economies of scale.

Now, the Valladolid plant is located close to FASA-Renault Palencia. The latter factory also improved its network position within the Renault hierarchy recently, due to obtaining leading factory status with respect to the Mégane Classic and Coupé. The fact that Renault built a supplier park next to FASA-Renault Palnecia can first of all be attributed to the fact that FASA-Renault Palencia displays leading factory features with respect to two Mégane variants. Second, the fact that, for the time being, they are not both given their own supplier park can also be interpreted as a result of the fact that supplier location processes are embedded in multiple client relationships.

In retrospective, the non-creation of a supplier park in the vicinity of FASA-Renault Valladolid can also be explained by the fact that recently the status of the Valladolid plant as an important Clio production centre was truncated by the decision to dedicate it fully to the Renault Modus. This arrested product line continuity and as a consequence, also continuity in certain supplier relationships come to a halt. Moreover, the Modus did not sell as well as expected, prompting the decision to devote part of FASA-Renault Valladolid's production capacity to a second model from 2006 onwards.

7.2.2 *Longevity of buyer–supplier relationships*

With regard to the question as to how representative our findings are in terms of evolution in the actor composition of business networks, we are confronted with a two-fold situation. On the one hand, we have the findings with respect to the Renault case indicating a relative stability. In principle, these need no further confirmation as they are strongly in line with what has been observed as the standard situation in almost all empirical b2b and network studies. On the other hand, we have the findings from the Volkswagen case indicating substantial supplier substitutions. It is worthwhile to see whether the findings with respect to this case can be confirmed and further explored by means of additional empirical analyses.

In this respect, we can point at the following recent phenomenon, which suggests that supplier substitution (is likely to) occur(s) on a broader scale. We refer to the way more and more supplier parks around car manufacturing subsidiaries throughout Europe are being set up and exploited today. Increasingly supplier parks are run by logistics service providers or by the car constructors themselves, housing facilities and services that can be rented and contracted by suppliers during the lifetime period of a supply contract. Examples of supplier parks that are (partly) conceived on this basis are the ones dedicated to Ford Genk and Volvo Car Ghent, both in Belgium, and to Saab Trollhättan in Sweden.

After the contract of a certain supplier expires (mostly coinciding with the production time of a certain model), the facilities are rented to the next supplier. This may or may not be the same one. This formula is not only aimed at reducing real estate costs for suppliers or providing on-site facilities for suppliers that otherwise would not invest in on-site assets on the location in question, with a corresponding loss of flexibility on the part of the car constructor. It is also meant to enable the car constructor to cope with possible supplier changes. The logistics service provider, contracted to take care of the final deliveries, may also be substituted. Although this kind of supplier parks predominantly house pre-assembly, warehousing and sequencing activities (which are only part of the activities carried out by the suppliers we observed in our case studies – most of the suppliers in our case studies also carried out genuine manufacturing activities), it clearly underlines the existence of the supplier substitution phenomenon or the prospect that it may take place.

Again, we are aware that these additional findings are obtained from the same sector where our empirical research was conducted. We also acknowledge that the above represents additional inductive proof obtained via static analysis that should be complemented by proof obtained through longitudinal analysis on a larger sample.

Clearly, evolutions in actor compositions of business networks should be tested through data that cover a longer time period. This, as we experienced with our own empirical case studies, implies genuine puzzle work with data from company reports that are primarily aimed at informing a select group of actors. The fact that our insights in this respect are to some extent at odds with the viewpoints currently being held by mainstream network theory, may also be due to difficulties in acquiring the necessary data to evaluate the degree of longevity and discontinuity in the actor composition of business networks.

We are convinced that our findings with respect to the VW case are not isolated or unique. We argue that the factors that produced the many supplier substitutions in that particular case are not case-specific, but rather generic. Also the lessons that can be derived from the way the supplier parks indicated previously have been conceived support the argument that supplier substitutions are, or will be, more than a marginal phenomenon.

To conclude with, we emphasize the need for additional empirical research on this topic, ideally cross-sectoral. The fact that our findings indicate that such substituting processes also bear on the location dynamics of business networks further underlines the importance of this research line.

7.2.3   *Closing word on predictive validity*

We are conscious of the fact that our research has focused on satellite business networks in peripheral regions. Consequently, we have attempted to reason to what extent our findings – with respect to geographical articulations and evolutions with regard to actor composition – can be applied to international business networks in general. It seems that especially as regards the geographical articulation and co-location degrees of business networks, it is recommendable to assess to what extent our conclusions are valid for international business networks in general, and for those networks whose point of gravity is situated in the home base of a focal buyer firm in particular. This should therefore be a concern for further research.

In general, as was also argued in Section 1.2, we are aware that in certain cases and certainly in regions or countries that form the 'home base' of the network's focal firm, certain local heritage, particular business cultures, regional or national economic and industrial policies and path dependence factors can play a strong flanking role in explaining the geographical and actor composition evolutions of business networks. Although we have consciously abstained from explicitly focusing on these contextual factors, they have been highlighted on several occasions in the case study descriptions. Especially the trajectory of the FASA-Renault Valladolid plant was to a considerable extent influenced by such factors. Consequently, we dedicated ample attention to them and they formed no obstacle to come to integrated reasonings (i.e. based on our own-developed conceptual framework) for our ultimate findings.

Although there is always the need to put one's own findings into perspective, we believe that our findings are highly valid and are based on solid theoretical foundations. First of all, through extensive cross-referencing with relevant publications of other scholars, the construct validity of our conceptual framework, its key variables and the underlying relationships was safeguarded. Consequently, we avoided the construction of a subjective and 'blinkered' conceptual framework. Secondly, as we employed a longitudinal research approach it can be argued that those determinants that matter most in the long run should become evident. As our conceptual framework proved to be able to analyse and foresee the trajectories of the research cases to a large extent, its validity and the ultimate findings to which it leads appear to be highly robust.

7.3 Further theoretical and conceptual contributions

Both the N&I approach, the network view on the IPM and the F/5P model wrestle with the question whether buyer–supplier relationships are generally characterized by (a)symmetry and (in)dependence. Whereas the first two assume b2b relationships (and internationalization moves) to depend on multiple b2b relationships governed by symmetrical and mutual resource dependencies, the third assumes that supplier internationalization moves are conditioned by asymmetrical dependencies on flagship firms, to which they are supposedly exclusively (and indefinitely – Rugman and D'Cruz, 2000, p. 86) dedicated.

7.3.1 Dependence and (a)symmetry aspects of international b2b relationships

Especially the F/5P model's claim that key suppliers are expected to give near or total exclusivity to a flagship firm, that is, regarding internationalization issues, raises some questions. Our research reveals that this may be true on certain occasions from a supply plant-basis view (when a supplier decomposes its assets and resources in such a way that each of them turn into 'dedicated assets' vis-à-vis certain networks or clients). But it rarely seems to be the case at a corporate level. Whereas it is already hard to conceive how suppliers would submit themselves completely to the mercy of one client (cf. lock-in dangers and dependence on one client), our research shows that car manufacturing firms rather have their suppliers working for multiple clients so that these suppliers can also bring in experiences from elsewhere. In addition, we also found several examples of what seem to be industry-wide suppliers (see also, Lieberman and Montgomery, 1988), like TRW, Faurecia, Bosch and Siemens. These suppliers act as key suppliers to various car constructors, providing the latter with strategic inputs for their respective networks. As a consequence, the validity of the exclusivity thesis is hard to hold. At best, it is (or was) valid for business networks around large US or Canadian buyer companies as it coincides with the way North American buyer–supplier relationships and production systems in the automobile industry have been characterized in the past (see for example, Lamming, 1993). However, in line with Boyer (1991), Boyer and Freyssenet (1995, 2000) and Chanaron and Lung (1999), our research shows that buyer-supplier relationships are more multiform in terms of inter-firm dependence and distribution of competences. Furthermore, we believe that the archetypical way the North American production model has often been characterized will also experience (or may already have experienced) disruptions of dedicated b2b relationships, a rise of industry-wide suppliers and cases of supplier substitutions in subsequent rounds of product generations. Thus, it is plausible that the exclusivity feature of North American automotive buyer–supplier relationships belongs to the past as well. In this regard, Liker and Choi (2004) registered how today American car constructors want myriad suppliers for everything (p. 109). At the same time, they play out vendors against each other and then do business with the last supplier standing (p. 110). That way, leaving little room for continuity in relationships.

As far as the F/5P model acknowledges suppliers' possibilities to influence car manufacturing firm strategies, one encounters the following pitfall. From Rugman (1999) and Rugman and D'Cruz (2000) it can be understood that the difference between key and non-key suppliers in an automotive industry setting is the difference between first tier and lower tier suppliers (see for example, Rugman and D'Cruz, 2000, pp. 36–37, 86, 94 and notably pp. 166–170). They argue that first tier suppliers deliver key inputs to the network in terms of products. Likewise, they may be able to exert influence on the strategies of car manufacturing firms to some extent. Curiously, in this respect all first tier suppliers are treated in the same way. As a result, also a paint manufacturer is considered a key supplier to an automobile constructor (Rugman and D'Cruz, 2000, p. 94) or a supplier of parts, seals and devices (p. 169). However, based on our findings we argue that there must exist different leagues of suppliers as regards possibilities to influence car constructor firm strategies. Some suppliers can be termed 'influential suppliers' (Lamming, 1993; Grohn, 2002) whereas others – in spite of being first tier suppliers – have a rather weak impact on the strategies of car manufacturing firms (for instance, a supplier of seals). One may even wonder whether some of the examples Rugman and D'Cruz (2000) cite as first tier suppliers are indeed tier one suppliers or will continue to be so, as they are not system integrators. In brief, one can indeed expect that high-technology component suppliers like Bosch, Siemens and even commodity suppliers like Alusuisse exert significant influence on the strategies of car manufacturing firms. However, one should expect suppliers responsible for the delivery of, for instance, rear mirrors, seals and window panes to do so to a far lesser degree.

As regards the statement of the F/5P model that key suppliers are more asymmetrically and exclusively dependent on flagship firms for their internationalization patterns than non-key suppliers, one is confronted with the following difficulty. Many of the firms that are conceived as key suppliers by the F/5P model are in fact multidivisional and multisectoral actors.

Consequently, they do not depend as much on automobile flagship firms (see for example, Hodges and Van Tulder, 1994) as will be the case for first or lower tier suppliers totally dedicated to the automotive industry. The internationalization patterns of key suppliers that are multidivisional and multisectoral will therefore probably not coincide with that of a single (important) client to such a large extent. Likewise, the group of pure automotive industry firms – in the F/5P model these can both be key and non-key suppliers – must in fact be more dependent on flagships firms from the automotive industry and should, consequently, show a stronger coherence with the internationalization patterns of automobile flagship firms (as is also illustrated on p. 182 of Rugman and D'Cruz, 2000).

Based on our research, an overall conclusion would be that the distinction between key and non-key suppliers in the F/5P model is not in accordance with the generic categorization of different tiers of suppliers as commonly used with respect to the automotive sector. This is remarkable as the design of the F/5P model is partly grounded in analyses of this specific sector. On the whole, the supplier categorization as used in the F/5P model leads us to unrealistic conclusions regarding features of (a)symmetry, (in)dependence and exclusivity in buyer–supplier relationships in the automotive industry.

In fact, suppliers that are active in more than one industry have commitments to several sectors and actors and they are thus more likely to pursue strategies that are embedded in multiple relationships. This means their location and internationalization behaviour and overall strategies are less likely to be conditioned by one relationship. This also supports the argument that single b2b relationships should be understood amidst the conjoint of b2b relationships a firm maintains (Johanson and Mattsson, 1987; Forsgren, 1989; Laage-Hellman, 1997).

Through Rugman and D'Cruz's (2000) acknowledgement that many members of F/5P networks are multidivisional and multisectoral, and by emphasizing inter – rather than intra – industry relations, it becomes all the more risky to sustain that asymmetry governs b2b relationships within the F/5P model. In fact, the buyer firms we analysed admitted in a very straight-forward way that technologically they are coming to depend more and more on certain suppliers. Especially on those that deliver and supply them with inputs they themselves are not capable of providing (anymore). What is more, being aware of this, they design and deploy outsourcing strategies aimed at containing this dependence.

Based on our findings we claim that firms that act as business network gatekeepers to a final consumer market maintain different kinds of relationships with their suppliers in terms of power equality and resource dependence. One-way dependence of the latter on a focal buyer firm is certainly not in line with reality. Instead, more plurality can be observed, including relationships in which the focal buyer firm can depend on certain input providers. The latter situation occurs especially when multidivisional and multisectoral suppliers bring in vital knowledge from what is considered to be outside the core business of automotive industry and which is not under control (anymore) of a buyer firm. Such a situation is also likely to be the case when industry-wide suppliers and suppliers that hold a near-monopoly position in their product niche are involved. With regard to suppliers that are only active in the automotive business and or only work for one buyer firm or only a few of them, a much more pronounced power asymmetry can be observed.

Consequently, instead of assuming a straightforward dependence of suppliers on buyer firms, we propose an action–reaction sequence in which the suppliers' (internationalization and assignment) actions are analysed in the light of buyer firms' moves. That is, independently of the power symmetry involved in the respective b2b relationships. With regard to the analysis of internationalization patterns of firms, our own empirical research indeed points out that the focal buyer firms of networks serve best as the actor of departure. We refer explicitly to focal buyer firms in plural here, as the context in which this sequence is embedded is one of multiple suppliers–multiple buyers. Whereas the F/5P model stresses asymmetric relationships between one flagship firm and its suppliers and dedicates relatively little attention to other, for example (inter-firm) relationships and contextual parameters that may co-determine the internationalization pattern and sequence of suppliers, our research results are in line with the N&I approach and the network view on the IPM. They emphasize that the overarching structures and the environment in which networks and b2b relationships are embedded, also determine firms' b2b and internationalization decisions and actions.

7.4   Conceptual positioning of research findings

To position the concept of business networks we developed through the present research amidst existing views on business networks as organization sets, we refer to Table 7.1. It compares our own concept of business networks – placed in the right column–with the others on a variety of structuring parameters of b2b relationships and networks.[44–47]

For further details and a discussion of the 'standing' views on business networks as organization sets, and on the grounding of our own view, see Chapters 1, 2, 3 and 4 respectively.

Our own view is termed 'kaleidoscopic organization sets', accentuating the changes that business networks can go through.

Apart from positioning it amidst standing views in Table 7.1 on a number of parameters, we visually synthesize our main findings in Figure 7.1. It indicates that changes can be set in motion from the centre of an international business network and can affect all incumbent members (see also Chapter 3). For instance through a sequence whereby 'the strategy of the focal buyer firm of a network with regard to subsidiary competence assignment and location' influences 'suppliers' location and competence assignment decisions'. Or alternatively, through a action–reaction process in which 'centralization of decisions within the hierarchy of the focal buyer firm of the network' has an impact on 'the choices of suppliers for specific subsidiaries'. They can also take place as a consequence of moves undertaken by actors and changes induced by elements in the less central part of the conceptual framework: like rival buyer firms and rival suppliers, reacting to or anticipating possible changes in their business environment, be it sectoral or macro-economic contextual events, postures of buyer firms or the behaviour of rival supplier firms. By all means, the principal actors with regard to the formation and evolution of business networks (notably the incumbent actors and the organizations aspiring to become incumbents) not only anticipate and react to all kinds of changing circumstances. Also, they themselves create and set in motion circumstances for a further evolution of business networks.[48] To highlight the change provoking events and circumstances that appear to be most relevant for international business networks and the way they can ultimately provoke changes to the deep structures of networks, Figure 7.1 includes a specific exhibit dedicated to this matter.

Our view on the interactions and dynamics between actors and events in a business network setting strongly resembles the one presented by Shackle on economic interaction and decision-making (1969, 1974). He analyses the way firms can cope with (potential) surprise and (expected) events in their environments and how this leads to a changing and swirling reality. He used the metaphor of the 'kaleidoscope' for his theories. Our findings also indicate that change is a regularly recurring, if not constant, factor when monitoring the deep structure of international business networks. This explains why we baptized our view as 'kaleidoscopic organization sets'.

7.5 Suggestions for further research

As regards recommendations for further research, what should stand out is the need for additional empirical research into the evolution of actor compositions of business networks over time. For that is the only way our observations regarding substantial supplier substitutions can be validated.

Moreover, especially as regards the geographical articulation and co-location degrees of business networks it is recommendable to assess to what extent our conclusions are valid for international business networks in general, and for networks whose locational point of gravity is situated in the home base of the focal buyer firm in particular.

Also, exploration in a profound way of the fundamental factors and mechanisms that intervene in actor substitutions and that drive such processes is highly recommended. In this respect, the case in which we detected a substantial number of substitutions would provide a good starting point. Consequently, this should lead to a conceptual framework, which underlying elements and relationships can then be tested more systematically

Table 7.1 Comparison of conceptual views on key structural parameters of b2b relationships and business networks

	IDs, learning region, cluster theories	TCE, AT, PRA	RBV, core competences	Network and interaction approach	Network view on the IPM	Flagship/Five Partners Model	Kaleidoscopic view on organization sets
Binding mechanism	Business cultural, linguistically, historical and/or geographical proximity	Efficiency; business economic rationality and short-term rent generating potential	Resources complementarity; business economic rationality, strategic positioning and long-term rent generating potential	Resources complementarity and bonding through time of cooperation	Resources complementarity and bonding through time of cooperation	Strategic leadership of focal firm	Business economic rationality: rent generating potential and search for learning effects
Objects of analysis	Amorphous/non-nominative groups of organizations	Dyads	Dyads	Dyads and networks with consideration of multiclient relations' implications for dyad and network	Dyads and networks with consideration of multiclient relations' implications for dyad and network	Networks without consideration of multiclient relations' implications for network	Dyads and networks with consideration of multiclient relations' implications for dyad and network
Actors involved	Local	Local/international	Local/international	Local/international	Local/international	International	Local/international
Involved capital involved	Local	Local/international	Local/international	Local/international	Local/international	International	Local/international
Decision taking power of actors	Sovereign	Sovereign	Sovereign	Sovereign/subordinated	Sovereign/subordinated	Sovereign	Sovereign/subordinated

Geographical locus	Home base of main member(s)	Home base/abroad/cross-border	Home base/abroad/cross-border	Home base/abroad/cross-border	Home base/abroad/cross-border	Home base/abroad/cross-border	Home base/abroad/cross-border
Resources division	Symmetry	Asymmetry	Symmetry	Symmetry	Symmetry	Asymmetry	Irrelevant
Continuity of partner composition	Continuity	Irrelevant	Irrelevant	Continuity	Continuity	Continuity	Discontinuity
Representative Scholars and Publications	Becattini, 1979; Brusco, 1982; Pyke et al., 1992; Harrison, 1992; Storper, 1992; Florida, 1995; Morgan, 1997; Cooke and Morgan, 1998; Porter, 1990; Krugman, 1991; Saxenian, 1994	Williamson, 1975, 1985, 1991; Fama, 1980; Langlois, 1988; Langlois and Robertson, 1989, 1995; Powel and Smith-Doerr, 1994; Fama and Jensen, 1983; Jensen and Meckling, 1976; Holmström and Roberts, 1998; Grossman and Hart, 1986; Hart and Moore, 1990	Wernerfelt, 1984; Barney, 1991; Mahoney and Pandian, 1992; Amit and Shoemaker, 1993; Dyer and Singh, 1998; Prahalad and Hamel, 1990	Håkansson, 1982, 1987, 1989; Håkansson and Shehota, 1995; Håkansson and Johanson, 1988; Johanson and Mattsson, 1987; Laage-Hellman, 1997	Forsgren, 1989; Forsgren and Johanson, 1992; Forsgren, et al., 1992; Forsgren and Holm, 1992; Holm 1993; Holm et al., 1995; Andersson and Pahlberg, 1997; Andersson and Forsgren, 2000	Lorenzoni and Baden-Fuller, 1993, 1995; Rugman, 1999; Rugman and D'Cruz, 2000	Present study

Source: Author's elaboration.

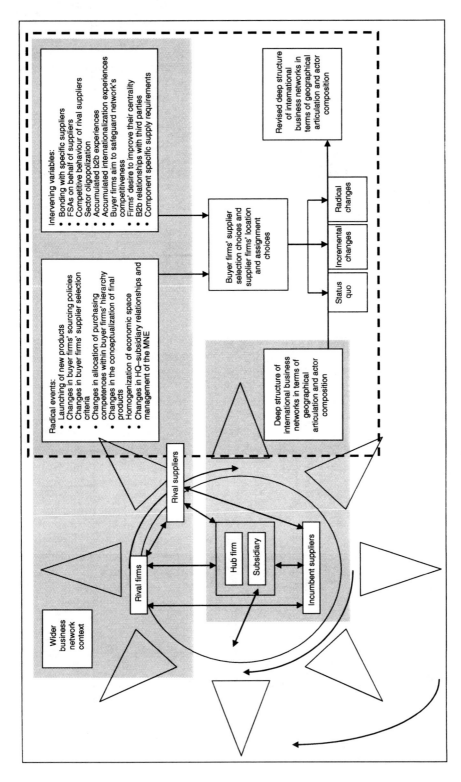

Intervening variables:
- Bonding with specific suppliers
- FSAs on behalf of suppliers
- Competitive behaviour of rival suppliers
- Sector oligopolization
- Accumulated b2b experiences
- Accumulated internationalization experiences
- Buyer firms aim to safeguard network's competitiveness
- Firms' desire to improve their centrality
- B2b relationships with third parties
- Component specific supply requirements

Radical events:
- Launching of new products
- Changes in buyer firms' sourcing policies
- Changes in buyer firms' supplier selection criteria
- Changes in allocation of purchasing competences within buyer firms' hierarchy
- Changes in the conceptualization of final products
- Homogenization of economic space
- Changes in HQ-subsidiary relationships and management of the MNE

Revised deep structure of international business networks in terms of geographical articulation and actor composition

Buyer firms' supplier selection choices and supplier firms' location and assignment choices

Radical changes

Incremental changes

Status quo

Deep structure of international business networks in terms of geographical articulation and actor composition

Rival suppliers

Hub firm

Subsidiary

Incumbent suppliers

Rival firms

Wider business network context

Figure 7.1 International business networks as Kaleidoscopic organization sets.

Source: Author's elaboration.

through, for instance, a large-scale survey of business networks. Eventually, the modelling of these elements and relationships and their large-scale and detailed testing can be done computationally based on models of complex dynamic systems (see for example, Kaufmann, 1992, 1995).

In line with the former, our research results can be interpreted as support for the claim that when firms are confident in their own b2b relationship management qualities, and in the resource potential and the agility of new partners in order to equal or surpass current partners' technological and logistics performances, trust built up with current partners will not prevent firms from changing partners. Certainly not, if rival firms promise to do better than current partners when conquering the network positions currently not under their control. This is a related hypothesis that should play a role in future research.

In addition to the former recommendations we want to formulate the following suggestions.

To set up research that allows testing whether the geographical articulation and actor composition patterns we found are country-specific (for instance, whether the Renault case is representative for the French car makers and the VW case is representative for the German ones, and so on.), in line with findings of, for example, Maurice *et al.* (1986) and Lane (1989), or whether they can be categorized in terms of certain business philosophies that cross national borders. For example, analogous to the way in which automotive buyer–supplier relationships and car constructor management philosophies of productive models (such as: Toyotism, Hondaism, Sloanism and Fordism) have been distinguished, for example, by Boyer (1991), Boyer and Freyssenet (1995, 2000) and Chanaron and Lung (1999).

Furthermore, whether the (varieties of) patterns that can be established with respect to automotive buyer–supplier networks are car industry-specific or whether they are more universal, through similar research in other sectors.

Appendix A

Assessment of longevity, change types and nationalities involved in the research cases

In Chapters 5 and 6 we assessed the longevity and the kinds of changes in the supplier networks surrounding the VW Navarra plant at Landaben and the FASA-Renault plant at Valladolid.

In what follows, we present the way the calculations and the assessments took place.

Whether a change is valued as a whole change, half a change or, for instance, a quarter of a change, depends on the fact whether – on average – over the time period considered, the car constructor practiced single sourcing, double or multiple sourcing for the component in question or whether it sourced in separate parts that make up the component.

Table 5.4 Changes in the actor composition of VW Navarra's supplier network

(A) oligopoly-related substitutions	(B) competitiveness-oriented substitutions	(C) first-time externalization	(D) re-internalization
7	$8\frac{1}{2}$	$\frac{3}{4}$	0

Source: Author's elaboration.

Table A.1 Oligopoly-related substitutions around VW Navarra

No. Substitutions	Past experiences with new owner
1 Entry of Expert components, front-end supplier, into VEAS (joint venture between Expert and Peguform) in 2001	Yes
2 Takeover of Dynoplast, fuel tank supplier, by Walbro in 1995	No
3 Takeover of Industrias Esteban, supplier of seats, by Archter und Ebels + RHW (Bertrand Faure) late 1980s	No
4 Takeover of Unicables, supplier of cabling and cockpits, by Delphi in 1995	No
5 Takeover of Lignotock, supplier of cockpits, by Sommer Allibert Siemens in 1999	Partial
6 Takeover of Heidemann Novel Ibérica, supplier of gearsticks, by Adwest Plc in 1997	No
7 Takeover of Adwest Plc, supplier of gearsticks, by Dura in 1999	No

Source: Author's elaboration.

Table A.2 Competitiveness-related substitutions

No.	Substitutions	Valued as
1	Switch from 100% exhaust delivery by Arvin to 50–50 between Arvin and Faurecia in 2001	$\frac{1}{2}$ a substitution
2	Switch from Dynamit Nobel Ibérica to Mecaplast for rear end bumpers in 2001	1 (whole) substitution
3	Switch from Walbro to Kautex for fuel tanks in 2001	1 (whole) substitution
4	Switch from partial supply of cabling by Bordnetze to partial supply of cabling by Unicables in the late 1980s	$\frac{1}{2}$ a substitution
5	Switch from exclusive supply of cabling by Unicables to exclusive supply by Bordnetze in 2001	1 (whole) substitution
6	Switch from Delphi to Lignotock for cockpits in 1997	1 (whole) substitution
7	Switch from Dynamit Nobel Ibérica to Mecaplast for interior trims and consoles in 2001	1 (whole) substitution
8	Switch from Küster as lead supplier and Irausa as second supplier for door and roof panels to the inverse situation in 2001	$\frac{1}{2}$ a substitution
9	Switch from MAESA-Hella to Yorka for lights in 2001	1 (whole) substitution
10	Switch from Lunke to ATESO for pedals in 2001	1 (whole) substitution

Source: Author's elaboration.

Table A.3 First-time externalizations

No.	Substitutions	Valued as
1	Switch from shared supply of steering systems by VW and TRW to 100% supply by TRW in 2001	$\frac{1}{2}$ an externalization
2	Outsourcing of VW Navarra's share of power train assembly to Expert in 1998	$\frac{1}{4}$ of an externalization

Source: Author's elaboration.

Table 6.9 Changes in the actor composition of FASA-Renault Valladolid's supplier network

(A) oligopoly-related substitutions	(B) competitiveness-oriented substitutions	(C) first-time externalizations	(D) re-internalizations
15	3.57	2.08	1

Source: Author's elaboration.

Table A.4 Oligopoly-related substitutions around FASA-Renault Valladolid

No.	Substitutions	Past experiences with new owner
1	Takeover of Ekin and PCG, exhaust suppliers, by ECIA in 1996	Yes
2	Entry of ECIA, exhaust supplier, into Faurecia (merger between Bertrand Faure and ECIA) in 1999	Yes
3	Entry of Solvay fueling systems, fuel tank supplier, into Inergy (joint venture between Solvay and Plastic Omnium) in 2000	Yes
4	Takeover of Inerga, front and rear end supplier, by Peguform in 1996	Yes
5	Adhesion of Sommer Allibert, supplier of front and rear ends, floor coverings and door and roof panels, to Faurecia in 2001	Yes
6	Entrance of Peguform, front and rear end supplier, into VEAS (joint venture between Expert and Peguform) in 2001	Partial
7	Creation of a joint venture between Plastic Omnium and Inoplast around 2000, to take care of the front and rear end supplies that were previously delivered by Plastic Omnium	Partial
8	Takeover of Trety, seat supplier, by Johnson Controls in the mid-1990s	No
9	Takeover of CETASA, cabling supplier, by Delphi in the mid-1990s	No
10	Takeover of MAISA, cabling supplier, by UTA in the 1990s	No
11	Sale of MAISA, cabling supplier, by UTA to Lear in the 1990s	No
12	Takeover of Reydel, cockpit supplier, by Plastic Omnium in 1995	Yes
13	Takeover of cockpit division of Plastic Omnium by Visteon in 1999	No
14	Takeover of Gunasa, supplier of floor coverings, by Sommer Allibert in the mid-1990s	Yes
15	Takeover of Valeo's motor and electricity activities by Siemens in 1995 (engine propulsion parts)	No

Source: Author's elaboration.

Table A.5 Competitiveness-related substitutions

No.	Substitutions	Valued as
1	Switch from shared supply of exhausts by Norma and Ekin (ECIA) to 100% supply by ECIA in 1996	$\frac{1}{2}$ a substitution
2	Switch from Draft. Airex + Carbureibar to Bundy/ IT Group for fuel alimentation in 1996	$\frac{1}{2}$ a substitution
3	Substitution of Fagor-MCC's share in front and rear end supply, by Sommer Allibert in 1996	$\frac{1}{3}$ of a substitution
4	Switch from shared supply of cabling by MAISA and CETASA/Delphi to exclusive supply by Delphi in 2001	$\frac{1}{2}$ a substitution
5	Substitution of Simoldes' share in door and roof panels supply, by Plastic Omnium in 1996	$\frac{1}{3}$ of substitution
6	Including Delphi-Lucas Varity for supplies of engine propulsion parts in 2001	$\frac{1}{4}$ of a substitution
7	Switch from Yorka's part of lighting supply to Hella-Maesa in 1996	$\frac{1}{2}$ a substitution
8	Switch from shares of Mikalor, Alumalsa, Inyectametal and Acenor in small metal device supplies to *Estampaciones Bizkaia* in 1996	$\frac{1}{3}$ of a substitution
9	Substitution of Bendiberica's share in brakes supply, by Fagor Ederlan and Bundy/TI Group in 1996	$\frac{1}{3}$ of a substitution

Source: Author's elaboration.

Table A.6 First-time externalizations

No.	Substitutions	Valued as
1	Outsourcing of FASA-Renault Valladolid's share of steering system assembly to TRW in 1996	$\frac{1}{2}$ an externalization
2	Outsourcing of SMI's (Renault) share of steering system assembly to Koyo in 1996	$\frac{1}{2}$ an externalization
3	Outsourcing of (FASA-)Renault's share of transmission assembly to NTN	$\frac{1}{2}$ an externalization
4	Outsourcing of (FASA-)Renault's share of motor propulsion part assembly to NTN	$\frac{1}{4}$ of an externalization
5	Outsourcing of shares of Funfrap (Renault) in small metal device supplies to Sofedit Ibérica in 1996	$\frac{1}{3}$ of an externalization

Source: Author's elaboration.

Table A.7 Re-internalizations

No.	Substitutions	Valued as
1	Parts of front and rear end bumper components at FASA-Renault Valladolid as of 2001	$\frac{1}{4}$ of a re-internalization
2	Substitution of Ayra Durex and Ascometal shares in transmission supplies, by in-house FASA-Renault/Renault France (incl. ACI) production in 1996	$\frac{1}{2}$ a re-internalization
3	Substitution of Fagor's share in motor propulsion part supplies, by in-house FASA-Renault/Renault France (incl. ACI) production in 1996	$\frac{1}{4}$ of a re-internalization

Source: Author's elaboration.

Table 5.5 Origin of capital of supplier sample for VW Navarra

Nationality	1984–1994	1994–2001	2001 *and beyond*
D	16.75	13.125	10
F	0.25	0.625	3.5
USA	0.5	2.75	3.25
E	2.5	2.5	1.75
NO	0	0.5	0
I	0	0	0.5
UK	0	0.5	0
CZ	0	0	1
Total	20	20	20

Source: Author's elaboration.

Similarly, in Chapters 5 and 6 we assessed the evolution of the nationality of the capital behind the supplier involved in the supplier networks surrounding the VW Navarra plant at Landaben and the FASA-Renault plant at Valladolid.

In what follows, we present the way the counting and the assessments took place.

Whether a nationality is valued as a whole, half or, for instance, a quarter of a change, depends on the capital structure behind the supplier in question (it may be a joint venture between companies from different countries), or on the number of component-specific suppliers: single sourcing or multiple sourcing. It may also depend on the question whether during a certain time period, for instance 1984–1994 for VW Navarra or 1990–1996 for FASA-Renault, there was a switch from one supplier to another.

Table A.8 Breakdown of nationalities behind suppliers to VW Navarra

Component	1984–1994	1994–2001	2001 and beyond
Exhaust pipe	D	USA	$\frac{1}{2}$ USA, $\frac{1}{2}$ F
Rear end bumper	D	D	F
Front-end bumper	$\frac{1}{2}$ D, $\frac{1}{2}$ E	D	$\frac{1}{2}$ D, $\frac{1}{2}$ USA
Fuel tank	D	$\frac{1}{2}$ No, $\frac{1}{2}$ USA	D
Seats	$\frac{1}{2}$ E, $\frac{1}{4}$ D, $\frac{1}{4}$ F	$\frac{1}{2}$ D, $\frac{1}{2}$ F	$\frac{1}{2}$ D, $\frac{1}{2}$ F
Steering system	$\frac{1}{2}$ USA, $\frac{1}{2}$ D	$\frac{1}{2}$ USA, $\frac{1}{2}$ D	USA
Cabling	$\frac{1}{2}$ E, $\frac{1}{2}$ D	$\frac{1}{2}$ E, $\frac{1}{2}$ USA	D
Cockpit	D	$\frac{1}{4}$ E, $\frac{1}{4}$ USA, $\frac{1}{4}$ E, $\frac{1}{8}$ D, $\frac{1}{8}$ F	$\frac{1}{2}$ D, $\frac{1}{2}$ F
Isolating floor coverings	D	D	D
Interior trims and consoles	D	D	F
Door and roof panels	$\frac{1}{2}$ E, $\frac{1}{2}$ D	$\frac{1}{2}$ E, $\frac{1}{2}$ D	$\frac{1}{2}$ E, $\frac{1}{2}$ D
Lights	D	D	$\frac{1}{2}$ E, $\frac{1}{2}$ I
Stamping of small metal devices	$\frac{1}{2}$ E, $\frac{1}{2}$ D	$\frac{3}{4}$ E, $\frac{1}{4}$ D	$\frac{3}{4}$ E, $\frac{1}{4}$ D
Gearbox	D	D	D
Engine	D	D	D
Brake devices	D	D	D
Transmission	D	D	D
Engine propulsion group (power train)	D	D	$\frac{3}{4}$ D, $\frac{1}{4}$ USA
Gearstick	D	$\frac{1}{4}$ D, $\frac{1}{4}$ E, $\frac{1}{4}$ UK, $\frac{1}{4}$ USA	1
Pedals	D	D	CZ

Source: Author's elaboration.

Table 6.10 Origin of capital of supplier sample for FASA-Renault Valladolid

Nationality	1990–1996	1996–2001	2001 and beyond
D	0.58	1.23	1.02
F	6.23	7.25	6.25
USA	0.17	2.67	5.16
E	7.63	3.68	1.79
J	—	0.5	1.2
P	0.74	0.33	0.33
B	0.33	0.33	0.25
UK	0.32	—	—
Total	16	16	16

Source: Author's elaboration.

Table A.9 Breakdown of nationalities behind suppliers to FASA-Renault Valladolid

Component	1990–1996	1996–2001	2001 *and beyond*
Exhaust pipe	$\frac{1}{2}$ E, $\frac{1}{2}$ F	$\frac{1}{3}$ E, $\frac{2}{3}$ F	F
Front end and rear end bumper	$\frac{1}{3}$ F, $\frac{1}{3}$ E, $\frac{1}{3}$D	$\frac{1}{3}$ E, $\frac{1}{3}$ F, $\frac{1}{3}$ F	$\frac{1}{4}$ F, $\frac{1}{8}$ E, $\frac{1}{8}$ F, $\frac{1}{4}$ F, $\frac{1}{8}$ D, $\frac{1}{8}$ USA
Fuel tank	$\frac{1}{6}$ E, $\frac{1}{3}$ B, $\frac{1}{4}$ F, $\frac{1}{4}$ E	$\frac{1}{6}$ E, $\frac{1}{3}$ B, $\frac{1}{2}$ USA	$\frac{1}{4}$ B, $\frac{1}{4}$ F, $\frac{1}{2}$ USA
Seats	$\frac{1}{2}$ E, $\frac{1}{2}$ F	USA	USA
Steering system	$\frac{1}{4}$ E, $\frac{1}{4}$ F, $\frac{1}{2}$ F	$\frac{1}{2}$ J, $\frac{1}{2}$ USA	$\frac{1}{2}$ J, $\frac{1}{2}$ USA
Cabling	$\frac{1}{3}$ E, $\frac{1}{3}$ E, $\frac{1}{3}$ E	$\frac{1}{4}$ E, $\frac{1}{4}$ USA, $\frac{1}{4}$ E, $\frac{1}{4}$ USA	USA
Cockpit	$\frac{1}{8}$ E, $\frac{1}{8}$ F, $\frac{1}{4}$ F, $\frac{1}{4}$ F, $\frac{1}{4}$ E	F	USA
Isolating floor coverings	$\frac{1}{4}$ E, $\frac{1}{4}$ F, $\frac{1}{4}$ E, $\frac{1}{8}$ E, $\frac{1}{8}$ F	F	F
Interior trims, consoles, door and roof panels	$\frac{1}{3}$ E, $\frac{1}{3}$ P, $\frac{1}{3}$ F	$\frac{1}{3}$ F, $\frac{1}{3}$ F, $\frac{1}{3}$ E	$\frac{1}{3}$ F, $\frac{1}{3}$ F, $\frac{1}{3}$ E
Lights	$\frac{1}{4}$ E, $\frac{1}{4}$ F, $\frac{1}{2}$ E	$\frac{1}{2}$ D, $\frac{1}{4}$ E, $\frac{1}{4}$ F	$\frac{1}{2}$ D, $\frac{1}{2}$ F
Stamping of small metal devices	$\frac{1}{7}$ E, $\frac{1}{14}$ P, $\frac{1}{14}$ F, $\frac{1}{7}$ E, $\frac{1}{7}$ E, $\frac{1}{7}$ E, $\frac{1}{7}$ E, $\frac{1}{7}$ UK	$\frac{1}{3}$ F, $\frac{1}{3}$ E, $\frac{1}{3}$ E	$\frac{1}{3}$ F, $\frac{1}{3}$ E, $\frac{1}{3}$ E
Gearbox	$\frac{1}{6}$ E, $\frac{1}{6}$ F, $\frac{1}{6}$ P, $\frac{1}{6}$ F, $\frac{1}{3}$ F	$\frac{1}{6}$ E, $\frac{1}{6}$ F, $\frac{1}{6}$ P, $\frac{1}{6}$ F, $\frac{1}{3}$ F	$\frac{1}{6}$ E, $\frac{1}{6}$ F, $\frac{1}{6}$ P, $\frac{1}{6}$ F, $\frac{1}{3}$ F
Engine	$\frac{1}{6}$ E, $\frac{1}{6}$ F, $\frac{1}{6}$ P, $\frac{1}{6}$ F, $\frac{1}{3}$ F	$\frac{1}{6}$ E, $\frac{1}{6}$ F, $\frac{1}{6}$ P, $\frac{1}{6}$ F, $\frac{1}{3}$ F	$\frac{1}{6}$ E, $\frac{1}{6}$ F, $\frac{1}{6}$ P, $\frac{1}{6}$ F, $\frac{1}{3}$ F
Brake devices	$\frac{1}{6}$ E, $\frac{1}{6}$ F, $\frac{1}{6}$ USA, $\frac{1}{6}$ E, $\frac{1}{3}$ E	$\frac{1}{6}$ E, $\frac{1}{6}$ F, $\frac{1}{6}$ USA, $\frac{1}{6}$ E, $\frac{1}{3}$ E	$\frac{1}{3}$ F, $\frac{1}{3}$ E, $\frac{1}{3}$ USA
Transmission	$\frac{1}{6}$ E, $\frac{1}{6}$ UK, $\frac{1}{6}$ E, $\frac{1}{6}$ F, $\frac{1}{3}$ F	$\frac{1}{2}$ F, $\frac{1}{2}$ F	$\frac{1}{2}$ F, $\frac{1}{2}$ J
Engine propulsion group (power train)	$\frac{1}{8}$ E, $\frac{1}{8}$ F, $\frac{1}{4}$ E, $\frac{1}{8}$ F, $\frac{1}{8}$ D, $\frac{1}{8}$ E, $\frac{1}{8}$ D	$\frac{1}{10}$ E, $\frac{1}{10}$ F, $\frac{1}{5}$ F, $\frac{1}{5}$ F, $\frac{1}{5}$ D, $\frac{1}{5}$ D	$\frac{1}{5}$ F, $\frac{1}{5}$ J, $\frac{1}{5}$ D, $\frac{1}{5}$ USA, $\frac{1}{5}$ D

Source: Author's elaboration.

In Chapters 5 and 6 we also assessed the geographical developments of the supplier network surrounding the VW Navarra plant at Landaben and the FASA-Renault plant at Valladolid.

In what follows, we present the way the counting and the assessments took place.

Whether a settlement in Castilla y Leon or Valladolid is valued as a whole, half or, for instance, a quarter of a change, depends on the number of component-specific suppliers: single sourcing or multiple sourcing. It may also depend on the question whether during a certain time period, for instance 1984–1994 for VW Navarra or 1990–1996 for FASA-Renault, there was a switch from one supplier to another.

Table A.10 Geographical developments of the supplier network surrounding VW Navarra

Component	Supply site 1984–1994	Supply site 2001 and beyond	Approximation, status quo or removal
Exhaust pipe	Germany (1)	Landaben area (1)	Approximation (incl. 1 on-site investment)
Rear end bumper	Germany + Navarra ($\frac{1}{2}$)	Madrid	'Intermediate' approximation
Front end bumper	Germany + Landaben area ($\frac{1}{4}$) + Catalonia	Landaben area (1)	Approximation (incl. 1 on-site investment)
Fuel tank	Germany	Landaben area (1)	Approximation (incl. 2 on-site investments)
Seats	Landaben area (1)	Landaben area (1)	Status quo (incl. 1 on on-site investment)
Steering system	Landaben area ($\frac{1}{2}$) + Germany	Landaben area (1)	Approximation
Cabling	Germany + Landaben area ($\frac{1}{2}$)	Landaben area (1)	Approximation (incl. 1 on-site investment)
Cockpit	Germany + Landaben area ($\frac{1}{2}$)	Landaben area (1)	Approximation (incl. 1 on-site investment)
Isolating floor coverings	Landaben area (1)	Landaben area (1)	Status quo (incl. 1 on-site investment)
Interior trims and consoles	Landaben area ($\frac{1}{2}$) + Navarra ($\frac{1}{2}$)	Madrid	Removal
Door and roof panels	Germany + Castilla y Leon	Landaben area ($\frac{3}{4}$) + Germany	Approximation (incl. 1 on-site investment)
Lights	Germany	Catalonia	'Intermediate' approximation
Stamping of small metal devices	Landaben area ($\frac{1}{4}$) + Germany + rest of Spain	Landaben area ($\frac{3}{4}$) + Madrid	Approximation (incl. 4 on-site investments)
Gearbox	Germany	Catalonia	'Intermediate' approximation
Engine	Germany	Germany	Status quo
Brake devices	Germany	Germany	Status quo
Transmission	Germany	Landaben area (1)	Approximation
Engine propulsion group (power train)	Germany	Germany + Landaben area ($\frac{1}{4}$)	Approximation
Gearstick	Germany	Landaben area (1)	Approximation (incl. 1 on-site investment)
Pedals	Catalonia + Landaben area ($\frac{1}{4}$)	Czech Republic	Removal (incl. 1 on-site investment)

Source: Author's elaboration.

Table A.11 Geographical developments of the supplier network surrounding FASA-Renault Valladolid

Component	Supply site 1990–1996	Supply site 2001 and beyond	Approximation, status quo or removal
Exhaust pipe	Euskadi + France	Madrid	Approximation
Front end and rear end bumper	Castilla y Leon ($\frac{2}{3}$) + Bizkaia	Valladolid ($\frac{1}{4}$) + Castilla y Leon ($\frac{1}{2}$) + Madrid	Approximation
Fuel tank	Valladolid ($\frac{1}{2}$) + France + Bizkaia	Valladolid ($\frac{1}{2}$) + Palencia ($\frac{1}{2}$)	Approximation
Seats	Valladolid (1)	Valladolid (1)	Status quo
Steering system	Valladolid ($\frac{1}{2}$) + France	France + Navarra	Removal
Cabling	Aragon + Portugal + Catalonia	Aragon	Status quo
Cockpit	Valladolid ($\frac{1}{2}$) + Catalonia	Valladolid (1)	Virtual approximation through tiering: status quo
Isolating floor coverings	Madrid + France + Catalonia + Valladolid ($\frac{1}{4}$)	Valladolid (1)	Virtual approximation through tiering: Status quo
Interior trims, consoles, door and roof panels	Castilla y Leon ($\frac{1}{6}$) + Valladolid ($\frac{1}{6}$) + Portugal + France + Madrid	Castilla y Leon ($\frac{1}{3}$) + Valladolid ($\frac{1}{6}$) + Madrid + Valladolid ($\frac{1}{3}$)	Approximation
Lights	Andalusia + Catalonia	Valladolid ($\frac{1}{2}$) + Andalusia	Approximation
Stamping of small metal devices	Valladolid ($\frac{1}{4}$) + rest of Spain + Portugal	Valladolid ($\frac{1}{3}$) + Castilla y Leon ($\frac{1}{3}$) + Madrid	Approximation
Gearbox	Andalusia + Portugal + France	Andalusia + Portugal + France	Status quo
Engine	Valladolid ($\frac{1}{3}$) + Portugal + France	Valladolid ($\frac{1}{3}$) + Portugal + France	Status quo
Brake devices	Valladolid ($\frac{2}{3}$) + Cantabria	France + Gipuzkoa + Castilla y Leon ($\frac{1}{3}$)	Removal
Transmission	Gipuzkoa + Valladolid ($\frac{1}{3}$) + France	France + Castilla y Leon ($\frac{1}{6}$)	Removal
Engine propulsion group (power train)	Valladolid ($\frac{1}{4}$) + rest of Spain + France	Castilla y Leon ($\frac{1}{10}$) + rest of Spain + France	Removal

Source: Author's elaboration.

Notes

1 Introduction

1 The value system of the automotive industry can broadly speaking be split into a part upstream and a part downstream of the 'detachment' point where a car leaves the assembly line and enters the distribution and commercial stages of the value system. Due to the fact that the assembler acts as a 'hinge' between production and sale of the final product and therefore as the 'gate' to the market, this actor can be considered the gatekeeping party in the value system.

2 The difference between stand-alone screwdriver factories which import all their components from somewhere far away, on the one hand, and locally concentrated Marshallian or Becattinesque complexes of manufacturers centred around a homogeneous range of products with their own R&D facilities on the other hand, is very illustrative in this respect. Likewise, whether a satellite branch plant is busy with ensuring a firm's international sales, or with more added value activities such as R&D and manufacturing, also makes a significant difference.

3 This policy issue is also a matter of concern in the traditional heartlands of mature industries (e.g. in the North of Europe, as is testified by the 'Standort' and delocalization debates that have been held in the last decades of the twentieth century and the start of the twenty-first century. There, the debates are normally centred around the question: '(How) can we maintain an industry here?' See, for example Bloch (1999); Wolff (1996) and Brenner (2000).

4 As an illustration: by the end of the twentieth century the typical manufacturing firm in the USA purchases 55% of the value of each product it produces, whereas this figure is 69% in Japan (Dyer and Singh, 1998, p. 660). In Europe, on average some 60% of the value of a new car comes from suppliers, according to the European Monitoring Centre on Change (2004, p. 8). Moreover, it is foreseen that the share of suppliers in the total added value of the automotive industry will increase to approximately 75% by 2015 (Mercer/Fraunhofer Institute, 2005).

5 As a matter of fact, whereas the suppliers are multiple, there is only one principal buyer (the hub or 'focal' firm) around which b2b relationships are centred and which renders a network character to the whole. Although the network may have some kind of cobweb appearance due to (b2b) relationships among suppliers of this same principal buyer, the general appearance is that of a one hub-multiple suppliers image and not of a radially and concentrically plus core–peripherally connected texture. Of course, suppliers may well have relationships with other focal firms as well and form nodes in different networks at the same time. The same holds true for the principal buyer firms of networks.

6 For our research approach, therefore, discussions on: 'what is temporary?' or: 'when is a network replaced by a hierarchy or a market relation?' – as in transaction cost economics – are beside the point. Independent of the question whether networks may be temporary, we focus on network interactions and dynamics while they last.

7 Either in countries or areas that form the home base of networks build up around large MNEs (Porter, 1990; Ohmae, 1993; Saxenian, 1994; Florida, 1995), or in areas made up of small and medium-sized enterprises in particular mature industries (e.g. Brusco, 1982; Piore and Sabel, 1984; Scott and Storper, 1986; Scott, 1988; Pyke *et. al.*, 1992; Storper, 1992).

8 Although GM and Ford have European headquarters, the fact that their respective mother companies are from the USA makes these cases less appropriate for our research, as the transcontinental dimension could easily interfere with the intra-Triad region headquarters–subsidiary relationships and network formation dynamics on which we focus.

2   Theoretical and empirical research literature review

9 See for example, Barley *et. al.*, 1992.

10 In this respect, it can be argued that the strength of the individual organization depends not on organization-specific strengths or advantages, but on links with network partners such as customers, suppliers, competitors, and regulatory agencies (Alchian and Demsetz, 1972; Cook and Emerson, 1982; Perry, 1989; Oliver, 1990; McKiernan, 1992; Dyer, 1996, 1997; Dyer and Singh, 1998).

11 'The network is in constant flux as suppliers, buyers and customers may enter and exit' (McKiernan, 1992, p. 106).

12 This point-of-view can also be found in literature on barriers to imitation (e.g. Mahoney and Pandian, 1992; Amit and Schoemaker, 1993), on the relational view of inter-organizational competitive advantage (Dyer and Singh, 1998) and on inter-firm specialization (Dyer, 1996).

13 Whereas frequency is a measure for determining the adequacy of internalization (hierarchization) of markets for TCE, in the N&I approach it is a measure for adaptation, trust and bonding processes between firms. By no means it is an omen for inter-nalization of or mergers between firms. See also the parallel with the issues highlighted in Ford (1980, 1997), as presented in Section.

14 Whereas AT, TCE and PRA focus on control measures and contracts to regulate uncertainty in exchange processes, the N&I approach stresses that uncertainty can be regulated via frequency of exchanges and the bonding, mutual adaptation and trust this produces. In addition, firms can of course formalize their relationship through contracts and other control mechanisms. See again the parallel with the issues highlighted in Ford (1980, 1997), as presented in Section.

15 The N&I approach has this point in common with the RBV and with Dyer and Singh's relational view (1998).

16 In this sense, the network approach postulates that notably the longevity of relationships and the specificity of a relationship, lead to a preference of actors to use 'voice' instead of 'exit' (Hirschman, 1970) in case of conflicts within relationships.

17 *OLI* stands for: Ownership-specific advantages, Location-specific advantages and Internalization incentive advantages.

18 The TCE and RBV approaches discussed earlier can also be considered as static IB approaches.

19 According to Devinney (2001), Rugman and D'Cruz offer their approach as an alternative to the more familiar five-forces model of Porter, involving an integration of network theories, the resource-based theory of the firm, and transaction cost economics. Just as Porter attempted to "managerialize" industrial organization, Devinney (2001) observes how Rugman and D'Cruz also attempt to explain the complex structures operating around multinational enterprises by means of a loose collection of theories.

3 Conceptual framework and hypotheses

20 It is this behaviour that is emphasized by scholars in the tradition of the N&I approach (e.g. Håkansson, 1987) and the F/5P model (e.g. Rugman and D'Cruz, 2000). They argue that b2b relationships, therefore, tend to have a long-lasting or unlimited character.

21 This can for example be understood through the aim of a specific buyer to tap into additional supplier learning effects due to experiences with other b2b relations.

5 Empirical results with respect to Volkswagen Navarra

22 The other part of the deal, was to produce 30,000 Passats and Santanas a year in SEAT plants in Catalonia.

23 In the following, we will use the terms 'Volkswagen Navarra' and 'the Landaben plant' as synonima.

24 The choice of a certain plant as the leading plant for a VW car model is made through a kind of business case competition whereby plants can take part and enter their business plans and cost calculations (Busto, 1997; Grohn, 2002).

25 From the French word 'filialisation', which stands for: '... *la création d'une structure juridique indépendante pour acceuillir une division, un département ou une activité nouvelle naisante qui, jusqu'alors, était intégrée au sein de la structure juridique de la maison mère.*' (Quintard and De Rongé, 1992).

26 A breakdown of total purchasing values in annual figures would reveal that 80% is 'productive': automotive parts and pieces and 20% is generic purchasing (maintenance of buildings etc.). In 2000, for instance, generic purchasing accounted for approximately €8.5 billion vis-à-vis a total purchasing sum of approximately €60 billion (Grohn, 2002).

27 The supplementary part was produced in Wolfsburg, Germany.

28 The additional badge of Polo production was carried out in Bratislava, Slovakia.

29 See the Appendix A – Table 5.4 for the way we arrived at the numbers presented in the present paragraph.

30 During the A03/GP99 period this figure was even higher.

31 During the A03/GP99 period this figure was also higher.

32 See Appendix A for the way we arrived at the content of this table.

33 See Appendix A for the way we arrived at the content of this table.

6 Empirical results with respect to FASA-Renault Valladolid

34 The increased figure for 2000 is due to Renault's alliance with Nissan at the turn of the century (Renault, 2000, pp. 2, 27, 31–34, 2001, pp. 30–32, 36, 2002, pp. 37–42; Parnière, 2001).

35 A breakdown of total annual purchasing values would reveal that 75–80% is 'productive': automotive parts and pieces, and 20–25% has to do with generic

purchasing goods, such as industrial equipment and facilities, tooling and after-sales (Renault, Atlas économique, various editions).

36 See the respective articles 15 and 19 of the financial appendices of the FASA-Renault Memorias y Balances for the 1980s and the 1990s.

37 Inputs acquired by Renault's headquarters and transferred to the FASA-Renault subsidiary – a practice that stems from the centralization of purchasing competences in the second half of the 1980s – were directly booked as external procurements for FASA-Renault (both in the previous table – third column – and the blocks 'value of third parties' inputs outside Spain' in 6.2. Of course, these represent net purchasing for the company as a whole as well and, therefore, also served as input for Figure 6.1 (see also Mandos 26, p. 7).

38 Take note that the figures in column 3 and 4 for the year 1994 are slightly different from those in Table 6.4, as in Table 6.4 the sum of Renault Clio and Renault Supercinq were presented.

39 The values of external purchasing in MPTAS for 2000 and 2001 are estimations.

40 See Appendix A for the way we arrived at the numbers forwarded in the present paragraph.

41 See Appendix A for the way we arrived at the content of this table.

7   Discussion of research results and conclusions

42 Apparently, cancellation or non-prolonging of b2b relationships on behalf of a buyer does not lead to a prohibitively negative reputation of that buyer or mistrust among rival suppliers. In fact, it was observed that substitute suppliers engage again in co-located supply sites. The go/no-go decision behind this is apparently based on rational economic calculations and well-founded estimations regarding profit and supplementary business opportunities. Confidence in achieving long-lasting clientele from the prime buyer should first of all be seen as an intervening factor in these calculations and estimations.

43 This can, for example, be understood as it allows a buyer to tap into additional supplier learning effects due to suppliers' experiences with other b2b relationships.

44 Each organization involved depends on another organization's resources (see Column 4 Row 7 of Table 7.1, i.e. 'symmetry').

45 It is the sequence of actions between partners that matters (See Column 8 Row 7 of Table 7.1, i.e. 'irrelevant').

46 Shifts in governance structure are considered, not shifts of partners (See Column 3 Row 8 of Table 7.1, i.e. 'irrelevant').

47 Due to not taking into account the time dimension (See Column 4 Row 8 of Table 7.1, i.e. 'irrelevant').

48 For a further exposition of our views on the causal structures between key forces and events, on the one hand, and the behaviour of key actors of organization sets, on the other hand, see Chapters 3 and 4.

Bibliography

Adam-Ledunois, S. and S. Renault, Mouvement de création de parcs fournisseurs: Le cas de Renault Sandouville, Cockeas working paper, Bordeaux, 30–31 March 2001

Aláez, R., Bilbao, J., Camino, V. and J.C. Longas, *El sector de automoción: Nuevas tendencias en la organizacion productiva*, Madrid: Civitas, 1996

Aláez, R., Bilbao, J., Camino, V. and J.C. Longás, New tendencies in inter-firm relations in the automotive industry and their impact on European periphery suppliers – lessons from Spain, In: *European Urban and Regional Studies*, 1999, 6 (3), pp. 255–264

Albinski, M. (Ed.), *Onderzoekstypen in de sociologie*, Assen, the Netherlands: Van Gorcum, 1981

Alchian, A.A. and H. Demsetz, Production, information costs and economic organization, In: *American Economic Review*, 1972, 62, pp. 777–795

Alderson, W., *Dynamic Marketing Behavior: A Functionalist Theory of Marketing, Homewood*, IL: Richard D. Irwin, Inc., 1965

Aldrich, H.E., An Organization-environment perspective on cooperation and conflict in the manpower training system, In: Negandhi, A. (Ed.), *Conflict and Power in Complex Organizations*, Ohio: CARI, Kent State University, 1972, pp. 11–37

Aldrich, H.E., Resource dependence and inter-organizational relations: Local employment service offices and social services sector organizations, In: *Administration and Society*, 1976, 7 (4), pp. 419–454

Aldrich, H.E., *Organizations and Environments*, Englewood Cliffs, NJ: Prentice Hall, 1979

Alter, C. and J. Hage, *Organizations Working Together*, Newbury Park, CA: Sage, 1993

Altersohn, C., *De la sous-traîtance au partenariat industriel*, Paris: L'Harmattan, 1992

Amin, A. and J. Goddard (Eds), *Technological Change, Industrial Restructuring and Regional Development*, London: Allen & Unwin, 1986

Amin, A. and I. Smith, Vertical integration or disintegration? The case of the UK car parts industry, In: Law, C. (Ed.), *Restructuring the Automobile Industry: National and Regional Impacts*, London, 1991, pp. 169–199

Amit, R. and P.J.H. Schoemaker, Strategic assets and organizational rent, In: *Strategic Management Journal*, 1993, 14 (1), pp. 33–46

Anderson, E., Two firms, one frontier: On assessing joint venture performance, In: *Sloan Management Review*, 1990, 31 (2), pp. 19–30

Anderson, M. and J. Holmes, High-skill, low-wage manufacturing in North America. A case study from the automotive parts industry, In: *Regional studies*, 1995, 29, pp. 655–671

Andersson, U., Subsidiary network embeddedness – Integration, control and influence in the Multinational Corporation, Published dissertation No. 66, Department of Business Studies, Uppsala University, 1997

Andersson, U. and M. Forsgren, In search of centre of excellence: Network embeddedness and subsidiary roles in multinational corporations, In: *Management International Review*, 2000, 40 (4), pp. 329–350

Andersson, U. and C. Pahlberg, Subsidiary influence on strategic behaviour in MNCs: An empirical study, In: *International Business Review*, 1997, 6 (3), pp. 319–334

Automotive Information Centre – MIRA, *The MIRA Interiors Review*, May 1998

Automotive News Europe, *Guide to Purchasing, Supplement to Automotive News Europe*, 2000, 5 (8), Detroit: Crain Communications Inc.

Automotive News Europe, *Guide to Purchasing.*

Autorevista, *La industria de Castilla y Leon demanda personal mejor cualificado*, No. 2.126, Febrero 2001, pp. 50–62

Axelsson, B. and G. Easton (Eds), *Industrial Networks: A New View of Reality*, London: Routledge, 1992

Baker, D., Epstein, J. and B. Pollin, *Globalization and Progressive Economic Policy*, Cambridge: Cambridge University Press, 1998

Balcet, G. and A. Enrietti, Entre stratégies globales et régionales: Les investissements directs de Fiat Auto et de ses fournisseurs en Pologne, In: *Mondes en developpement*, 1996, pp. 24–95

Balcet, G. and A. Enrietti, Partnership and global production: Fiat's strategies in Turkey, Cockeas working paper, Bordeaux, 30–31 March 2001

Barley, S.R., Freeman, J. and R. Hybels, Strategic alliances in commercial biotechnology, In: Nohria, N. and R.G. Eccles (Eds), *Networks and Organizations: Structure, Form, and Action*, Boston, MA: Harvard Business School Press, 1992, pp. 311–345

Barney, J.B., Firm resources and sustained competitive advantage, In: *Journal of Management*, 1991, 17 (1), pp. 99–120

Bartlett, C.A., Multinational structural change: Evolution versus reorganization, In: Otterbeck, L. (Ed.), *The Management of Headquarters–Subsidiary Relationships in Multinational Corporations*, Aldershot, UK: Gower, 1981

Bartlett, C.A. and S. Ghoshal, Tap your subsidiaries for global reach, In: *Harvard Business Review*, 1986, 64 (6), pp. 87–94

Bartlett, C.A. and S. Ghoshal, *Managing Across Borders: The Transnational Solution*, Boston, MA: Harvard Business School Press, 1989

Becattini G., Dal settore industriale al distretto industriale, In: *Rivista di Economia e Politica Industriale*, 1979, 1, pp. 7–21

Becattini, G., El distrito industrial marshalliano como concepto socioeconomico, In: Pyke, F., Becattini, G. and W. Sengenberger (Eds), *Los distritos industriales y las pequeñas empresas I: Distritos industriales y cooperacion interempresarial en Italia*, Madrid: Ministerio de Trabajo y de Seguridad social, 1992, pp. 7–21

Beije, P., The role of international subcontracting in European corporate strategy, In: Dijck, J.J.J. Van and J.P.M. Groenewegen (Eds), *Changing Business Systems in Europe*, Brussel: VUB Press, 1994, pp. 45–60

Bélis-Bergouignan, M.-C., Bordenave, G. and Y. Lung, Hiérarchie et multinationalisation. Une application à l'industrie automobile, In: *Révue d'économie politique*, Sept.–Oct. 1994, 104 (5), pp. 739–762

Bélis-Bergouignan, M.-C., Bordenave, G. and Y. Lung, Global strategies in the automobile industry, In: *Regional Studies*, February 2000, 34 (1), pp. 41–55

Berkhofer, R.F., *A Behavioural Approach to Historical Analysis*, New York: Free Press, 1969

Bertrand Faure, Annual Report, Boulogne, various years

Best, M., *The New Competition, Institutions of Industrial Restructuring*, Cambridge: Polity Press, 1990

Birkinshaw, J.M., How multinational subsidiary mandates are gained and lost, In: *Journal of International Business Studies*, Third Quarter 1996, pp. 467–495

Birkinshaw, J.M. and N. Hood, An empirical study of development processes in foreign owned subsidiaries in Canada and Scotland, In: *Management International Review*, 1997, 37 (4), pp. 339–364

Birkinshaw, J.M. and N. Hood (Eds), *Multinational Corporate Evolution and Ssubsidiary Development*, London, 1998a

Birkinshaw, J.M. and N. Hood (Eds), Multinational subsidiary evolution: Capability and charter change in foreign-owned subsidiary companies, In: *Academy of Management Review*, 1998b, 23 (4), pp. 773–795

Bish, R.L., Intergovernmental relations in the United States: Some concepts and implications from a public choice perspective, In: Hanf, K. and F.W. Scharpf (Eds), *Interorganisational Policy Making: Limits to Coordination and Central Control*, London: Sage, 1978, pp. 19–36

Blau, P.M., *Exchange and Power in Social Life*, New York: John Willey and Sons Inc., 1964

Bloch, B., Globalization and downsizing in Germany, In: *M@n@gement*, 1999, 2 (3), Special Issue: Organization Downsizing, pp. 287–303

Bonzemba, E.L. and H. Okano, The effects of target costing implementation on an organizational culture in France, Paper presented at the 2nd Asian Interdisciplinary Research in Accounting Conference Osaka City University, Japan, 4–6 August 1998

Bordenave, G. and Y. Lung, Les nouvelles configurations de l'espace automobile européen, Bordeaux, 1993

Bordenave, G. and Y. Lung, New spatial configuration in the European automobile industry, In: *European Urban and Regional Studies*, 1996, 3, pp. 305–321

Boston Consulting Group, The evolving challenge for the European automotive components industry, Brussels, 1993

Boyer, R., New directions in management practices and work organizations. General principles and national trajectories, Paris, 1991

Boyer, R. and M. Freyssenet, The emergence of new industrial models, In: *Actes du GERPISA*, No. 15, 1995, pp. 75–142

Boyer, R. and M. Freyssenet, *Les modèles productifs*, Paris: La Découverte, 2000

Boyer, R. and M. Freyssenet, Les uns fusionnent, les autres pas. Quelles recompositions de l'industrie automobile mondiale?, Paper presented at the 9th GERPISA International colloquium, Paris, 2001

Brenner, N., Building 'Euro-regions': Locational politics and the political geography of neoliberalism in post-unification Germany, In: *European Urban and Regional Studies*, October 2000, 7 (4), pp. 319–347

Brinberg, D. and J. McGrath, *Validity and the Research Process*, Beverly Hills, CA: Sage Publications, 1985

Brucker, K. De, Verbeke, A. and W. Winkelmans, Sociaal-economische evaluatie van overheidsinvesteringen in transportinfrastructuur: Kritische analyse van het bestaande instrumentarium – Ontwikkeling van een eclectisch evaluatie-instrument, Leuven/Apeldoorn: Garant, 1998

Brusco, S., The Emilian model: Productive decentralisation and social integration, In: *Cambridge Journal of Economics*, 1982, 6, pp. 167–184

Buckley, P.J. and M. Casson, *The Future of the Multinational Enterprise*, London: MacMillan, 1976

Bueno Lastra, J. and A. Ramos Barrado, *La industria de automoviles de turismo*, Madrid: Servicio de Estudios Bolsa de Madrid, 1981

Busto, 1997: Interview with Mr. P. Busto Lacabe, Chief co-ordinator of serial production launchments at Volkswagen Navarra, 17 July 1997, Pamplona

Busto, 2000: Interview with Mr. P. Busto Lacabe, Chief co-ordinator of serial production launchments at Volkswagen Navarra, 16 November 2000, Pamplona

Cabus, P., De auto-industrie in België: Een reus op lemen voeten? In: *Planologisch nieuws*, 1997, 17, pp. 21–52

Caniëls, M.C.J., The geographic distribution of patents and value added across European regions, Paper presented at the 37th European ERSA Conference, Rome, 25–29 August 1997, Maastricht, 1997

Carillo, J. and S. Gonzalez Lopez, Relaciones cliente-proveedor de empresas auto-motrices alemanas en Mexico, In: *Actes du GERPISA*, février 1999, pp. 65–76

Carlson, S., *International Business Research*, Uppsala: Acta Universitatis Uppsaliensis, Studiae Oeconomiae Negotiorum, 1966

Carreras, A. and S. Estapé-Triay, Entrepreneurship, organization and economic performance among Spanish firms, 1930–1975. The case of the motor industry, DIGES Paper PB96-0301, Barcelona, 1998

Carrincazeaux, Chr. and Y. Lung, La proximité dans l'organisation de la conception des produits de l'automobile, In: *Actes du GERPISA*, No. 19, février 1997

Castells, M., *The Rise of the Network Society*, Oxford: Blackwell Publishers, 1996

Caves, R.E., International corporations: The industrial economics of foreign investment, In: *Economica*, 1971, 38 (February), pp. 1–27

CEC (Commission of the European Community), European Automobile Industry 1996, 1996, COM (96), 327, CEC, Brussels

CEC (Commission of the European Community) DG XXIII, Newsletter 122/NL, Brussels, October 1999

CEIN (Centro Europeo de Empresas e Innovacion de Navarra), 97 Navarr@ 1.800 empresas: Directorio e informe economico financiero, Pamplona, 1997

Chamber of Commerce of Valladolid, Actualidad economica, Del 30 de octubre al 5 de noviembre de 2000, pp. 236–237

Chanaron, J.-J., Globalisation-Spécialisation-Concentration, In: *La lettre du GERPISA*, No. 116, Octobre 1997

Chanaron, J.-J., Globalisation, division internationale du travail et relations constructeurs-fournisseurs, In: *Actes du GERPISA*, No. 25, 1999, pp. 5–23

Chanaron, J.-J. and Y. Lung, *L'économie de l'automobile*, Paris: La Découverte: Ashgate Publishing Co., 1995

Chanaron, J.-J. and Y. Lung, Product variety, productive organization and industrial models, In: Lung, Y., Chanaron, J.-J., Fujimoto, T. and D. Raff (Eds), *Coping with Variety: Flexible Productive Systems for Product Variety in the Auto Industry*, Aldershot: Ashgate Publishing Co., 1999, pp. 3–31

Child, J., Information technology, organization and the response to strategic challenges, In: *California Management Review*, Fall 1987, pp. 33–50

Cidaut, Informe de situacion del sector automocion en Castilla y Leon, Boecillo, Octubre 2000

Cidaut, 1993–2000, Boecillo, 2001

Contractor, F.J. and P. Lorange (Eds), *Cooperative Strategies in International Business*, San Francisco, CA: Pergamon, 1988

Cook, K.S. and R.M. Emerson, Power, equity and commitment in exchange networks, In: *American Sociological Review*, 1978, 43 (October), pp. 721–739

Cook, K.S. and R.M. Emerson, Exchange networks and the analysis of complex organization, In: *Research in the Sociology in Organizations*, 1984, 3, pp. 1–30

Cooke, Ph. and K. Morgan, *The Associational Economy: Firms, Regions, and Innovation*, Oxford: Oxford University Press, 1998

Cox, R.W., Global restructuring: Making sense of the changing international political economy, In: Stubbs, R. and G.R.D. Underhill (Eds), *Political Economy and the Changing Global Order*, Oxford: Oxford University Press, 2000, pp. 25–38

Cunningham, M.T., International marketing and purchasing of industrial goods: Features of a European research project, In: *European Journal of Marketing*, 1980, 14 (5/6), pp. 322–338

Cunningham, M.T. and K.L. Culligan, Competition and competitive groupings: An exploratory study in information technology markets, In: *Journal of Marketing Management*, 1988, 4, pp. 148–174

Cyert, R.M. and J.G. March, *A Behavioural Theory of the Firm* (2nd edn), Malden, MA: Blackwell Publishers Inc., 1963

DeBresson, C. and F. Amesse, Networks of innovators. A review and introduction to the issue, In: *Research Policy*, 1991, 20, pp. 363–379

Devinney, T.M., Book review of: Multinationals as flagship firms, by Alan M. Rugman and Joseph R. D'Cruz, In: *Academy of Management Review*, 2001, 26 (3), p. 462

Dicken, P., *Global shift: Transforming the World Economy*, New York: Guilford Press, 1998

Dicken, P. and S. Oberg, The Global Context: Europe in a world of dynamic economic and population change, In: *European Urban and Regional Studies*, 1996, 3 (2), pp. 101–120

Doz, Y.L. and G. Hamel, *Alliance Advantage: The Art of Creating Value through Partnering*, Boston, MA: Harvard Business School Press, 1998

Dudley, J.W., *Strategies for the Single Market*, London: Kogan Page, 1989

Dunning, J.H., Explaining changing patterns of international production: In defense of the eclectic theory, In: *Oxford Bulletin of Economics and Statistics*, 1979, 41, pp. 269–296

Dunning, J.H., *International Production and the Multinational Enterprise*, London: Allen and Unwin, 1981

Dunning, J.H., *Multinationals, Technology and Competitiveness*, London: Unwin Hyman, 1988

Dunning, J.H., The globalization of firms and the competitiveness of countries, In: Dunning, J.H., Kogut, B., and M. Blomstrom (Eds), *Globalization of Firms and Competitiveness of Nations*, Lund: Institute of economic research, Lund University Press, 1990, pp. 9–58

Dunning, J.H. and J. Cantwell, Directory of statistics of international investment and production, London: Macmillan, 1987

Dyer, J.H., Specialized supplier networks as a source of competitive advantage: Evidence from the auto industry, In: *Strategic Management Journal*, 1996, 17, pp. 271–291

Dyer, J.H., Effective interfirm collaboration: How firms minimize transaction costs and maximize transaction value, In: *Strategic Management Journal*, 1997, 18, pp. 535–556

Dyer, J.H. and W. Chu, *The Determinants and Economic Outcomes of Trust in Buyer–Supplier Relations*, Boston, MA: MIT/IMVP Publications, 1997

Dyer, J.H. and H. Singh, The relational view: Cooperative strategy and sources of interorganizational competitive advantage, In: *Academy of Management Review*, 1998, 23 (4), pp. 660–679

Dyer, J.H., Sung Cho, D. and W. Chu, Strategic supplier segmentation: The next 'Best Practice' in supply chain management, In: *California Management Review*, 1998, 40 (2), pp. 57–77

Easton, G., Industrial networks – a review, In: Wilson, D.T., Han, S.-L. and G.W. Holler (Eds), Proceedings of the 5th IMP Conference, Pennsylvania State University, 1989, pp. 161–182

Easton, G. and H. Håkansson, Markets as networks: Editorial introduction, In: *International Journal of Research in Marketing*, 1996, 13, pp. 407–413

Easton, G. and A. Lundgren, Changes in industrial networks as flow through nodes, In: Axelsson, B. and G. Easton (Eds), *Industrial Networks – a New View of Reality*, London: Routledge, 1992, pp. 88–104

Easton, G., Wilkinson, I. and Chr. Georgieva, Towards evolutionary models of industrial networks, In: Gemünden, H.G., Ritter, Th. and A. Walter (Eds), *Relationships and Networks in International Markets*, Oxford: Elsevier, 1997, pp. 273–293

Echo, L'., Un constructeur dont la production est chère, est en perte de vitesse sur la concurrence, Samedi 1er au lundi 3 mars 1997, p. 2

ECIA, Annual Report, Paris, various years

ECIA, Consolidated financial statements, Paris, various years

ECIA, Press release, Paris, various editions

Egelhoff, W.G., Strategy and structure in multinational corporations: A revision of the Stopford and Wells model, In: *Strategic Management Journal*, 1988, 9, pp. 1–14

Ellison, D.J., Clark, K.B., Fujimoto, T. and Y.-S. Hyun, Product development performance in the auto industry: 1990s update, Working paper, Harvard Business School, 1995

El Norte de Castilla, FASA paraliza su produccion por la falta de piezas a consecuencia de la huelga, 4 de octubre de 2000

El Norte de Castilla, FASA para por falta de motores diesel, 21 de noviembre de 2000

El Norte de Castilla, La cadena de montaje de FASA volvera a parar los dias 7 y 11, 3 de diciembre de 2000

El Norte de Castilla, FASA se paraliza de nuevo el lunes por falta de motores para vehiculos diesel, 9 de diciembre de 2000

El Norte de Castilla, Varias lineas de produccion de FASA vuelven a parar por falta de piezas, 11 de diciembre de 2000

El Norte de Castilla, La falta de piezas para los motores diesel impide reanudar el trabajo en FASA, 3 de enero de 2001

El Norte de Castilla, Proveedores mas cercanos, 14 de abril de 2002, p. 11

El País, Volkswagen adquiere la fabrica de SEAT en Pamplona, viernes 18 de marzo de 1994, p. 67

El País, La 'germanizacion' de la marca, domingo 15 de septiembre de 1996, suplemento Negocios, p. 3

El País, Herencia de tuercas y tornillos, domingo 2 de febrero de 1997a, suplemento Negocios, p. 10

El País, Volkswagen invertira 25.000 millones en Navarra el proximo año, lunes 1 de diciembre de 1997b, p. 67

El País, Renault aumenta su produccion en España en un 25%, domingo 31 de mayo de 1998, suplemento Negocios, p. 9

Emerson, R.M., Power-dependence relations, In: *American Journal of Sociology*, 1962, 27 (1), pp. 31–41

Emory, C., *Business Research Methods*, Homewood, IL: Richard D. Irwin Inc., 1985

Entreprises Rhône-Alpes, Inoplast passe le vitesse supérieure, septembre 2000 – No. 1439

Erro, J.L., 2001, In: Autorevista, Entrevista con José Luis Erro, director general de la factoria de Volkswagen Navarra, No. 2.142 Segunda quincena de septiembre 2001, pp. 36–40

Estall, R.C., Stock control in manufacturing: The just-in-time system and its locational implications, In: *Area*, 1985, 17 (2), pp. 129–133

European Monitoring Centre on Change, Trends and drivers of change in the European automotive industry: Mapping report, Dublin, 2004

Evan, W.M., The organization set: Towards a theory of interorganizational relations, In: Thomson, J. (Ed.), *Approaches to Organizational Design*, Pittsburgh, MA: University of Pittsburgh Press, 1966, pp. 175–190

Evan, W.M., An organizational-set model of interorganizational relations, In: Tuite, M.F., Radnor, M. and R.K. Chisholm (Eds), *Interorganizational Decision-Making*, Chicago, IL: Aldine Publishers, 1972, pp. 181–200

Evan, W.M., *Organization Theory*, London, 1974

Excal, La exportacion de Castilla y Leon: Una radiografia por productos y empresas, Valladolid, 1995, pp. 278–281

Expert Components Pamplona S.A.: Written correspondence with Mr. Vicente Bernad Coves (director gerente), 23 March 2000

Fama, E.F., Agency problems and theory of the firm, In: *Journal of Political Economy*, April 1980, 88, pp. 288–307

Fama, E.F. and M.C. Jensen, Agency problems and residual claims, In: *Journal of Law and Economics*, 1983, 26 (June), pp. 327–349

FASA (Fabricacion de Automoviles Sociedad Anonima), Memorias correspondientes a los ejercicios economicos de 1952–1964, Valladolid, 1953–1965

FASA Calidad: FASA-Renault, Direccion de Comunicacion, Calidad '92 Proveedores de FASA-Renault, Valladolid, 1989

FASA-Renault, Memorias y Balances/Informes Anuales correspondientes a los años 1965–2002, Madrid, 1966–2003

Faurecia, Annual Report, Boulogne, various years

Fernandez Arrufe, J.E. and R. Pedrosa Sanz, El impacto de FASA Renault en la economia de Castilla-Leon, In: Vazquez Barquero, A., Garofoli, G. and J.-P. Gilly (Eds), *Gran empresa y desarrollo economico*, Madrid: Síntesis, 1997, pp. 215–235

FET (Financieel-Economische Tijd), Mokerslag onder de viaduct, Zaterdag 1 maart 1997, p. 1 van Bijlage 'Zaterdag Tijd'

Fina, E. and A.M. Rugman, A test of internalization theory and internationalization theory: The Upjohn Company, In: *Management International Review*, 1996, 36 (3), pp. 199–213

Fine, Ch.H., Clockspeed: *Winning Industry Control in the Age of Temporary Advantage*, Reading, MA: Perseus Books, 1998

Fine, Ch.H. and D.E. Whitney, *Is the Make-Buy Decision Process a Core Competence?* Boston, MA: MIT/IMVP Publications, 1996

Florence, A., Supply chain interactions and supplier relationships, Paper presented at the 'Colloquium on Regional strategies for innovation and competitiveness in the automotive industry', Cardiff, 25–26 January 1996

Florida, R., Toward the learning region, In: *Futures*, 1995, 27 (5), pp. 527–536

Ford, D. (Ed.), *Understanding Business Markets*, London: Dryden Press, 1997

Ford, D., Developments of buyer-supplier relationships in industrial markets, In: *European Journal of Marketing*, 1980, 14, pp. 339–353

Forsgren, M., *Managing the Internationalisation Process: The Swedish Case*, London: Routledge, 1989

Forsgren, M., Some critical notes on learning in the Uppsala Internationalization Process Model, Working Paper Uppsala Universitet, 2000

Forsgren, M. and U. Holm, Internationalization of management – Dominance and distance, In: Buckley, P.J. and P.N. Ghauri (Eds), *The Internationalization of the firm – A reader*, London: Academic Press, 1993, pp. 337–349

Forsgren, M. and J. Johanson, *Managing Networks in International Business*, Philadelphia: Gordon & Breach, 1992

Forsgren, M., Holm, U. and J. Johanson, Internationalization of the second degree: The emergence of European-based centres in Swedish firms, In: Young, S. and J. Hamill (Eds), *Europe and the Multinationals*, Aldershot: Edward Elgar, 1992, pp. 235–253

Forsgren, M., Hägg, I., Håkansson, H., Johanson, J. and Mattsson, L.G., Firms in networks: A new perspective on competitive power, studia oeconomiae Negotiorum #38, Uppsala: Acta Universitatis Upsaliensis, 1995

Forsgren, M., Pedersen, T. and N.J. Foss, Accounting for the strengths of MNC subsidiaries: The case of foreign-owned firms in Denmark, In: *International Business Review*, 1999 (8), pp. 181–196

Freyssenet, M., The recomposition of the economic and political environment, In: La Lettre du GERPISA, No. 106, Octobre 1996

Freyssenet, M. and Y. Lung, Entre mondialisation et régionalisation: Quelles voies possibles pour l'internationalisation de l'industrie automobile? In: *Actes du GERPISA*, No. 18, Novembre 1996

Frigant, V. and Y. Lung, Geographical proximity and supplying relationships in modular production, In: *International Journal of Urban and Regional Research*, December 2002, 26 (4), pp. 742–755

Fujimoto, T., A note on the origin of the 'black box parts' practice in the Japanese motor vehicle industry, In: Shiomi, H. and K. Wada (Eds), *Fordism Transformed: The development of Production Methods in the Automobile Industry*, Oxford: Oxford University Press, 1995, pp. 184–216

Gadde, L.-E. and H. Hakansson, *Professional Purchasing*, London: Routledge, 1993

Gadde, L.-E. and L.-G. Mattsson, Stability and change in network relationships, In: *International Journal of Research and Marketing*, 1987 (4), pp. 29–41

Generalitat de Catalunya, Dossier: El rol estratègic de les filials catalanes de multinacionals industrials estrangeres, Barcelona, 2001

Gersick, C.J.G., Revolutionary change theories: A multilevel exploration of the punctuated equilibrium paradigm, In: *Academy of Management Review*, 1991, 16 (1), pp. 10–36

Ghoshal, S. and C.A. Bartlett , The multinational corporation as an interorganizational network, In: *Academy of Management Review*, 1990, 15 (4), pp. 603–625

Ghoshal, S. and C.A. Bartlett, Multinational corporation as an interorganizational network, In: Ghoshal, S. and D.E. Westney (Eds), *Organization Theory and the*

Multinational Corporation, London: Macmillan and New York: St Martins Press, 1993, pp. 77–104

Ghoshal, S. and N. Nohria, Internal differentiation within multinational corporations, *Strategic Management Journal*, 1989, 10, 323–337

Gilodi, 2001: Interview with Mr. A. Gilodi, Member of Renault's Corporate Purchasing Management, 7 June 2001, Technocentre Renault Guyancourt

Gobierno Foral de Navarra, export.navarra.net – automocion (website), Pamplona, 1998

Gobierno Foral de Navarra, www.navarra.net/industria – Fabricacion de partes, piezas y acesorios no electricos para vehiculos de motor (website), Pamplona, 2000a

Gobierno Foral de Navarra, Catalogo Industrial de Navarra – automotive index, Pamplona, 2000b

Gomes-Casseres, B., Group versus group: How alliance networks compete, In: *Harvard Business Review*, 1994, 4, pp. 62–74

Gonzalez de la Fé, P., SEAT: Desarrollo y privatización de una empresa automovilística española en un contexto de internacionalización creciente, Paper presented at the 'VII Congreso de la Asociacion de Historia Economica, Sesión: La automoción en la industrialización española: Aspectos de demanda y oferta', Zaragoza, 19 de septiembre de 2001

Gonzalez Lopez, S., Estrategias corporativas y espacios locales: Las empresas automotrices en la zona de Toluca, Mexico, In: *Actes du GERPISA*, No. 29, avril 2000, pp. 67–90

Gorgeu, A. and R. Mathieu, Les liens de Renault avec ses fournisseurs: Equipementiers et sous-traîtants, In: *Actes du GERPISA*, No. 14, 1995, pp. 41–58

Grabher, G., (Ed.) *The Embedded Firm: On the Socio-Economics of Industrial Networks*, London: Routledge, 1993

Granovetter, M., Economic action and social structure: The problem of embeddedness, In: *American Journal of Sociology*, 1985, 91, pp. 481–510

Grant, R.M., *Contemporary Strategy Analyses: Concepts, Techniques, Application*, Cambridge, MA: Harvard University Press, 1991

Groenewegen, J. and J.J. Vromen, A case for theoretical pluralism, In: Groenewegen, J. (Ed.), *Transaction Cost Economics and beyond*, Dordrecht: Kluwer Academic Publishing, 1996, pp. 365–380

Grohn, 2002: Interview with Mr. F. Grohn, Member of Volkswagen's corporate management for global and forward sourcing, 21 March 2002, Wolfsburg

Grossman, S. and O. Hart, The costs and benefits of ownership: A theory of vertical and lateral integration, In: *Journal of Political Economy*, 1986, 94 (August), pp. 691–719

Grupo Antolín, Retos y oportunidades de los suministradores, Presentation by Francisco Cervera from Grupo Antolín at 'Seminario sobre Modelos de agrupamiento de proveedores de automocion', Parque Tecnologico de Castilla y Leon (Boecillo), 19 de Septiembre 2000

Hadjikhani, A. and H. Håkansson, Political actions in business networks: A Swedish case, In: *International Journal of Research in Marketing*, 1996, 13, pp. 431–447

Hägg, I. and J. Johansson (Eds), *Företag i nätverk – en ny syn på konkurrenskraft*, Stockholm: SNS, 1982

Hakanson, L., Towards a theory of location and corporate growth, In: Hamilton, F.E.I. and G.J.R. Linge (Eds), *Spatial Analysis, Industry and the Industrial Eenvironment. Vol. I. Industrial Systems*, Chichester: John Wiley and Sons, 1979, pp. 115–138

Håkansson, H. (Ed.), *International Marketing and Purchasing of Industrial Goods: An Interaction Approach*, Chichester: John Wiley and Sons, 1982

Håkansson, H. (Ed.), *Industrial Technological Development: A Network Approach*, Kent: Croom Helm, 1987

Håkansson, H., *Corporate Technological Behaviour. Co-operation and Networks*, London: Routledge, 1989

Håkansson, H., Networks as mechanism to develop resources, In: Beije, P., Groenewegen, J. and O. Nuys (Eds), *Networking in Dutch Industries*, Leuven/Apeldoorn: Garant/Siswo, 1993, pp. 207–223

Håkansson, H. and B. Henders, Network dynamics: Forces and process underlying evolution and revolution in business networks, In: Moller, K. and D. Wilson (Eds), *Business Marketing: An Interaction and Network Perspective*, Boston, MA: Kluwer, 1995, pp. 139–156

Håkansson, H. and J. Johanson, Formal and informal cooperation strategies in international industrial networks, In: Contractor, F.J. and P. Lorange (Eds), *Cooperative Strategies in International Business*, San Francisco, CA: Pergamon, 1988

Håkansson, H. and J. Johanson, The network as a governance structure: Interfirm cooperation beyond markets and hierarchies, In: Grabher, G. (Ed.), *The Embedded Firm*, London: Routledge, 1993, pp. 35–51

Håkansson, H. and I. Shehota, No business is an island: The network concept of business strategy, In: *Scandinavian Journal of Management*, 1989, 5 (3), pp. 187–200

Håkansson, H. and I. Shehota, *Developing Relationships in Business Networks*, London: Routledge, 1995

Håkansson, H., Johanson, J. and B. Wootz, Influence tactics in buyer-seller processes, In: *Industrial Marketing Management*, 1977 (5), pp. 319–332

Halinen, A., Salmi, A. and V. Havila, From dyadic change to changing business networks: An analytical framework, In: *Journal of Management Studies*, 36 (6), November 1999, pp. 779–794

Harrison, B., Industrial districts: Old wine in new bottles, In: *Regional studies*, 1992, 26 (5), pp. 469–483

Hart, O. and J. Moore, Property rights and the nature of the firm, In: *Journal of Political Economy*, 1990, 98, pp. 1119–1158

Heckscher, E., The effect of foreign trade on the distribution of income, In: *Economisk Tidskrift*, 1919, 21, pp. 497–512

Hedlund, G., Autonomy of subsidiaries and formalization of headquarters-subsidiary relationships in Swedish MNCs, In: Otterbeck, L. (Ed.), *The Management of Headquarters–Subsidiary Relations in Multinational Corporations*, Aldershot: Gower, 1981

Hedlund, G., The hypermodern MNC – a heterarchy? In: *Human Resources Management*, Spring 1986, 25 (1), pp. 9–35

Helper, S., Supplier relations and innovation: Theory and application to the US auto industry, Thesis, Harvard University, 1987

Helper, S., How much has really changed between US auto-makers and their suppliers?, In: *Sloan Management Review*, Summer issue 1991, pp. 15–28

Hertz, S., Towards more integrated industrial networks, In: Axelsson, B. and G. Easton (Eds), *Industrial Networks: A New View of Reality*, London: Routledge, 1992, chapter 6

Hertz, S., The internationalization process of freight transport companies, Thesis, Stockholm School of Economics, The Economic Research Institute, Stockholm, 1993

Hirschmann, A., *Exit, Voice and Loyalty*, Cambridge, MA: Harvard University Press, 1970

Hodges, U.W. and R. Van Tulder, The chemistry of dependence: Cars, chemicals and technological change in the United States, Germany and Japan, Working paper 69, Berkeley, CA, 1994

Hofer, C.W. and D. Schendel, *Strategy Formulation: Analytical Concepts*, St. Paul, MN: West Publishing, 1978

Holm, U., Internationalization of the second degree, Thesis, Uppsala University, 1994

Holm, U., Johanson, J. and P. Thilenius, Headquarters' knowledge of subsidiary network contexts in the multinational corporation, In: *International Studies of Management and Organization*, Spring–Summer 1995, 25 (1/2), pp. 97–119

Holmström, B. and J. Roberts, The boundaries of the firm revisited, In: *Journal of Economic Perspectives*, Fall 1998, 12 (4), pp. 73–94

Hood, N. and J.E. Vahlne (Eds), *Strategies in Global Competition*, New York: Croom Helm, 1988

Hoover's Online Europe Ltd, Sylea SA (internet source), 2002

Hudson, R. and E.W. Schamp (Eds), *Towards a New Map of Automobile Manufacturing in Europe? New Production Concepts and Regional Restructuring*, Frankfurt am Main: Axel Springer Verlag, 1995

Hymer, S.H., *The International Operations of National Firms: A Study of Direct Investment*, Cambridge, MA: The MIT Press, 1976 (original: 1960)

IFA: Invest in France Agency North America, Johnson Controls activities report 1st quarter 1999 (internet source), 1999

ITEC, A industria automovel em Espanha, Noticias, semana 1, 1998, Dossier 04

Jarillo, J.C., On strategic networks, In: *Strategic Management Journal*, 1988, 9, pp. 31–41

Jarillo, J.C., *Strategic Networks: Creating the Borderless Organization*, Oxford: Butterworth-Heinemann Ltd, 1993

Jarillo, J.C. and J. Martinez, Different roles for subsidiaries: The case of multi-national corporations, In: *Strategic Management Journal*, 1990, 11, pp. 501–512

Jensen, M. and W. Meckling, Theory of the firm: Managerial behavior, agency cost, and capital structure, In: *Journal of Financial Economics*, October 1976, 3, pp. 305–360

Johanson, J. and L.-G. Mattsson, Interorganizational relations in industrial systems – a network approach compared with the transaction cost approach, working paper, Uppsala, 1984

Johanson, J. and L.-G. Mattsson, Interorganizational relations in industrial systems: A network approach compared with the transaction cost approach, In: *International Studies of Management and Organization*, 1987, XVII (1), pp. 34–48

Johanson, J. and L.-G. Mattsson, Internationalisation in industrial systemsa network approach, In: Hood, N. and J.E. Vahlne (Eds), *Strategies in Global Competition*, New York: Croom Helm, 1988, pp. 287–314

Johanson, J. and L.-G. Mattsson, Interorganizational relations in industrial systems: A network approach compared with the transactions-cost approach, In: Thompson, G., Frances, J., Levacic, R. and J. Mitchell (Eds), *Markets, Hierarchies and Networks*, London: Sage, 1991, pp. 256–264

Johanson, J. and L.-G. Mattsson, Network positions and strategic action – an analytical framework, In: Ford, D. (Ed.), *Understanding Business Markets: Interaction, Relationships and Networks* 2, 1997, London: The Dryden Press, pp. 176–193

Johanson, J. and J. Vahlne, The internationalization process of the firm – a model of knowledge development and increasing foreign market commitment, In: *Journal of International Business Studies*, 1977, 8 (1), pp. 23–32

Johanson, J. and J. Vahlne, The mechanism of internationalization, In: *International Marketing Review*, 1990, 7 (4), pp. 11–24

Johanson, J. and F. Wiedersheim-Paul, The internationalization of the firm – four Swedish cases, In: *Journal of Management Studies*, 1975, 12 (3), pp. 305–322

Johnson Controls, Automotive market leadership, Milwaukee, WI, 2001

Johnston, R. and P.R. Lawrence, Beyond vertical integration – The rise of the value added partnership, In: *Harvard Business Review*, July–August 1988, pp. 94–101

Jong, G. De and B. Nooteboom, *The Causal Structure of Long-Term Supply Relationships*, Deventer: Kluwer, 2000

Junta de Castilla y Leon, www.hinter-land.com: capitulos 1–3 y anexo, Valladolid, 2000

Junta de Castilla y Leon - CEH D.G. de Estadistica, Resultados de la Consulta de la Base de Datos de Comercio Exterior, Valladolid, 2001

Jüttner, U. and L.E. Schlange, A network approach to strategy, In: *International Journal of Research in Marketing*, 1996, 13, pp. 479–494

Kalawani, M. and N. Narayandas, Long-term manufacturer–supplier relationship: Do they pay off for supplier firms? In: *Journal of Marketing*, 1995, 59 (1), pp. 1–16

Kamp, B.P.G., Catalunya: Quo vadis? Unpublished Master Thesis, Department of Policy and Organization Science, Tilburg, 1994

Kamp, B.P.G., A visionary approach on the evolution of buyer–supplier relationships in conception and commercialisation of automobiles – implications of car assembly plants' and component manufacturers' philosophies and postures, Paper presented at the 8th GERPISA International colloquium, Paris, 2000

Kaufmann, S., *Origins of Order: Self Organisation and Selection in Evolution*, New York: Oxford University Press, 1992

Kaufmann, S., *At Home in the Universe*, Oxford: Oxford University Press, 1995

Kerlinger, F., *Foundations of Behavioural Research*, London: Rinehart and Winston, 1977

Kesseler, A., Evolution of supplier relations in European automotive industry: Product development challenge for a first tier supplier, In: *Actes du GERPISA*, No. 19, 1997, Article 6

Kindleberger, C.P., *American Business Abroad*, New Haven, CT: Yale University Press, 1969

King, G., Keohane, R. and S. Verba, *Designing Social Inquiry: Scientific Interference in Qualitative Research*, Princeton, NJ: Princeton University Press, 1994

Knoke, D. and J.H. Kuklinski, *Network Analysis*, Beverly Hills, CA: Sage, 1982

Kochan, T.A., Determinants of power boundary units in an interorganizational bargaining relation, In: *Administrative Science Quarterly*, 1975, 20, pp. 435–452

Kogut, B., Joint ventures: Theoretical and empirical perspectives, In: *Strategic Management Journal*, 1988, 9, pp. 319–332

Kogut, B. and U. Zander, Knowledge of the firm and the evolutionary theory of the multinational corporation, In: *Journal of International Business Studies*, 1995, 24 (4), pp. 625–645

Kotler, Ph., *Marketing Management*, Englewood Cliffs, NJ: Prentice-Hall, 1980

Krugman, P., *Geography and Trade*, Leuven: Leuven University Press, 1991

Laage-Hellman, J., *Business Networks in Japan: Supplier–Customer Interaction in Product Development*, London: Routledge, 1997

Lagendijk, A., The impact of internationalisation and rationalisation of production on the Spanish automobile industry, 1950–90, In: *Environment and Planning A*, 1994, 27 (2), pp. 321–343

Lagendijk, A., The foreign takeover of the Spanish automobile industry: A growth analysis of internationalization, In: *Regional Studies*, 1995, 29 (4), pp. 381–393

Laigle, L., The trajectories of internationalization of French suppliers: The trajectory of Valeo, In: *Actes du GERPISA*, No. 22, février 1997, pp. 55–68

La Lettre du GERPISA, No. 115–162, juillet 1997 – Septembre–Octobre 2002, Evry

Lamming, R., *Beyond Partnership: Strategies for Innovation and Lean Supply*, London: Prentice-Hall, 1993

Lamming, R. and A. Cox (Eds), *Strategic Procurement Management in the 1990s*, London: Earlsgate Press, 1995

Lane, Chr., *Management and Labor in Europe: The Industrial Enterprise in Germany*, Britain and France, Hants: Edward Elgar, 1989

Lane, P.J. and M. Lubatkin, Relative absorptive capacity and interorganizational learning, In: *Strategic Management Journal*, 1998, 19 (5), pp. 461–477

Langlois, R.N., Economic change and the boundaries of the firm, In: *Journal of Institutional and Theoretical Economics*, 1988, 144, pp. 635–657

Langlois, R.N. and P.L. Robertson, Explaining vertical integration: Lessons from the American automobile industry, In: *Journal of Economic History*, 1989, XLIX (2), pp. 361–375

Langlois, R.N. and P.L. Robertson, *Firms, Markets, and Economic Change: A Dynamic Theory of Business Institutions*, London: Routledge, 1995

Larsson, A., The changing geographical structure of the domestic supplier-system of Volvo Automotive in Sweden, Paper presented at the 8th International colloquium GERPISA Paris, 2000

La Vanguardia, VW compra a SEAT la planta de Landaben por 98.000 millones, viernes 18 de marzo de 1994

Layan, J.-B., Transformacion y resurgimiento de los fabricantes franceses: Renault y PSA, In: *Economia Industrial*, 1997, 315 (III), pp. 139–150

Layan, J.-B., Existe-t-il un modèle d'intégration Hispanique? In: *Actes du GERPISA*, No. 28, février 2000

Layan, J.-B. and Y. Lung, Péricentralité ou centralité périphérique: La globalisation de l'industrie automobile laisse-t-elle une place aux intégrations régionales périphériques, In: Célimène, F. and C. Lacour (Eds), *L'intégration régionales des espaces*, Paris: Economica, 1995, pp. 255–270

Leborgne, D. and A. Lipietz, L'après-fordisme et son espace, In: *Les temps modernes*, 1988, 501, pp. 75–114

Leborgne, D. and A. Lipietz, Idées fausses et questions ouvertes de l'après-fordisme, In: *Espaces et sociétés*, 1991, pp. 39–68

Le Monde, Renault réorganise sa production européenne et ferme son usine belge, Samedi 1er mars 1997, p. 20

Levine, S. and P.E. White, Exchange as a conceptual framework for the study of interorganizational relationships, In: *Administrative Science Quarterly*, 1961, 5, pp. 583–601

Levitt, B. and J.G. March, Organizational learning, In: *Annual Review of Sociology*, 1988, 14, pp. 319–340

Lieberman, S., *The Contemporary Spanish Economy: A Historical Perspective*, London: George Allen & Unwin, 1982

Lieberman, M.B. and D.B. Montgomery, First-mover advantages, In: *Strategic Management Journal*, 1988, 9 (1), pp. 41–58

Liker, J.K. and Th.Y. Choi, Building deep supplier relationships, In: *Harvard Business Review*, December 2004, 82 (12), pp. 104–112

Lipietz, A., *Le capital et son espace*, Paris: Maspéro, 1977

Lipietz, A., *Mirages et miracles. Problèmes de l'industrialisation dans le tiers monde*, Paris: La Découverte, 1985

Lloyd, De, VW centraliseert Polo-productie in Spanje, Antwerpen, 23 Juni 1998

Lloyd, De, Peugeot-dochter Faurecia neemt Sommer Allibert over, Antwerpen, 26 Oktober 2000

Logistica Navarra, 1996: Interview with Mr. J. Goñi and Mr. J.A. Prieto, Executives of the Human Resources and Production department, 16 July 1996, Pamplona

Longás, J.C., *Organización productiva y localización. La industria del automóvil en Navarra*, Pamplona: Gobierno de Navarra, 1998

Longas, 2000: Interview with Mr. J.C. Longas, Professor at the Department of Economy, Universidad Pública de Navarra, 16 November 2000, Pamplona

Lorenzoni, G. and C. Baden-Fuller, Creating a Strategic Center to Manage a Web of partners, Working paper, June, University of Bath, School of Management, Bath BA2 7AY, 1993

Lorenzoni, G. and C. Baden-Fuller, Creating a strategic center to manage a web of partners, In: *California Management Review*, 1995, 37 (3), pp. 146–163

Ludvigsen Associates, Trends in the development of supplier parks in Western Europe, Presentation by Graham Sayles Cervera from Ludvigsen Associates at 'Seminario sobre Modelos de agrupamiento de proveedores de automocion', Parque Tecnologico de Castilla y Leon (Boecillo), 19 de Septiembre 2000

Lundgren, A., Technological innovation and the emergence and evolution of industrial networks: The case of digital image technology in Sweden, *Industrial Networks*, Vol. 5, Greenwich Connecticut: JAI Press, 1993, pp. 145–170

Lung, Y., Modèles industriels et géographie de la production, Cahiers de la recherche de l'IERSO, Pessac, 1995

Lung, Y., The co-ordination of competencies and knowledge: A critical issue for regional automotive systems, In: *Actes du GERPISA*, No. 31, 2001, pp. 91–108

Lung, Y. and V. Frigant, Modularisation et concentration de l'industrie équipementière en Europe, Paper presented at the 9th International colloquium GERPISA Paris, 2001

Lunke Navarra S.A., Written correspondence with Mr. Luis Rodriguez Carrillo (director gerente), 24 March 2000

Luostarinen, R., *Internationalization of the firm*, Helsinki: Helsinki School of Economics, 1979

Luostarinen, R. and L.S. Welch, *International Business Operations*, Helsinki: Kyriiri Oy, 1990

Macaulay, S., Non-contractual relations in business, In: *American Sociological Review*, 1963, 28, pp. 55–70

McKiernan, P., *Strategies of growth: Maturity, Recovery and Internationalization*, London: Routledge, 1992

Mahoney, J.T. and J.R. Pandian, The resource-based view within the conversation of strategic management, In: *Strategic Management Journal*, 1992, 13 (5), pp. 363–380

Mair, A., Just-in-time manufacturing and the spatial structure of the automobile industry, Working paper Department of Geography – University of Durham, NC, 1991a

Mair, A., The just-in-time strategy for local economic development, Working paper Department of Geography – University of Durham, NC, 1991b

Mandos: FASA Renault, Direccion de Comunicacion, Comunicacion Mandos / Info Mandos, Nos. 6–129, Diciembre 1989–Abril 2001, Valladolid

Manero Miguel, 1997: Interview with Prof. Dr. F. Manero Miguel, Professor of Department of Geografía y Ordenación del Territorio, Universidad de Valladolid, 21 July 1997, Valladolid

Manero Miguel, F. and H . Pascual Ruiz de Valdepeñas, Castilla y Leon ante el cambio industrial: Ajustes productivos y estrategias de desarrollo, In: *Junta de Castilla y Leon Consejería de Economia y Hacienda, La economia de Castilla y Leon ante el siglo XXI*, Valladolid: Junta de Castilla y Leon, 1998, pp. 109–166

Markusen, A., Studying regions by studying firms, In: *Professional Geographer*, 1994, 46, pp. 477–490

Marrodan, H. 1996: Interview with Mr. H. Marrodan, Director of logistics at Volkswagen Navarra, 16 July 1996, Pamplona

Marrodan, H., 1999: In: Volkswagen Navarra, S.A., Apunto, Nuestros proveedores, cada vez mas cerca, Numero 21, pp. 34–37

Marx, R., Zilbovicius, M. and M.S. Salerno, The 'modular consortium' in a new VW truck plan in Brazil: New forms of assembler and suppliers relationship, In: *Integrated Manufacturing Systems*, 1997, 8 (5), pp. 292–298

Mattsson, L.-G., An application of a network approach to marketing: Defending and changing market positions, In: Dholakia, N. and J. Arndt (Eds), *Changing the Course of Marketing: Alternative Paradigms for Widening Marketing Theory, Research in Marketing*, Greenwich Connecticut: JAI Press, 1985, pp. 263–288

Mattsson, L.-G., Indirect relations in industrial networks – A conceptual analysis of their strategic significance, Paper presented at the 3rd International I.M.P. Research Seminar on International Marketing, 1986

Mattson L.-G. and S. Hultén (Eds), *Företag och marknader i förändring, dynamik i nätverk*, Stockholm: Nerenius and Santérus Förlag, 1994

Maurice, M., Sellier, F. and J.-J. Sylvestre, *The Social Foundations of Industrial Power: A Comparison of France and Germany*, London: MIT Press, 1986

Meeus, M.Th. and L.A.G. Oerlemans, Economic network research: A methodological state of the art, In: Beije, P., Groenewegen, J. and O. Nuys (Eds), *Networking in Dutch Industries*, Leuven/Apeldoorn: Garant/Siswo, 1993, pp. 37–67

Melin, L., Internationalization as a strategy process, In: *Strategic Management Journal*, 1992, 13, pp. 99–118

Mercer/Fraunhofer Institute, FAST 2015, Stuttgart: Fraunhofer Institute, 2005

Mill, J.S., *Principles of Political Economy*, London, 1848

Miller, R., Global R&D networks and large-scale innovations: The case of the automobile industry, In: *Research Policy*, 1994, 23, pp. 27–46

Mitchell, W. and K. Singh, Business survival of firms using hybrid relationships in The American hospital software systems industry, 1961–1991, In: *Strategic Management Journal*, 1996, 17 (3): 169–195

Montgomery, C.A., Of diamonds and rust: A new look at resources, In: Montgomery, C.A. (Ed.), *Resource-based and Evolutionary Theories of the Firm: Towards a Synthesis*, Norwell, MA: Kluwer Academic Publishing, 1995, pp. 251–268

Morgan, K., The learning region: Institutions, innovation and regional renewal, In: *Regional Studies*, 1997, 31 (5), pp. 491–503

Morris, J. and R. Imrie, *Transforming Buyer–Supplier Relations*, London: Macmillan, 1992

Muruzabal, 2000: Interview with Mr. F.J. Muruzabal, Commercial Director of Lingotes Especiales, 15 November 2000, Valladolid

Navarra empresarial, La industria del automóvil en Navarra: La locomotora que tira de la economia navarra, Burlada, diciembre 1994, pp. 11–38

Nishiguchi, T., Governing competitive supplier relations: New auto-industry evidence, Cape Cod, MA: MIT/IMVP Annual sponsors' briefing meeting, 1993

Nohria, N., Introduction, In: Nohria, N. and R.G. Eccles (Eds), *Networks and Organizations: Structure, Form, and Action*, Boston, MA: Harvard Business School Press, 1992, pp. 4–8

Nohria, N. and R.G. Eccles (Eds), *Networks and Organizations: Structure, Form, and Action*, Boston, MA: Harvard Business School Press, 1992

Noorderhaven, N.G., *Strategic Decision Making*, Wokingham: Addison-Wesley Publishing Company, 1995

Nooteboom, B., Trust, opportunism and governance: A process and control model, In: *Organization Studies*, 1996, 17 (5), pp. 985–1010

Nooteboom, B., *Management van Partnerships*, Schoonhoven: Academic service, 1998

Nooteboom, B., A Balanced Theory of Sourcing, Collaboration and Networks, ERIM Report Series Reference No. ERS-2002-24-ORG, March 2002

Nooteboom, B., Berger, J. and N.G. Noorderhaven, Effects of trust and governance on relational risk, In: *Academy of Management Journal*, 1997, 40 (2), pp. 308–338

Ohlin, B., *Interregional and International Trade*, Cambridge, MA: Harvard University Press, 1933

Ohmae, K., *Triad power: The Coming Shape of Global Competition*, New York: Free Press, 1985

Ohmae, K., Managing in a Borderless World, In: *Harvard Business Review*, 1989, May–June, pp. 152–161

Ohmae, K., The rise of the region state, In: *Foreign Affairs*, 1993, pp. 78–87

O hUallachain, B., Vertical integration in American manufacturing: Evidence for the 1980s, In: *Professional Geographer*, 1996, 48, pp. 343–356

O hUallachain, B., Restructuring the American semiconductor industry: Vertical integration of design houses and wafer fabrications, In: *Annals of the Association of American Geographers*, 1997, 87, pp. 217–238

O hUallachain, B. and D. Wasserman, Vertical integration in a lean supply chain: Brazilian automobile components parts, In: *Economic Geography*, 1999, 75 (1), pp. 21–43

Oliver, Chr., Determinants of interorganizational relationships: Integration and future directions, In: *Academy of Management Review*, 1990, 15, pp. 241–265

Ortiz-Villajos, J.M., Evolucion historica de la industria de equipos y componentes de automocion, Paper presented at the 'VII Congreso de la Asociacion de Historia Economica, Sesión: La automoción en la industrialización española: Aspectos de demanda y oferta', Zaragoza, 19 de septiembre de 2001

Pallarès-Barbera, M., *Changing Production Systems and Spatial Reaction: The Automobile Industry in Spain*, Bellaterra: Universitat Autonoma de Barcelona, Department of Geography, 1996

Pallarès-Barbera, M., Changing production systems: The automobile industry in Spain, In: *Economic Geography*, 1998, 74 (4), pp. 344–359

Parnière, 2001: Interview with Mr. P. Parnière, Vice Président Stratégie – direction des achats, 6 June 2001, Boulogne Billancourt

Pedrosa Sanz, R., Aproximación al estudio del capital extranjero en Castilla y León, Valladolid: Institución Cultural Simancas, 1983

Pedrosa Sanz, R., Les effets indirects sur l'emploi de FASA-Renault à Valladolid (Espagne), In: Dupuy, C. and J. Savary (Eds), *Les effets indirects des entreprises multinationales sur l'emploi des pays d'accueil*, Bureau international du Travail, Programme des entreprises multinationales, Document de travail No. 72, Genève, 1993, pp. 98–117

Pedrosa Sanz, R., 1997: Interview with Prof. Dr. R. Pedrosa Sanz, Professor at the Faculty of Economics, University of Valladolid, 21 July 1997, Valladolid

Péran Gonzalez, 1997: Interview with Mr. J. R. Perán González, Director of Cartif-UVA (Technology Park of Boecillo), 21 July 1997, Valladolid

Perfiles 3, p. 3: Nuevo Renault Clio, In: Factoria Carroceria-Montaje Valladolid, Perfiles, No. 3, Junio 2001, p. 3

Perfiles 3, p. 11: Taller de pintura de paragolpes, In: Factoria Carroceria-Montaje Valladolid, Perfiles, No. 3, Junio 2001, p. 11

Perlmutter, H.V., L'entreprise internationale – trois conceptions, In: *Revue économique et social*, 1965, 23, pp. 151–165

Perry, M.K., Vertical Integration, In: Schmalensee, R. and R. Willig (Eds), *Handbook of Industrial Organization*, Amsterdam: North-Holland Press, 1989, pp. 185–255

Pettigrew, A.M., Longitudinal field research on change: Theory and practice, In: *Organization Science*, 1990, 1 (3), pp. 267–292

Pfeffer, J., *Organizational Design*, Arlington Heights, 1978

Pfeffer, J. and G.R. Salancik, *The External Control of Organizations: A Resource Dependence Perspective*, New York: Harper & Row Publishers, 1978

Phelps, N.A. and C. Fuller, Multinationals, intracorporate competition, and regional development, In: *Economic Geography*, 2000, pp. 224–243

Pilorusso, F., *Finding a Place in the Automotive Supplier Hierarchy in the year 2000 and Beyond*, IMVP, Boston, MA: MIT/IMVP Publications, 1997

Piore, M. and Ch. Sabel, *The Second Industrial Divide*, New York: Basic Books, 1984

Plastic Omnium, Annual Report, Paris-Levallois, various years

Plastic Omnium, Shareholders Letter No. 7, Paris-Levallois, June 2001

Porter, M.E., *The Competitive Advantages of Nations*, New York: Free Press, 1990

Porter, M.E. and V.E. Millar, How information gives you competitive advantage, In: *Harvard Business Review*, July–August 1985, 4, pp. 149–160

Powell, W.W., Neither market nor hierarchy: Network forms of organization, In: *Research in Organizational Behaviour*, 1990, 12, pp. 295–336

Powell, W.W. and L. Smith-Doerr, Networks and economic life, In: Smelser, N.J. and R. Swedberg (Eds), *The Handbook of Economic Sociology*, Princeton NJ, 1994, pp. 368–402

Prahalad, C.K. and Y.L. Doz, An approach to strategic control in MNCs, In: *Sloan Management Review*, Summer 1981, pp. 5–13

Prahalad, C.K. and G. Hamel, The core competence of the organization, In: *Harvard Business Review*, 1990, pp. 79–91

Pries, L., The dialectics of automobile assemblers and suppliers restructuring and globalization of the German 'big three', In: *Actes du GERPISA*, février 1999, pp. 77–92

PSA Peugeot Citroën, Comptes consolidés, Paris, various years

Pyke, F., Becattini, G. and W. Sengenberger, Los distritos industriales y las pequeñas empresas I, Madrid: Ministerio de Trabajo y de Seguridad Social, 1992

Quintard, A. and Y. De Rongé (Eds), *Filialisation d'activities d'enterprises – Stratégie et gestion*, Bruxelles, 1992

Renault, Annual Report/Rapport Annuel 1985–2002, Paris, 1986–2003

Renault, Atlas économique éditions 1990–2001, Paris, 1991–2003

Renault, Financial Report 1985–2002, Paris, 1986F–2003F

Renault, Global Magazine, Nos. 1–11 (Febrero 2001–Marzo 2002), Madrid, 2001–2002

Renault, R & D – La route de l'innovation, Nos. 18–19 (Octobre 2000–Janvier 2001), Paris, 2000–2001

Renfe, 2000, In: Diario de Navarra, Renfe triplica en seis meses el transporte de componentes de automocion desde Landaben, jueves 24 de agosto de 2000

Rey del Castillo, C.M., La industria española del automovil y la globalizacion, In: *Economia Industrial*, 1994, pp. 121–132

Rhys, G., 2000, In: Financial Times Survey – Industry briefs, 'Supplier parks: Economies of scale play a vital role', *FT Auto 0200/Outsourcing*

Ricardo, D., *The Principles of Political Economy and Taxation*, Baltimore, MD, 1817

Richardson, G.B., The organisation of industry, In: *The Economic Journal*, 1972, September, pp. 883–896

Richardson, H.W., *Economia regional. Teoria de la localizacion, estructuras urbanas y crecimiento regional*, Barcelona, 1973

Richardson, H.W., *Politica y planificacion del desarrollo regional en España*, Madrid: Alianza Universidad, 1976

Richardson, H.W., *Regional and Urban Economics*, Penwin: Harmontsworth, 1978

Rivas, 2001: Interview with Mr. L. Rivas, Director General de compras de FASA-Renault, 9 May 2001, Valladolid

Rombo: FASA-Renault, Rombo, Numeros 48 – 178 (Otoño 1984–Diciembre 2000), Valladolid, 1984–2000

Rugman, A.M., *Inside the Multinationals: The Economics of Internal Markets*, New York: Columbia University Press, 1981

Rugman, A.M., Multinational enterprises and the end of global strategy, Oxford University working paper, Oxford, 1999

Rugman, A.M. and J.R. D'Cruz, *Multinationals as Flagship Firms*, New York: Oxford University Press, 2000

Rugman, A.M. and A. Verbeke, *Global Corporate Strategy and Trade Policy*, London/New York, 1990

Rugman, A.M. and A. Verbeke (Eds), Global competition and the European community, In: *Research in Global Strategic Management*, Vol. 2, Greenwich Connecticut: JAI Press, 1991

Rugman, A.M. and A. Verbeke (Eds), *Research in Global Strategic Management: Corporate Response to Change*, Greenwich, Connecticut: JAI Press, Vol. 3, 1992

Rugman, A.M. and A. Verbeke, Subsidiary-specific advantages in multinational enterprises, In: *Strategic Management Journal*, 2001, 22, pp. 237–250

Rugman, A.M. and A. Verbeke, Multinational enterprises and clusters, In: *Management International Review*, 2003, Special Issue 3, pp. 151–169

Rutherford, T.D., Japanese investment and buyer–supplier relations in the Canadian automotive industry, In: *Regional Studies*, 2000, 34 (8), pp. 739–751

Sadler, D., Internationalization and Specialization in the European Automotive Components Sector: Implications for the Hollowing-out Thesis, In: *Regional Studies*, 1999, 33 (2), pp. 109–119

Sadler, D. and A. Amin, 'Europeanisation' in the automotive components sector and its implications for state and locality, In: Hudson, R. and Schamp, E. (Eds), *Towards a New Map of Automobile Manufacturing in Europe? New Production Concepts and Spatial Restructuring*, Frankfurt and Main: Axel Springer Verlag, 1995, pp. 39–61

Sadler, D. and A. Swain, State and market in Eastern Europe: Regional development and workplace implications of direct foreign investment in the automobile industry in Hungary, *Transactions of the Institute of British Geographers New Series*, 1994, 19 (4), pp. 387–403

Sako, M., *Prices, Quality and Trust: Inter-firm Relations in Britain and Japan*, Cambridge: Cambridge University Press, 1992

Sako, M. and M. Warburton, Preliminary report of European research team Modularization and outsourcing project, Boston, MA: MIT/IMVP Annual forum, 1999

Samuelson, Paul A. International trade and the equalisation of factor prices, *Economic Journal* 58, June 1948, pp. 163–184

Sanchez Jauregui, 2001: Interview with Mr. P. Sanchez Jauregui, Miembro de la oficina de direccion of Volkswagen Navarra, 11 July 2001, Pamplona

Sanchez Jauregui, P. and M.A. Royo Vicente, La adaptacion del sector del automovil navarro a los proces de globalizacion, In: Gobierno de Navarra – Departamento de Economia y Hacienda, La internacionalizacion de la economia navarra (Actas del Segundo Congreso de Economia de Navarra, Pamplona, 22 and 23 October 1997), Pamplona, 1997, pp. 189–202

Saxenian, A., *Regional Advantage: Culture and Competition in Silicon Valley and Route 128*, Cambridge, MA: Harvard University Press, 1994

Schoenberger, E., The corporate interview as a research method in economic geography, in: *Professional Geographer*, 1991, 43, pp. 180–189

Scott, A.J., *New Industrial Spaces*, London: Pion, 1988

Scott, A.J. and M. Storper, High technology industry and regional development, Reading Geographical Papers No. 95, Department of Geography, University of Reading, 1986

SEAT (Sociedad Española de Automoviles de Turismo) S.A., Memoria y Balance ejercicios 1976–1986, Madrid, 1977–1987

Seidler, E., *Olé, Toledo! The saga of SEAT and the car which is giving it a new dimension*, Lausanne: Editions J.R. Piccard, 1991

Shackle, G.L.S., *Decision, Order and Time in Human Affairs*, 2nd edition, Cambridge UK: Cambridge University Press, 1969

Shackle, G.L.S., *Keynesian Kaleidics, the Evolution of a General Political Economy*, Edinburgh UK: Edinburgh University Press, 1974

Shimokawa, K., *Reorganization of Automobile Industry and Structural Change of the Automobile Component Industry*, Boston, MA: MIT/IMVP Publications, 1999

Siemens Automotive Corporation – Communications Department, Siemens and Sommer-Allibert form JV to supply vehicle cockpit modules to global car industry, Document No. 1109, Auburn Hills, News release of 06–08–1996

Siemens Automotive France, Du rêve à la réalité, Toulouse, 1999

Skinner, W., The focused factory, In: *Harvard Business Review*, 52 (3), May–June 1974, pp. 113–121

Sleuwaegen, L., The restructuring of European manufacturing industries, In: Rugman, A.M. and A. Verbeke (Eds), *Research in Global Strategic Management*, Vol. 2, Greenwich Connecticut: JAI Press, 1991, pp. 81–103

Smith, A., *An Inquiry into the Nature and Causes of the Wealth of Nations*, New York, 1776

Smith, K.G., Caroll, S.J. and S.J. Ashford, Intra- and interorganizational cooperation: Toward a research agenda, In: *Academy of Management Journal*, 1995, 38 (1), pp. 7–23

Sodena, www.sodena.com – Companies with foreign capital

Sodena/Conway, Navarre, Spain investment guide (internet source), 1997

Solvay S.A., Annual Report, Brussels, various years

Solvay S.A., *Towards Sustainable Development*, Brussels, 2002

Sölvell, Ö., Porter, M.E. and I. Zander, Creation of competitive firms and industries in Sweden – The role of domestic rivalry, Paper presented at the 10th Annual SMS Conference, Stockholm, 24–27 September 1990 (IIB Research Paper 90/6)

Sölvell, Ö. and I. Zander, Preface to special issue on 'The dynamic multinational firm', In: *International Studies of Management and Organization*, Spring–Summer 1995, 25 (1/2), pp. 3–16

Stalk, G. and Th.M. Hout, *Competing Against Time*, New york: Free Press, 1990

Stopford, J.M. and L.T. Wells, *Managing the Multinational Enterprise: Organizations of the Firm and Ownership of Subsidiaries*, New York: Basic Books, 1972

Stopford, J.M., Strange, S. and J.S. Henley, *Rival States, Rival Firms: Competition for World Market Shares*, Cambridge: Cambridge University Press, 1991

Storper, M., The limits to globalization: Technology districts and international trade, In: *Economic Geography*, 1992, 68 (1), pp. 60–93

Storper, M. and R. Walker, *The Capitalist Imperative. Territory, Technology and Industrial Growth*, Oxford: Blackwell Publishers, 1989

Sullivan, D. and A. Bauerschmidt, Incremental internationalization: A test of Johanson and Vahlne's thesis, In: *Management International Review*, 1990, 30 (1), pp. 19–30

Swain, A., Governing the workplace: The workplace and regional development implications of automotive foreign direct investment in Hungary, In: *Regional studies*, 1998, 32(7), pp. 653–671

Telecyl, Guia empresarial de Castilla y Leon edicion 1998–1999, Valladolid, 1998

Thompson, J.D., *Organizations in Action*, New York: McGraw-Hill, 1967

Thorelli, H.B., Networks: Between markets and hierarchies, In: *Strategic Management Journal*, 1986, 7, pp. 37–51

Torrico, 2002: Interview with Mr. J. Gonzalez Torrico, Director General de la Direccion de Relaciones Proveedores España at Renault-España S.A., 11 April 2002, Valladolid

Toyne, B., International exchange: A foundation for theory building in international business, In: *Journal of International Business Studies*, 1989, 20 (1), pp. 1–17

TPV Johnson Controls d.o.o., Company presentation, Novo Mesto, 2001

Trends, Focus artikel: 'Help, de autofabriek verdwijnt', 4 April 2002, pp. 38–42

TRW, Vector, Boletin Informativo No. 8, Pamplona, Abril 1996

Tuite, M.F., Toward a theory of joint decision-making, In: Tuite, M.F., Radnor, M. and R.K. Chisholm (Eds), *Interorganizational Decision-Making*, Chicago, IL: Aldine Publishers, 1972, pp. 9–19

Turnbull, P.W. and J.-P. Valla (Eds), *Strategies for International Industrial Marketing: The Management of Customer Relationships in European Industrial Markets*, London: Croom Helm, 1986

Uzzi, B., Social structure and competition in interfirm networks: The paradox of embeddedness, In: *Administrative Science Quarterly*, 1997, 42 (1), pp. 35–67

Valeo, 2000, In: Financial Times Survey – Industry briefs, 'Supplier parks: Economies of scale play a vital role', *FT Auto 0200/Outsourcing*

Ven, A.H. Van de, Suggestions for studying strategy process: 'A research note', In: *Strategic Management Journal*, 1992, 13, pp. 169–188

Ven, A.H. Van de and M.S. Poole, Explaining development and change in organizations, In: *Academy of Management Review*, 1995, 20, pp. 510–540

Vernon, R., International investments and international trade in the product cycle, In: *Quarterly Journal of Economics*, 1966, 80 (May), pp. 190–207

Vickery, G., Globalisation in the automobile industry, In: *Globalisation of Industry, Overview and Sector Reports*, Paris: OECD, 1996

Volkswagen AG, Geschäftsbericht/Annual Report 1980–2002, Wolfsburg, 1981–2003

Volkswagen Navarra S.A., Vocacion de Calidad, Pamplona, 1995

Volkswagen Navarra S.A., Direccion Logistica, Aufteilung (%) Materialherkunft 1989, 1994, 2001, Pamplona, 1989, 1995, 2001

Volkswagen Navarra S.A., Apunto, Numeros 1–37, Pamplona, Marzo 1996 – Marzo 2002

Volkswagen slide show, 2002: Volkswagen AG, Wissensstafette in der Beschaffung (Powerpoint presentation), Wolfsburg, 2002

Volpato, G., Fiat Auto and Magneti Marelli: Toward globalization, In: *Actes du GER-PISA*, No. 22, février 1997, pp. 69–98

Vries, G. De, *De ontwikkeling van wetenschap*, Groningen: Wolters-Noordhof, 1985

Wallerstein, I., *The Modern World System I: Capitalist Agriculture and the Origins of the European World-Economy in the Sixteenth Century*, New York: Academic Press, 1974

Welch, L.S. and R. Luostarinen, Internationalization: Evolution of a concept, In: *Journal of General Management*, 1988, 14 (2), pp. 34–55

Wells, P. and M. Rawlinson, New procurement regimes and the spatial distribution of suppliers: The case of Ford in Europe, In: *Area*, 1992, 24 (4), pp. 380–390

Wells, P. and M. Rawlinson, *The New European Automobile Industry*, Basingstoke: Macmillan, 1994

Wernerfelt, B., A resource-based view of the firm, In: *Strategic Management Journal*, 1984, 5 (2), pp. 171–180

White, P.E., Intra and interorganizational studies, In: *Administration and Society*, 1974, 6, pp. 105–152

Williamson, O.E., *Markets and hierarchies: Analysis and Antitrust Implications*, New York: Free Press, 1975

Williamson, O.E., Transaction-cost economics: The governance of contractual relations, In: *Journal of Law and Economics*, 1979, 22, pp. 233–261

Williamson, O.E., The organization of work: A comparative institutional assessment, In: *Journal of Economic Behaviour and Organization*, March 1980, I (1), pp. 6–38

Williamson, O.E., The economics of organization: The transaction cost approach, In: *American Journal of Sociology*, November 1981, 87 (3), pp. 548–575

Williamson, O.E., *The Economic Institutions of Capitalism*, New York: Free Press, 1985

Williamson, O.E., Comparative economic organization: The analysis of discrete structural alternatives, In: *Administrative Science Quarterly*, 1991, 26, pp. 269–296

Williamson, O.E. and G. Ouchi, The markets and hierarchies program of research: Origins, implications, prospects, In: Ven, A.H. Van de and W.F. Joyce (Eds), *Perspectives on Organization Design and Behavior*, New York: Wiley, 1981, pp. 347–370

Wolff, B., Incentive-Compatiable change management in a welfare state: asking the right questions in the German Standort-Debate, working paper 6.4, center for European studies, Harvard University, 1996

Womack, J.P., Jones, D.T. and D. Roos, *The Machine that Changed the World*, New York: Rawson Associates, 1990

Yéboles, 1997: Interview with Mr. Carlos Yéboles, Member of Dirección de Ingeniería de Vehículo at FASA-Renault, 22 July 1997, Palencia

Yin, R.K., *Case Study Research: Design and Methods* (2nd edition), Beverly Hills, CA: Sage, 1994

Yuchtman, E. and S. Seashore, A system resource approach to organizational effectiveness, In: *American Sociological Review*, 1967, 32, pp. 891–903

Zabalo, 2000: Interview with Mr. J. Zabalo, General director of Sodena, 17 November 2000, Pamplona

Index